P9-DYJ-516

Value Investing in Real Estate

Value Investing in Real Estate

GARY W. ELDRED

John Wiley & Sons, Inc.

Published by John Wiley & Sons, Inc., New York
Published simultaneously in Canada.

Library of Congress Cataloging-in-Publication Data:
Eldred, Gary W.
Value investing in real estate / Gary Eldred.
p. cm.
Includes index.
ISBN 0-471-18520-5 (cloth : alk. paper)
1. Real estate investment—United States. 2. Real property—Valuation—United States. I. Title.
HD255 .E3753 2002
332.63′24—dc21 2001046885

Printed in the United States of America.

10 9 8 7 6 5 4 3 2 1

About the Author

Gary W. Eldred, Ph.D., combines a thorough academic grounding in finance and real estate with more than 20 years of practical experience. He has been involved in more than 100 real estate projects as either an investor or a consultant. His clients have included regional and national development companies as well as Fortune 500 corporations such as Georgia Pacific, Wells Fargo, and Century 21 International. Dr. Eldred also has served on the graduate business faculty at the University of British Columbia, The University of Virginia, and Stanford University.

A well-regarded author, Dr. Eldred has written or co-written three college textbooks, several dozen articles for academic and professional journals, and numerous successful books for home buyers and real estate investors. As a media commentator, he has contributed to many articles for such publications as the *New York Times*, *Business Week*, *Barron's*, *Kiplinger's Personal Finance*, *Reader's Digest*, and *Money*.

Contents

Preface

Throughout the past 10 years, the financial-planning establishment, personal finance magazines, and dozens of best-selling books (especially Jeremy Siegel's *Stocks for the Long Run*) have served as head cheerleaders for the stock market. These stock market enthusiasts have encouraged more than 50 million Americans to place all (or nearly all) of their long-term savings into stocks. Saving a down payment for a home? Saving for your children's college education? Saving for retirement? Then put your money into stocks, they say. You'll never find a better investment.

According to the stock market enthusiasts, stocks will protect you against inflation; stocks will provide you a higher return with little or no long-term risk; and should the stock market stall, hang tight—it's sure to quickly bounce back and regain its climb to even greater heights. Indeed, in their book *Dow 36,000*, Glassman and Hassett celebrate the fact that the public has at last learned the (supposed) wisdom of these cheerleader pep talks. On this final point, Glassman and Hassett are most certainly correct. Recent surveys do show that most of the investing public maintains an unwavering faith in stocks.

But is this faith truly justified by the facts? Absolutely not. As Robert Shiller perceptively notes in *Irrational Exuberance*, "When the facts are wrong, it can't be called learning. Someday investors will 'unlearn' these 'facts.' But before this happens, we must consider what we as individuals . . . should be doing."

Shiller is right. And in this book, I show you not only why the stock market enthusiasts err with their so-called facts, but also what you should be doing to diversify away from stocks. For when compared head-to-head on all risk and return attributes, value investors in income properties—even during the past 20 years—have outperformed the major stock market indexes. More importantly, in this book you will see why the future looks even better for real estate, and not just better in the contest for the highest risk-adjusted rate of return. Rather, you will see why real estate offers a safer, surer, and more definitive way than stocks to build the amount of wealth you will want and need for your longer-term financial goals.

Yet the lesson taught here is not the simplistic "buy real estate and the money will come" propaganda that appeals to the naive and the gullible. No, to succeed in real estate, to achieve high returns with low risk, you must follow those principles of investing that were spelled out best by Ben Graham in *The Intelligent Investor* and *Security Analysis*. Although originally developed for stocks and bonds, today Graham's principles of value investing apply even more so to real estate.

Why real estate? Because with real estate, individual investors can actually ferret out the facts they need. No intelligent real estate investor relies on analyst puff pieces that are passed off as unbiased research. No intelligent real estate investor can be misled by artificially created accounting numbers that bear no necessary relationship to a property's actual operating earnings or its asset value. Even better, real estate pays big dividends to human enterprise far better than stocks.

Can you lose money in real estate? Most assuredly, and many have. Can you lose money in real estate if you follow the principles of value investing? Not very likely. For the verdict of history rings clear: As long as the population and economy of the United States continue to grow, value investors in real estate will continue to reap their large and just rewards. And with this book, you will gain the know-how to join their ranks. I wish you the best.

Introduction

Rethink Your Financial Future

How do you plan to build wealth for your retirement? Stocks? Employer pension? Social Security?[1] If you answered yes to any or all of these choices, you *must* rethink your financial future. For unless we are blessed by a miracle, these resources will not and cannot fully deliver on their promises.[2] If, on the other hand, you answered "income properties," feel free to jump directly to Chapter 4. Unlike the sure-to-be-disappointed majority, you're already on the right track.

Why downplay stocks, Social Security, and pensions in favor of real estate? Because the coming age wave will overwhelm the capacity of these financial assets.[3] Too many people are counting on receiving too much. Certainly, it's true that a few million Americans can build wealth with stocks, pensions, and, yes, even Social Security. But what stands true for the few must prove false for the many.[4] By the time you read through the first four chapters of this book, you will understand perfectly why our national experiment with stocks for retirement must fail. Yet on the positive side, you also will learn how you (but certainly not the majority) can secure your financial future by value investing in property that will reliably yield and grow a generous stream of income.

The Coming Age Wave

As you have read many times, Americans must soon stand face-to-face against a demographic crisis. During the next three decades, the number of Americans over age 60 will mushroom from 45 million today to 87.5 million by the year 2030. Yet over this same three decades, the primary workforce population of persons age 25 to 60 will merely edge up from 132 million to 144 million in the year 2030.[5]

Now, carefully think through these age wave numbers. The population of potential workers will increase by just 12 million people, whereas the number of people crossing into their retirement years will grow by more than 40 million. In other words, for every person who enters the workforce, two or three more people will (hope to) leave it.[6]

Although demographers and statisticians may quibble over the precise numbers and ratio of workers to nonworkers—no one can perfectly predict the future—all do agree that this emerging age wave will bear heavily on the people who remain employed. For it is only the employed who will work to produce all of the economy's goods and services that are necessary to meet everyone's needs and wants. Stated bluntly, during the next 30 years, our society will grow the number of nonworking retired consumers far faster than we grow the number of working producers.

Therefore, with absolutely no doubt, a lot of us are going to get squeezed. Either tomorrow's workers must accept a lower standard of living; tomorrow's retirees must accept a lower quality of life; or, more likely, there will be some combination of both.[7] Moreover, this squeeze could really hurt if we experience an even more explosive growth of seniors due to breakthrough treatments for cancer, heart disease, or other illnesses that currently take their toll on the over-60 age group.[8]

The Age Wave, Retirement Income, and Real Estate

Unfortunately, few Americans yet recognize how these time-bomb demographics will impact their plans to save, invest, and live a comfortable, worry-free retirement. Most Americans still mistakenly believe that they will be able to count on their 401(k) or 403(b) plan; their IRAs, Keoghs, and mutual funds; Social Security; and maybe a pension.

In fact, though, in promoting these types of retirement or wealth-building plans, our society is blindly erecting a house of cards. We are failing to focus on the supreme critical question: How are we as a society going to produce enough goods and services to fulfill the American Dream for everyone? Instead, we are leading people to believe in illusionary wealth, wealth that consists of nothing more than inflated stock prices (at best) and empty promises in a so-called Social Security trust fund.

Consequently, as I will show throughout this book, your only firm foundation for a secure future lies with investment real estate: a hard asset that—if selected properly—will yield a continuing stream of increasing income. But first, here's why you (and 100 million other Americans) should not expect stocks, pensions, or Social Security to adequately and safely fund your retirement.

Danger: Illusionary Wealth

During the 2000–2001 fall in stock prices, journalists routinely reported stories with such headlines as "$4.2 Trillion of Wealth Evaporates." In doing so, these commentators confused illusionary wealth with real wealth. In fact, though, we only create illusionary wealth by inflating stock prices far beyond the actual increase in our real economy, namely, corporate profits, corporate dividends, and the total quantity of goods and services that we produce and consume. Likewise, the government creates illusionary wealth when it deposits government bonds into the so-called Social Security trust fund.

No one can live on illusionary wealth. You—and everybody else—can live only on the actual cars, houses, food, clothing, health care, and other items that working people produce in the course of their employment. Neither the stock market nor Social Security addresses this issue of production. Neither faces the fact that stock price increases and Social Security merely take from some people to provide for others. Neither seeks to increase the economic pie.

Of course, in some instances, a company initial public offering (IPO) or secondary stock offerings will put money into a corporate treasury that will be used to expand business production. But 99% of the time, your "investing" in stocks simply means a nonproductive trade between a stock buyer and a stock seller. Nothing is created. Gross domestic product (GDP) does not grow. Therefore, as you plan for your future years, you must decide: Do you want to mistakenly count on the illusionary wealth of stock trading and Social Security? Or do you want to count on the real wealth of income properties? Only with income property investments do you satisfy real human needs and wants (housing, commercial space) in a productive exchange: a service (space) for money (rent).

Illusionary Wealth: Stocks

If you've ever cashed out some stocks to buy a new car or maybe even a second home, you may think I'm foolish to call stocks illusionary wealth. But by using this term, I don't mean to say that all stocks at all times deserve such a label. Rather, I'm using it to point out two indisputable facts: (1) During the past 20 years, stock prices (in the aggregate) have shot up far faster than our real economy, and (2) cash dividends paid to corporate shareholders cannot come close to providing decent retirement incomes for the great majority of Americans.

Stock Prices versus the Real Economy

Table I.1 shows the past 21-year relationship between the GDP and various stock price indices as represented by the Dow Jones Industrial Average (DJIA), the Standard & Poor's (S&P) 500 index, and the NASDAQ, the "new economy" index that is heavily weighted with technology companies. Regardless of which stock market index you choose, the same exuberant relationship shows clearly: Stock prices have risen dramatically faster than our nation's output.[9] Whereas the nation's production of goods and services has risen by 281%, stock prices have risen by 916% to 1,400%.

Naturally, at the time you read this, the stock indexes may sit substantially higher or lower than shown here. But unless we suffer a catastrophic crash, these figures clearly reveal illusionary wealth.[10] If significant numbers of people could actually sell their stocks and use their cash proceeds to buy cars, homes, travel, health care, and other goods and services, we would experience massive inflation[11]—too many dollars chasing too few goods. As Table I.1 clearly shows, our real output has not risen anywhere near enough to satisfy all of this supposed stock market buying power.

Table I.1 **Growth Rate of Gross Domestic Product versus Selected Stock Indices***

	1980	*1990*	*2001*	*Increase (1980–2001)*
GDP	$2.7 trillion	$5.5 trillion	$10.3 trillion	281%
DJIA	891	2,678	10,500	1,070%
S&P 500	118	335	1,200	916%
NASDAQ	124	323	1,860	1,400%

*Yearly average from 1980 for DJIA and S&P 500. Yearly low from 1980 for NASDAQ.

That's why the term illusionary wealth aptly describes our present stock market. It's nice to imagine a future life of ease. But for the great majority of shareholders, stock market wealth does not, and cannot, reflect actual buying power. Over long periods (within the bounds of reason) inflation-adjusted, aggregate stock market wealth can't continue to increase faster than real economic growth.

For wealth to be real, it must be easily converted into goods and services. When only the relatively few wealthy and near-wealthy owned stocks, that was not a problem. But how do 50, 75, or 100 million Americans all reap these rewards when the nation's growth in output lags the growth in stock market wealth by a factor of three or more?

(This discussion begs another equally important question: What will happen to stock prices when tens of millions of seniors decide to sell? We shall address this issue in later chapters. Here I'm trying to emphasize that when as individuals we look at our stock portfolio balances, we imagine all of the things we can buy with that money. But when we as 50 or even 100 million stockholders look at our collective balance, it would be impossible for any substantial number of us to transform our stocks into goods and services—even if we could sell without pushing down the overall level of stock prices.)

Stock Prices versus Corporate Dividends

In days gone by, prudence dictated that stocks should pay dividends at a rate equal to or greater than the yield on risk-free bonds. In other words, if a benchmark $1,000 U.S. government bond paid $50 (5%) a year in interest, then $1,000 in stocks should pay at least $50 a year in cash dividends. In fact, in the late 1940s, the dividend yield for many stocks climbed above 8%. The interest rate on government bonds averaged less than 4%.

It was only in the late 1950s that dividend yields permanently fell below the interest rates on long-term bonds. Up until the modern era of stock pricing, investors believed that because of higher risk, stocks should reward shareholders with higher annual cash returns.

This higher reward was called the equity risk premium. It reflected the widely believed age-old axiom "the higher the risk, the greater the expected reward." Today, such prudence has been tossed into the dustbin of history. Dividend yields on stocks (S&P 500) now sit at near record lows. In contrast to long-term, high-grade bond yields of 5% to 7% per year (possibly a little more), the dividends paid on $1,000 worth of stocks would total the grand sum of $12.50 (a 1.25% return). This dramatic change in dividend yields is catastrophic for stocks as retirement income.[12]

Today, if you owned a $1,000,000 diversified portfolio of stocks, you could expect to receive (pretax) annual dividend checks of just $12,500. (And yet you've been told that becoming a stock market millionaire would give you financial independence.)

What good does it do to accumulate $1,000,000 in stocks if they won't even pay you a poverty-level income? In terms of buying actual goods and services, the dividend income produced by even a nice-sized portfolio of stocks won't get you very far. This is truly illusionary wealth.

"So sell them," you say. But who will buy? Set aside the price effect and simply ask, Why should investors continue to readily buy stocks according to the greater fool theory? How much longer will people continue to buy stocks simply on the belief that they can sell (a subperforming asset) at higher and higher prices? Once retirees and near-retirees begin to see the meager cash returns that stocks pay, the bloom on the rose will surely shrivel and fade.[13]

Dividends: Too Little to Go Around

Here's another way to think about dividends: There's too little to go around. In recent years, corporate dividends have averaged around 5% of total national income and less than 7% of total employee compensation.[14] In other words, within the complete picture of earnings and income, dividends count for a very small fraction of current household spending power. To say that corporate dividends could serve as any major source of wage replacement for tens of millions of retirees defies reality.

Even worse for the great majority, due to the heavily skewed distribution of wealth in the United States, 80% to 90% of the corporate dividends paid to individuals and families go to the top 10% of the population.[15] Thus, the actual amount of dividends available to those tens of millions of less well off households will make for slim pickings. In contrast to Wall Street promises, a majority of Americans cannot and should not reasonably expect their stock portfolios to provide them a generous (or even a satisfactory) retirement income. The relatively small amount of cash dividends paid (now and expected in the future) cannot adequately support the tens of millions of people who are currently accumulating stocks for retirement in their 401(k)s, 403(b)s, IRAs, Keoghs, and other similar stock-buying programs.

Stocks and Retirement Plans

As another related danger point, keep in mind, too, that most employer-sponsored defined-benefit retirement plans hold a majority of their assets in stocks. As recently as 20 to 30 years ago, many private and government defined-benefit retirement plans invested primarily in bonds. Stocks were considered too risky.

However, as tens of millions of Americans pushed stock prices higher and higher, employer retirement plans abandoned their cautious ways. They too wanted a larger piece of the stock market action. Today, many government and employer retirement plans hold 60% to 80% of their assets in stocks.[16]

In addition, during the late 1980s and throughout the 1990s, many employers began to tap into their retirement funds for use as a cash kitty to boost corporate earnings. As their realized returns on stock market holdings exceeded actuarial expectations, firms would withdraw the surplus gains and boost their forecast for future returns. In tandem, a higher assumed rate of return on a firm's retirement fund reduces the amount of annual corporate contributions. However, if those larger assumed rates of return don't continue, many retirement funds throughout the United States could quickly shift from overfunded to underfunded.

Even if you're not exposed directly to the vagaries of the stock market, your employer-sponsored retirement plan probably is. That puts your retirement income at risk. As a backup reserve, you too should definitely add at least a few investment properties to your retirement (or other) wealth-building and savings programs. You definitely need to diversify your portfolio of wealth and income.

Illusionary Wealth: Social Security

As most astute Americans now know, the Social Security program has become a giant Ponzi scheme. As the program is currently structured, the U.S. government promises to pay ever-increasing levels of benefits to successive generations of retirees. Yet to honor these promises, it must burden succeeding generations of workers with ever-higher Social Security taxes. Just since 1950, the maximum Social Security taxes paid per worker has skyrocketed from $60 per year to more than $12,000 per year.

Given the emerging age wave and resulting demographic imbalance of retirees to workers, here's the critical question: How much longer can this Ponzi scheme continue before the benefits promised crush the workers' ability (or willingness) to bear the necessary taxes?

Social Security program cheerleaders say, "No worries; we're putting aside monies right now in the Social Security trust fund. Everything's being taken care of." On the other hand, critics say, "At best, the program can last another 10 or 15 years before hitting a major cash crunch. To avoid this crisis, we need to give today's workers (and tomorrow's retirees) more personal control over their future. We must give them the right to invest (at least) part of their Social Security taxes into their own private, individual stock accounts."[17]

Does either of these positions make economic sense? No.

The Trust Fund Deception

In building its trust fund, the Social Security program is using a bookkeeping sleight-of-hand that would land an insurance company executive in jail. For this "trust fund" holds no real assets. The U.S. government is disposing of the excess Social Security money as fast as it comes in.[18] In exchange, the "trust fund" merely books an IOU from the federal government. Here's how the government budget report describes this accounting fiction.

> Trust fund balances are available to finance future benefit payments and other trust fund expenditures—but only in a bookkeeping sense. . . . They do not consist of real economic assets that can be drawn down to fund benefits. Instead, they are claims on the U.S. Treasury that, when redeemed will have to be financed by either raising taxes, more borrowing, or reducing benefits. . . . *The existence of large trust fund balances, therefore, does not give the Government any ability to pay benefits*. [italics added][19]

There you have it. The Social Security trust fund remains an illusion that gives the uninformed a sense of financial comfort. Once the age wave hits, Social Security will default unless it raises taxes, borrows from taxpayers, or slices promised benefits. Somebody is sure to get squeezed.

In typical political obfuscation and deceit, the "trust fund" does not address the central problem: Where will the government actually get the money to pay the fast-approaching avalanche of seniors? Who's really going to pay? Who's really going to get squeezed: Workers? Retirees? Or both? Politicians prefer to skirt these unpleasant questions. They would have you believe that we live in a world of free-lunch economics.

Social Security Private Accounts

In recognizing the trust fund illusion, critics (or, some might say, realists) do acknowledge that the Social Security program can't survive as it is currently structured. Regrettably, though, the critics' cure would only compound the problem of illusionary wealth. Most of these critics want to permit workers to begin placing at least a portion of their Social Security tax monies into private investment accounts.

Where would this money be invested? In the stock market! Such a solution is no solution at all. It merely substitutes one type of illusionary wealth (the fictional Social Security trust fund) with another illusion—a portfolio of stocks whose inflated prices and meager dividends do not and cannot represent real buying power for tens of millions of retirees.

The Galveston Experience

Some of the private-account stock market enthusiasts hold up Galveston, Texas, as exhibit 1.[20] In the early 1980s, the Galveston county government terminated its enrollment in Social Security and instead allowed its employees to contribute to individual accounts.[21] As you can imagine, given our recent 20-year bull economy, many Galveston employees did succeed in building up very nice sized private retirement accounts.

Nevertheless, this investment approach that (so far) has worked for a few thousand people during the greatest U.S. market gains in history cannot be extrapolated into the future on a much larger scale. Not only are today's stock and bond yields far lower than they were 20 years ago when the Galveston plan started, but we're talking about the retirement income needs of 60 to 80 million people—not just a few thousand.

As everyone must come to realize, the stock (or bond) market doesn't grow food or build houses. At today's low yields and high valuations, the stock market merely creates illusionary wealth untethered from the actual production of economic goods and services that people need and want to live their everyday lives, and, even worse, untethered from a supporting foundation of annual dividends.

The New Economy

Many stock market enthusiasts admit that the stock market still sits far above all reasonable measures that were applied in the past. Yet they claim that these high valuations can be justified because we've entered a new era with a new economy. According to this (now somewhat muted) view, emerging technologies, low inflation, and economic stability will bring us unbounded future prosperity. They have said the old rules no longer apply. We're leaving behind the age of scarcity and business cycles. Instead, we will enjoy unrelenting growth without pain or limits.

Claims of New Era Are Old Hat

In his excellent book *Irrational Exuberance*, Yale University economist Robert Shiller devotes 36 pages to debunking the new-era hyperbole.[22] In reality, the United States has repeatedly moved through cycles of both new-era and end-of-history overstatements.

The early 1900s, the late 1920s, and the early 1960s all gave us exaggerated pronouncements of glorious days and unbounded future. Most famous of all, perhaps, is the oft-quoted pronouncement of Irving Fisher. Celebrating an earlier so-called new era of permanent prosperity, Professor Fisher (a leading economist of the day) declared, "Stock prices have reached what looks like a permanently high plateau." The date: October 14, 1929, just two weeks before the fateful Black Thursday stock market crash and the ensuing 11 years of economic depression.[23]

In stark contrast, on the brink of recovery in 1939, University of Chicago economist Oscar Lange wrote, "The view is widely held that the American economy has lost its momentum of expansion and reached a stage of more or less permanent stagflation."[24] Likewise, in 1980, Massachusetts Institute of Technology professor Lester Thurow reflected the bleak views of that period in his best-selling book, *The Zero Sum Society*. There Thurow explained that U.S. economic growth and prosperity had ended. Our only hope was to learn to live on less.[25]

Cycles of History

Perhaps it's human nature, but we seem to swing from absurdly bleak outlooks to those displaying irrational optimism. The past supports neither view. Today, though, far too many Americans still believe that they can count on stocks, employer pensions, and Social Security to provide them a decent retirement income. They look at the high returns of the past two decades and unjustifiably extend them into the future. Even after the 2000–2001 swoon of the Dow and the crash of the NASDAQ, a *Wall Street Journal* survey revealed that investors still believed that during the next 20 years, stocks will yield an average return of 12% to 20% a year.[26] Most financial journalists still use 10% to 12% returns in advising their readers.[27]

In terms of illusionary wealth, perhaps such gains are possible. In terms of real spendable wealth for the great majority of Americans, they are absolutely impossible.

New era or not, we have seen no sustained evidence that our real economy will (or can) grow faster than its historical norm of 2.5% to 3.0% a year—some years better, other years lagging. Absent more robust (ebullient?) economic growth, aggregate stock market gains of even 8% a year cannot translate into a commensurate amount of buying power.

Dow 36,000

Among the most enthusiastic and well-publicized new-era advocates were James K. Glassman and Kevin Hassett. In their best-selling book, *Dow 36,000*, the authors argued that the old rules that governed stock price limits no longer apply.[28] They celebrated the fact that Americans have finally learned that over the long term stocks present virtually no risks worth worrying about. Thus, these authors predict that maybe by 2010, the Dow Jones Industrial Average will shoot up from 10,000 (its level when their book was published) to 36,000.

The Fatal Oversight

In putting forth their Dow 36,000 thesis, Glassman and Hassett stirred up a continuing debate over the "right" way to value stocks and whether the market is currently undervalued or overvalued. But nearly all critics and champions alike miss the implications of this and other theories of ever-rising stock market wealth.

Those implications are clearly stated in the first paragraph of *Dow 36,000*. The authors begin Chapter 1 with the following passage:

> Never before have so many people owned so much stock. They depend on their shares not just to enjoy a comfortable retirement, but also to pay college tuition, to buy a house or a car, to help their children, to take a long vacation, or simply to lead the good life . . . The stock market is a money machine: Put dollars in at one end, get those dollars back and more at the other end.[29]

All of this easy abundance sounds wonderful. And it's clearly a popular vision that many Americans continue to hold (although perhaps not so extreme): the stock market as a gigantic ATM backed up by a vault with unlimited amounts of cash, available on demand.

Yet nowhere in their book do these authors even mention the contradiction that their thesis generates—namely, that their stock market money machine does not create houses, cars, vacations, or those other goods and services that are necessary to yield the good life. This abundance is assumed to just magically appear as needed when these tens of millions of retiree-shareholders decide to cash in their soon-to-be multimillion-dollar portfolios.

The Hard Reality

Let's assume the authors have correctly apprehended the future. We conquer terrorism, experience solid economic growth, and as we close the year 2010, the Dow sprints across the 36,000 mark. Under the optimistic assumption of 3% per year of real economic growth, stock market wealth will have outpaced the real economy by a factor of three. Stock market wealth will have more than tripled. But the real economy will have grown by less than 50%.

So again, we face hard reality. How will people convert this extraordinary wealth into the ordinary goods and services that they plan to buy? The unrebuttable answer: They won't. They can't. The great majority will not be able to transform their illusionary stock market wealth into that good life that Glassman and Hassett promise for all Americans who continue to faithfully feed their supposed money machine.

Unfortunately, millions of Americans will learn sooner or later that the real machine analogy for stocks is a slot machine: Put money in, and if you're one of the lucky ones, you'll get even more back (at the expense of others). But the laws of mathematics and the laws of the economy mandate that in total, people cannot win (consume) from society more than we deposit (produce). Over a period of decades, aggregate stock market buying power can't persistently outpace a real economic growth.

What Does This Mean for You?

Throughout this book, we will expand on the critical points raised in this introduction. But for now, you should at least begin to question the national emphasis on stock market wealth, and especially to question stocks as the recommended and preferred retirement investment vehicle (either directly or indirectly) for most of the 130 million members of the current workforce.

No matter how high stock prices may climb, as a nation we still cannot consume more than we produce. Yes, some people will win the stock market game. They will discover the next Microsoft or Intel way ahead of the crowd. They will find those Ben Graham bargains. Or they will liquidate their holdings before the masses rush to the exit. But mathematically, the majority cannot achieve the promised wealth. Just as we all can't get rich taking in each other's laundry, neither can we all achieve material abundance simply by trading stocks with each other.

In addition, contrary to repeated affirmations by politicians in high places, the Social Security program is not sound. The "trust fund" is a deception. Like Wall Street, the government has promised far more than it can deliver.

So, these adverse facts of life leave you with two important questions. If you want to advance safer, surer, and faster than the herd, (1) where should you invest your money (asset allocation); and (2) what style of investing should you adopt? Is there realistic hope for a secure financial future? Yes, and the choice is investment real estate.

Asset Allocation

As you think out and plan your wealth-building and income requirements, you must think critically about what asset classes (stocks, bonds, money market, certificates of deposit, real estate, collectibles, etc.) offer the best return for the least risk. Today, nearly all financial planners still recommend and enthusiastically advocate stocks. In fact, many so-called financial experts advise that if you've got at least 10 years until you need the money, you've got no asset allocation problem. Simply put 100% (or more) of your investable funds in stocks because "over the long run, stocks can be expected to outperform all other types of investments."[30]

I beg to differ. As I will show in later chapters, smart investors should begin now to dramatically increase the percentage of their investments they hold in real estate. Based on current relative price levels, expected risks, and returns, real estate offers the far superior choice for value investors.

Investing Style

In addition to asset class(es), you also must consciously (or unconsciously) choose an investment style. Do you wish to emphasize value, growth, momentum, fads, speculation, gambling, or some other approach?

Too many investors never deliberately select their investment style (philosophy). Then, without discipline, they drift. They ricochet randomly, always searching in vain for that next big score, or that proverbial tenbagger. As often as not, such an undisciplined approach leads to disappointment, regret, and even financial ruin.

Does sticking to one style actually outperform all others? Yes, and that style is called value investing.[31] If you invest in real estate and follow the Ben Graham–Warren Buffet principles of value investing, you will not need to worry about the fate of the stock market or the solvency of Social Security.

Can everyone easily succeed with this approach? Unfortunately, no. Contrary to the advice of most so-called financial experts, real estate gurus, and stock market promoters, no investment program can work for everyone (easily or otherwise). But value investing in real estate will succeed for everyone who is willing to think and willing to work. Foolishly, a majority of investors want something easy, quick, or preferably both. That's what makes stocks so deceptively attractive—all gain, no pain. Just regularly put a few dollars in and voilà, pull out vast wealth in later years. Sorry, but the world will no longer oblige. What worked in the past for a few million people will not and cannot work in the future for 50 million people (or more). But if you are willing to pay a moderate price in terms of the research, thought, and effort that value investing requires, your rewards in real estate will multiply. You will achieve that Peter Lynch tenbagger—and possibly much more.[32]

Chapter 1

Value Investing
The One Best Way

Just as in the late 1920s, today we have damaged our future financial prosperity with the continual degradation of the word investment. People who wish to make a sale, earn a vote, or push a product know that by attaching the word investment to their pitch, they can cloak their agenda with an aura of wisdom, prudence, and good sense.

Think for a moment. Peddlers of financial products, purveyors of financial services, demagoguing politicians, and even new car dealers tell us to buy what they are selling because we would be making a good *investment*. We are told to invest in our children, invest in our health, and invest in our schools. I've seen vacations, commodities, clothing, jewelry, time-shares, baseball cards, remodeled kitchens, swimming pools, and old Mason jars all put forth as worthy *investments*.

Regrettably, the more broadly a term of language is spread, the more it loses its true meaning. Voltaire is supposed to have remarked, "Nothing is right or wrong; only thinking makes it so." To paraphrase Voltaire, I would observe that today, "Nothing is good or bad; only labeling makes it so." And if we label something—anything—an investment ipso facto, it must be good.

As a result of this semantic confusion and the power of words, we let others lie to us, and we lie to ourselves. We rely on the rubric of "investing" to justify and rationalize unwise consumption, fanciful acquisitions, high-risk speculation, and sure money losers.

Humpty-Dumpty, Ben Graham, and the Birth of Value Investing

On this point of semantic confusion you may recall the famous exchange between Humpty Dumpty and Alice from Lewis Carroll's *Through the Looking-Glass:*

> "And only *one* [day] for birthday presents, you know. There's glory for you!" [said Humpty].
>
> "I don't know what you mean by 'glory,'" Alice said.
>
> Humpty Dumpty smiled contemptuously. "Of course you don't—till I tell you. I meant 'there's a nice knock-down argument for you!'"
>
> "But 'glory' doesn't mean 'a nice knock-down argument,'" Alice objected.
>
> "When *I* use a word," Humpty Dumpty said, in rather a scornful tone, "it means just what I choose it to mean—neither more nor less."
>
> "The question is," said Alice, "whether you *can* make a word mean so many different things."
>
> "The question is," said Humpty Dumpty, "which is to be master—that's all."

Now, the question for you is this: What do you mean when you use the word invest? Have you even thought about it? Without a clear and distinct meaning, the word, not you, becomes the master. As Professor (and later U.S. Senator) S. I. Hayakawa warned in his widely acclaimed book *Language in Thought and Action*, too often we let language itself shape our thoughts and actions, rather than shaping our language and actions with clear, explicit, and distinctive thinking.

Ben Graham, the acknowledged father of value investing, pointed to the damage done with this semantic trap in his and David Dodd's 1934 magnum opus, *Security Analysis*.[1]

Ben Graham on Investing

In the early years of the Great Depression, when Graham was writing the first edition of *Security Analysis*, he was trying to fight two semantic battles: (1) speculation as investment, and (2) all stocks as speculation.

Speculation as Investment

Graham was quite disturbed that leading up to the 1929 stock market decline and subsequent crash, stock promoters and media pundits were "misusing the term 'investment' to cover the crassest and most unrestrained speculation." As a result, people who thought themselves investors were throwing money at the most foolish and unproven financial propositions. Stock prices reached record levels with no obvious firm foundation.[2]

All Stocks as Speculation

Yet after the crash, a fierce reaction set in that Graham also objected to. According to this constricted view, people should never fool themselves into believing that a purchase of common stocks qualifies as investing. In their popular book of the day, *Investment and Speculations*, Chamberlain and Hay wrote boldly,

> We have gone out of our way to emphasize that in theory and in fact, common stocks are not investments; that they are speculations; that the reasoning that tries to draw them into the category of investments is fallacious.[3]

In fairness to these authors, note that they did not wait until after the 1929–1932 crash to express their thesis that common stocks had become the focus of speculative frenzy, that far too may people were being "lulled into a false sense of price-security by the siren doctrine of 'common stocks as long-term investments.'"[4] As early as 1927, in a series of articles, Chamberlain and Hay rejected the widely-held view that

> Americans live in a chosen country to which has been vouchsafed a 'new era' in which all one has to do is buy 'well-selected' stocks at any time, at any price, and hold with sufficient patience in order to sell for more than one paid and thereby realize [a handsome return] on the investment.[5]

Graham and Dodd's Distinctions

Like Chamberlain and Hay, Graham and Dodd rejected the wholesale misuse of the term investment in the late 1920s. Nevertheless, they still believed that they could fashion a set of principles and techniques that not only would yield common stock buyers an attractive return, but also would provide them a margin of safety. For Graham and Dodd, a stock that met both of these two criteria would justly garner the title of investment.[6]

In tandem with these two criteria, though, runs the corollary: Stocks (or other financial outlays, including real estate) that violate their stated principles of investment should not win such high regard. Nevertheless, in developing these principles, Graham and Dodd did not mean to disparage all speculation, gambling, or the occasional "taking a flier." Rather, they wanted true *investors* to explicitly recognize the differences among these various ways of putting money on the line. Then each investor should choose intelligently according to one's goals, financial means, and need for capital preservation (avoiding loss).

The Pendulum Swings

For the better part of three decades, most Americans rejected Graham and Dodd. Throughout the 1930s and 1940s and up through the late 1950s, Americans lived in fear of stocks. The views of Chamberlain and Hay pervaded common attitudes: Common stocks were too risky. They were too speculative. It was far better for nonwealthy families to put their money in savings banks and government bonds.[7]

Rather than intelligently discriminate among stocks—as Graham had recommended—to find those with good returns *and* a margin of safety, Americans in the main dismissed stocks as merely gambling. Besides, who could trust that gang of Wall Street sharpies? Weren't they the ones who in the late 1920s persuaded Americans to throw caution to the wind and reach for pie in the sky?[8]

The 1960s: Late 1920s Redux

Eventually, though, memories of the crash and the Great Depression began to fade. Throughout the 1950s, an increasing number of average Americans began to take the plunge. At the start of the fifties, only 6.5 million individuals (about 5% of the adult population) owned stocks. By 1960, that number had almost doubled to 12.5 million. What created this dramatic turnaround? Here are four important factors that seem to have contributed to the shift in the public mind (though, of course, stock owners still constituted only a small minority of the population).

1. *New record high*. On March 5, 1954, the Dow crossed 300 for the first time since 1929. Then on November 17, 1954, the Dow broke through 381 to establish a new record high—surpassing the former high set in September of 1929. To many, this event signaled another new era of continuing prosperity.
2. *Walter Winchell touts stocks*. During the early to mid-fifties, Walter Winchell was one of America's top-rated commentators. So when he began touting stocks on his national radio show, he put a buzz in the ear of the middle class.
3. *Rise of mutual funds*. In tandem with a nationally oriented Wall Street publicity campaign, mutual fund salespeople began to spread throughout the country to persuade Americans that they could get rich in stocks.[9]
4. *Eisenhower prosperity*. Although the 1950s experienced its share of economic ups and downs, Americans overall did feel optimistic and prosperous. Accordingly, the decade of the fifties closed with the Dow Jones Industrial Average (DJIA) at nearly 700—up more than threefold from its level of 175 in 1950.

Notwithstanding these positives, Graham saw ominous signs. After applying time-tested valuation principles, he thought the late 1950s' stock market overvalued. Like other value investors, he derided the fact that by 1959, cash dividend yields on stocks had fallen below benchmark bond yields.[10] By this time, though, too many investors were again willing to believe that old standards no longer applied. They jumped into stocks with both feet. Yet, although the sixties had some hot moments (the Dow briefly crossed 1,000 for the first time), the decade of the 1970s opened with the Dow just a wee bit higher than it had been at the end of 1962.[11]

Yet stock buyers of the 1960s (by 1969 more than 30 million strong) had not embraced Graham-Dodd principles. Instead, they went directly from the excessive Chamberlain-Hay fear of the 1930s, 1940s, and early 1950s to the greed and speculative fervor of the "go-go" years of the late 1960s (as they had in the late 1920s). In the mid- to late 1960s, many top- (and briefly) performing mutual fund managers were known as "gunslingers." This new breed of cowboy was not about to follow an old horse like Ben Graham. But when the bull that these cowboys had been riding stumbled, they fell to the ground.[12] It was Graham whose shrewd analysis had once again proved that *investment* (properly defined) beats speculation.

The Boom-Bust Repeats: The Early 1970s

In the last edition of his book *The Intelligent Investor*, Graham once again turned to the investor-speculator distinction that he had originally noted nearly 40 years earlier. On the opening page of his introduction, Graham wrote,

> No statement is more true and better applicable to Wall Street than the famous warning of Santayana: "Those who do not remember the mistakes of the past are condemned to repeat them." [This book] is directed to investors as distinguished from speculators, and our first task will be to clarify and emphasize this now all but forgotten distinction.[13]

At the time Graham wrote those words, he was reacting to the euphoric mantra of "good stocks can only go up" that once again had taken hold on Wall Street and throughout the United States. Since its then-recent slide in 1969–1970, the stock market by 1972 was on target to reach 1,500 by 1975—or so most stock pundits and stock buyers thought.

Yet once again Graham steadfastly maintained that business fundamentals still would not support such a high price level. The overall market price-to-earnings ratio (P/E) stood at 22, and some popular stocks were selling with P/E ratios of 40, 50, 60, or higher.[14] Graham wisely remarked that such historically lofty multiples weren't just discounting the future; they were discounting the hereafter. "Hence," he concluded in 1973, "the [current] market level remains the same as it was some 7 years ago—i.e., that it is unattractive from the standpoint of conservative investment." He then mused, "Can such heedlessness go unpunished?"[15]

Within months, Graham's reflective query was answered. In the bear attack of 1973–1974, stocks fell by 43%. The high mark of 1973 was not achieved again for another 10 years.[16]

After Inflation, Big Losses

Although the stock market seemed as though it was going to march to a firm recovery in 1975, much of its gain soon evaporated. The market refused to advance to sustainable new heights. In fact, in 1982 the stock market sat below the 1000 level that it had briefly reached 16 years earlier in 1966.[17]

Adding insult to injury, this continuing poor performance of the stock market vanquished the longstanding Wall Street promise that stocks would protect shareholders against losses due to inflation. In inflation-adjusted dollars, the 1982 market level was not just below that of the 1960s—it was now below the level of 1928.

The Death of Equities

The popular mood against stocks (and toward real estate) had become so widespread by 1979 that *Business Week* ran a now-famous cover story entitled "The Death of Equities." To show how far public sentiment has now shifted from those dark days of 1979, consider these telling passages from that *Business Week* article:

- "The masses long ago switched from stocks to investments having higher yields and more protection from inflation. . . . Now [even] the pension funds have quit stocks for real estate. The death of equities looks like an almost permanent condition—reversible someday, but not soon."[18]

- "The problem is not merely that there are 7 million fewer shareholders today [1979] than in 1970. Younger investors [i.e., baby boomers] in particular are avoiding stocks."[19]
- "Wall Street has learned that there are more profitable things to sell than stocks, among them, options, futures, and real estate . . . "[20]
- "A decade ago [1969], the entire equity market was perceived as an inflation hedge. In the early 1970s, large growth stocks, especially the 'nifty fifty,' were in vogue as inflation fighters—until the 1974 recession dealt them a blow from which they have yet to recover."[21]
- "Today, the old attitude of buying solid stocks as a cornerstone for one's life savings and retirement has simply disappeared."[22]

Imagine: On the eve of the greatest bull run in U.S. history, relatively few wanted to own stocks. Real estate—and even gold, diamonds, and artwork—were judged superior to stocks. How sharp the contrast with recent attitudes. The almost uncontested view has been that "stocks for the long run" provide the best and safest cornerstone for one's savings and retirement. Even more astonishing, few of today's stock enthusiasts acknowledge that this same song has played many times before—only to end on very sour notes.

The Lessons of History

These quotations from *Business Week*, as well as the earlier stock market history, serve to emphasize three critical issues:

1. *Lessons of history*. Value investors must learn and then never forget the lessons of history. As Ben Graham instructed, the stock market has always swung back and forth like a pendulum. Excessive expectations periodically morph into dismal outlooks—and vice versa.
2. *Public moods*. Value investors must always remain alert to detect the public's manic or depressive moods. Each can signal, respectively, a warning of speculative fervor or true investment opportunity.
3. *Price matters*. Whether buying stocks, real estate, or other assets, value investors never accept market price (whether reflected by

expert opinion or popular sentiment) as the ultimate answer to the question of value.

As Graham and Dodd wrote, "The 'new-era' doctrine that 'good stocks' were sound investments regardless of how high the price paid for them—was at bottom only a means of rationalizing under the title of 'investment' the well-nigh capitulation to the gambling fever."[23] Extending this foundation point, Graham and Dodd wrote,

> The [investment] price is an integral part of every complete judgement. . . . In the field of common stocks the necessity of taking price into account is compelling because the danger of paying the wrong price is almost as great as buying the wrong issue. . . . [The] new-era theory of investment left price out of the reckoning, and this omission was of most disastrous consequences. . . . An investment in the soundest enterprise may be made on unsound and unfavorable terms.[24]

With respect to real estate—which, too, has suffered its downs and enjoyed its ups—Graham and Dodd illustrated the same point:

> The value of urban real estate has tended to grow steadily over a long period of years; hence it came to be regarded by many as the "safest" medium of investment. But the purchase of [an interest in] a New York City real estate development in 1929 might have involved *terms* of investment so thoroughly disadvantageous as to banish all elements of soundness from the proposition.[25]

Yet today, Graham and Dodd's most unarguable thesis—that price matters because investment markets routinely swing between gloom and boom—is seldom heard from the stock enthusiasts. To invest wisely and profitably, they say, you need learn only two words: buy stocks. Then hold for the long term.[26] Even worse, this overcrowded train of expert opinion dismisses real estate as inferior to stocks—without any point-by-point comparison of the *relative terms of investment* that now exist. The stock enthusiasts have decided that at all prices, in all times, and in all places, stocks not only outperform real estate, they outperform all other types of investment.

Long before Ben Graham, the Roman philosopher Cato the Elder spoke of the damage caused in mistaking investment for speculation:

> There must certainly be a vast Fund of Stupidity in Human Nature, else men would not be caught as they are, a thousand times over, by the same Snare, and while they yet remember past Misfortunes, they go on to embrace and encourage the Causes which will once again produce them.[27]

Such that you might choose the road less traveled—and consequently reap the rewards that evade the many—let's travel further into the philosophy of value investing.

All Investing Is Value Investing

Contrary to near universal misconception, Graham did not intend to father a school of value investing. Rather, he promoted a way of thinking, a discipline of analysis, that has become known as value investing. So what's the difference? Why does it matter? As you will soon see, the difference is critical, and it matters a great deal for us as individuals and as a nation.

The Difference

Recall that when Graham and Dodd wrote *Security Analysis*, in part they were trying to clear up a semantic confusion. They wanted to create a definition and methodology that would distinguish investment from speculation and gambling. Caught up in the euphoria of the late 1920s, too many people were taking uncharted risks as they sailed into stocks priced far above any historical standards of value.

Yet these stock buyers thought of themselves as investors. When they were subsequently wiped out, they were shell-shocked. Rather than face the fact that they were stock operators (as opposed to investors), they abandoned the market wholesale. Echoing Chamberlain and Hay, they concluded that the stock market was no place for investors. And for the rest of their lives, many never returned. Plus, even more tragic, perhaps, millions of other Americans who may have safely profited from stocks in the 1930s and 1940s were too scared to venture forward. Moreover, the nation needlessly languished in the Great Depression. A steadily advancing market during that period most certainly would have buoyed spirits and sparked the economy.

No, in writing *Security Analysis* and, later, *The Intelligent Investor*, Graham never intended to create a specialized school of investing called value investing. Instead, he aimed to educate, inform, and alert people to the universal criteria by which all true investments should be judged.

Not surprisingly, Graham failed to win the semantic battle. The term investment is misused today more than ever. Perhaps that's why Graham supposedly remarked, not long before his death, that, quite likely, "I have been the most read, yet least followed analyst on Wall Street." True or not, this quotation certainly reflects a truism. Even with value investing back in vogue, Graham's metrics of valuation hold little power.

Why It Matters

As philosophers and historians are wont to remind us, speculation can easily turn to calamity. Mass speculation can easily turn to mass calamity. Often, only those relatively few who foresee and prepare emerge whole (and possibly enriched). Perversely contrary to Graham's intent, his painstaking efforts to differentiate investing from more speculative techniques of making money are now mostly forgotten.

Instead, his insights, his careful calculations and contemplations, and his important warnings are either ignored or pigeonholed as just another style of investing called value investing—a term he never used and would have rejected, at least in its current usage. Without a doubt, the term value investing now works against Graham's purposes in that the "value" modifier seems to admit the equal validity of many different styles of investing.

Thus, we see all types of speculation masquerading as growth investing, dot-com investing, momentum investing, long-term investing, emerging markets investing, options investing, commodities investing, and an endless variety of others. To understand the confused and varied use of the term investing, look at these quotations taken from a recent *Wall Street Journal* special section on mutual fund performance (italics added for emphasis):[28]

- "The stock market has become a little less treacherous . . . but *investors* still couldn't be sure that stocks they picked one day wouldn't blow up the next."
- "The days of *investing* blindly in technology stocks and then coming up with winners are becoming a distant memory."
- "Let's face it, *investing* is complicated. If it were easy, all of those day traders would still be in business."
- "Some people think *investing* in the stock market is just another form of gambling."

So, even today, people still speak of treacherous investing, blind investing, day-trader investing, and investing as placing a bet or "gambling." The two dangers that Graham and Dodd first explored in 1934 still persist: First, lacking clear distinctions and methodology, far too many would-be investors fool themselves. They put their monies into speculation, gambling, and touted high-fliers. Yet because they refer to all of these ventures and schemes as investing, they dramatically understate risks while magnifying expected rewards. Second, extremely safety-conscious savers dismiss all (or nearly all) stocks, corporate bonds, real estate, and other potential investment media. These fearful folks buy a house, put savings in CDs or whole-life insurance policies, and perhaps accumulate some U.S. government bonds. With a broad brush they sweep other types of investments into a basket called gambling.

If this were 40 years ago, these mistakes of aggression or retreat wouldn't matter so much. Back then, most long-term employees could count on Social Security and employer (defined-benefit) pensions to see them through retirement. Personal savings (or investments) were merely icing on the cake. With company pensions and Social Security far less certain today, however, investment mistakes can easily make the difference between a later life of joy, comfort, and adventure versus one of penny-pinching and borderline destitution.

Are These Fears Realistic?

For the very reasons cited previously, studies routinely show that most Americans are not on track to safely and securely build wealth for retirement and the other good things that life can offer. "401(k) Accounts Are Losing Money: Investors' Errors Cited," headlines a recent *New York Times* front-page story.[29] The article reports, "Over the last decade, many people have grown overly dependent on stocks; do not contribute enough to retire when they expect; and place too much money in aggressive mutual funds or their own company's stock. . . . Others often with the most ability and longest time frames to withstand market shocks put too much in conservative investments such as G.I.C.s (guaranteed investment contracts), government bonds, and money market accounts."[30]

The Grand Experiment

During our late bull market, it didn't matter much where you placed your money. Account balances just seemed to magically grow larger. But with the shakeout of 2000–2001, experts and investors alike are rethinking their financial planning and favored investments.

"You could be stupid in the last ten years and still make a lot of money," says Continental Air pilot Mark Briggs in the previously cited *New York Times* article. But after losing 35% of his retirement savings, Briggs faces reality and admits, "Now you've got to buckle down and start learning all over again." Or maybe he should say, "Buckle down and begin to learn for the first time."[31] Data supplied by the Employee Research Benefits Council make perfectly plain that when it comes to *investing*, few Americans (including many who believe otherwise) really understand what they are doing, let alone what they really need to be doing to sensibly prepare for the future.

That's why William McNabb, who supervises retirement services for the Vanguard family of funds, muses forlornly, "Whether people have enough money when they retire is going to be the critical issue in determining whether this experiment [in personal financial responsibility] has worked."[32] Thus far, much evidence points to the high chance of failure.

What Is to Be Done?

To escape from this potential calamity, what can you do to protect against loss as well as safely and surely build wealth? First, as an intelligent investor, you must thoroughly understand the distinction between investing and other efforts to make money. You must come to understand that, properly understood, all true investing is value investing.

Second, you must learn to evaluate and select investments that will give you the best performance. Not just in terms of individual stocks, bonds, or properties, but perhaps even more importantly in terms of categorical asset allocation (stocks, bonds, real estate, life insurance products, money market accounts, etc.). You must abolish the foolish and self-contradicting idea that over the long run stocks will outperform all other types of investment.

Value Investing: Briefly Explained

In capitulation to contemporary practice, I will continue to use the term value investing. But once again I emphasize that Graham spoke of "investing," not "value investing." Thus, he defined investing as follows: "An investment operation is one which upon thorough analysis promises safety of principal and an adequate return."[33] In short, then, you can see that conducting an investment operation, requires (1) thorough analysis, (2) preservation of capital, and (3) an attractive yield.

Thorough Analysis

As a value investor, you must conduct a thorough analysis of the asset and the asset classification. Graham gave no quarter to fads, momentum, technical analysis, hunches, tips, broker recommendations, media touts, or any type of new-era rationalizations.

If you tend to jump on bandwagons, your chances for success are slim. If you merely follow what other people tell you, prepare to be led to slaughter. If you like to make quick decisions based on hunches or intuition, you are doomed as a value investor. If you want to reap the kinds of rewards gained by such famous value investors as Warren Buffet, John Templeton, John Neff, and, of course, Graham himself (who reputedly was earning $600,000 per year at age 23 in 1915), you must prepare to work for it.

As a value investor, you will run away from anyone who promises you easy profits if you just adopt their "surefire" system. That goes double for any system that's supposedly easy, simple, fast, and risk-free—for example, the no-money-down real estate courses pitched on late-night cable channels. Of course, those who do promise easy, simple, fast, and risk-free know the minds of their potential buyers. They know what most people want to hear. But the fact that most people hate thinking, studying, and making a concerted effort is what opens the door to superior profits for value investors.

Preservation of Capital (the Margin of Safety)

"Confronted with a challenge to distill the secret of investment into three words, we venture the motto MARGIN OF SAFETY," wrote Graham.[34] Essentially, this "motto" means that the price you pay for an asset must always lie significantly below its appraised value or, alternatively, its indicated (intrinsic) value. The price must be fully grounded in reason and experience. Likewise, imprudent borrowing to finance acquisitions vanquishes the margin of safety.

Reason and Experience

"A true margin of safety," writes Graham, "is one that can be demonstrated by figures, by persuasive reasoning, and by reference to a body of actual experience."[35] If you cannot justify current value based on proven figures previously demonstrated, then you are speculating (or worse).

When you pay for castles in the air, for dreams over reality, for sunny expectations that have never before been realized, you permit hope to triumph over experience. With both stocks and real estate, buyers again and again mistakenly forecast appreciation, earnings growth, or both at excessive rates that bear no relation to history or reason.

In stark contrast, value investors never pay for acorns at oak tree prices.

Dangerous Borrowing

There's no faster way to lose your capital than to pay (and especially overpay) for an asset with highly (dangerously) levered funds. In fact, Graham said, "In our conservative view, every nonprofessional who [borrows to buy stocks] is *ipso facto* speculating, and it is his broker's duty to so advise him."[36] (Of course, brokers seldom honor this duty, for to so advise would reduce margin fees and trading commissions.)

In real estate, obviously, borrowing purchase money is widely practiced and eminently sensible—*if a margin-of-safety rule is followed.* Yet realty investors routinely violate this stricture. That's why "get rich quick" when coupled with "nothing down" so often leads to financial ruin.

Indeed, the Texas real estate crash of the late 1980s proved nothing about the merits of real estate as an investment. Rather, it laid out proof as to how excessive expectations (those formulated during the oil boom years) when financed with leverage of 100% (or more) will most certainly bring about a speculative collapse.

Nothing destroys wealth building faster than a loss of capital. So, first and foremost, preserve your capital. Always secure a margin of safety. Though this would seem a basic, commonsense rule, it is one that investors regularly violate with reckless abandon—much to their regret.

Attractive Return

Obviously, if you were exclusively interested in preserving capital, your investment portfolio would include only the recently created, inflation-protected U.S. government bonds. Unfortunately, though, at a real rate of return of less than 4%, these bonds won't do much to help you build wealth. For that you need a much more attractive rate of return.

Yet it's not just the rate of return that value investors must consider. They must study as well the source of the return and its reasonable certainty.

Earning Power

Graham wanted investments to show a history of strong earnings and cash dividends. In both *Security Analysis* and *The Intelligent Investor*, he warned investors to avoid paying for pie-in-the-sky promises of earnings growth. If current earnings and dividends aren't enough to provide an attractive rate of return, then chances are your expected attractive return will never be realized.

Obviously, the buyer binge for tech stocks and, even more so, the dot-coms (or, as some wag remarked insightfully, the dot-*cons*), proved Graham's point. When you forgo current earnings and dividends for a future bonanza, you're not investing. Though on occasion your bet may pay off, more than likely it won't.

Reasonable Certainty

If you pay now for a future yield that fails to materialize, you not only lose income, but in addition the value of your asset will plummet. At one point, Amazon.com shares sold at more than $400. At that price, Amazon was valued far more highly than Borders, Books-A-Million, and Barnes and Noble combined. The amounts of future earnings necessary to support such a stratospheric valuation were not even within the realm of possibility, let alone reason. Naturally, as Amazon repeatedly failed to meet its profit-and-growth targets, its stock price went into a free fall.

In real estate, you can see similar results (although never of the same magnitude) when buyers expect to see—year after year—annual rent increases and appreciation rates of 6%, 8%, 10%, or 12%. Before the collapse of the Texas bubble in the 1980s, many foolish condo buyers were expecting an unbelievable 16% per year rate of appreciation—even though then-current market rent levels wouldn't cover even 60% of the monthly mortgage payment on a typically financed condo unit.

If you want a margin of safety, don't pay high prices for unattractive current yields. Such a rule does mean that you will miss the run-ups that occur during speculative frenzies. But it also means that you avoid major losses. As Graham repeatedly emphasized, value investors hate big losses far more than they love big gains. Big losses can set you back years. But even with modest wins, you still survive to continue building toward the future you want.

Value Investing versus Other Methods of Investing

As a universal principle, neither Graham nor Chamberlain and Hay had anything against speculation or other expenditures such as gambling, taking a flier, or even consumer spending. What they objected to was the failure of people to see a clear distinction among these various types of outlays such that they could consciously budget for them according to their needs, wants, and goals.

In addition, they condemned the stock enthusiasts, real estate promoters, life insurance salesmen, Madison Avenue slickers, and other hypesters and hucksters who lure people into tempting schemes. Rather than upfront disclosure, these various mountebanks entice with the purr word investment.

Value investors don't fall for such misrepresentations. Nor do they lie to themselves. On occasion they may take a flier on a hot stock, spend an hour at the roulette wheel, or splurge on a new car. But they know they're not investing. And they certainly don't risk the money they're building up for college tuition or a worry-free retirement.

Speculation

"There is intelligent speculation," said Graham, "as there is intelligent investing. But there are many ways that speculation may prove to be unintelligent. Of the foremost are these: (1) speculating when you think you are investing; (2) speculating seriously instead of as a pastime, when you lack proper knowledge and skill for it; and (3) risking money in speculation that you can ill afford to lose."[37]

The Intelligent Speculator

To speculate intelligently, you usually put up a sum of money for a position that you would like to pay a big return. But you also must be able to reasonably calculate the odds. Otherwise you can't know whether the hoped-for reward will outweigh the probable loss.

For example, assume you learn that a new high-tech manufacturing company is considering a building site near some farmland that's for sale. The farm's owner (who knows about the potential plant) is firm on his price of $2,500 per acre. As a farm, the land is worth $1,000 an acre. If the plant is built, you can sell the land to a subdivision developer for $20,000 an acre. The odds are 5 to 1 against this site being chosen. Should you buy?

The Difficulty of Speculating Intelligently

Assuming you can easily afford the loss, you definitely should buy. Here are how the probabilities of loss and reward (per acre) compute:

Expected value of reward (per acre)
20% (1 out of 5 chance) × $20,000 = $4,000

Expected value of loss (per acre)
80% (4 out of 5 chance) × ($2,500 – $1,000, or $1,500) = $1,200

According to the odds, this speculation is worth the high risk of loss. The expected payoff from winning greatly exceeds the amount of expected loss. But where do these odds come from? How can you tell for sure the potential selling prices of the land? This example shows why speculating intelligently is so difficult. You must be able to accurately calculate the odds for a variety of possible outcomes. And you must be able to attach expected dollar values to each possible result.

If you're thinking about speculating, ask yourself whether you can reasonably fill in all of the blanks that need to be filled in. Over the long run, intelligent speculators such as hedge-fund billionaire George Soros make tons of money. Unfortunately, though, over both the short and the long run, very, very few people can match the speculative success rate of George Soros. (Moreover, if we compare the accumulated wealth of Soros, perhaps the world's most successful speculator, to that of Warren Buffet, the world's most successful value investor, Buffet's net worth trumps that of Soros at least 10-fold.)

Gambling

Unlike intelligent speculating, gambling is a negative-sum game. In the aggregate, gamblers lose. The house odds are stacked against them. Las Vegas obviously comes to mind as the perfect example. But playing the market, engaging in day trading and commodities trading, and buying futures contracts also represent forms of gambling. Absolutely no evidence supports the widely held belief that one can make money trading in and out of positions on a short-term basis.

Quite the opposite is true. Researchers have studied this topic exhaustively, and the result remains unambiguous: traders lose.[38] Lady luck may smile upon such traders from time-to-time, especially in a bull market. But trading fees, taxes, and expenses will likely eat up any profits that they may be fortunate enough to win temporarily.[39]

Taking a Flier

Intelligent speculators bet with the odds showing potential gain. In contrast, gamblers bet with history showing near-certain losses. In both cases, the probabilities of winning or losing can be (more or less) estimated. But some bets don't lend themselves to any type of reasonable calculation. In those cases, you might as well admit that you're taking a flier. Realistically (and honestly), you don't have a clue as to why any particular outcomes should be expected. Not surprisingly, some people mistakenly call this mindless activity investing.

Growth versus Value

Before we leave this topic of investing style, I must draw attention to the simpleminded way that most financial writers and investment commentators explain the supposed contest between value stocks and growth stocks. According to this prevailing view, value stocks are beaten down and bargain-priced. They typically show low P/E ratios. In contrast, growth stocks typically carry high P/E ratios of 40, 60, or even 100 or more. These stocks represent the companies that will push our economy into the future. Frequently, these rising stars are a good buy at almost any price. Thus, even without earnings, a growth stock can presumably show promise even at a price of 2, 4, or, in some cases, 10 times sales.

In point of fact, of course, during bull markets, most growth stocks fail to meet any sensible definition of investing. The term "growth investor" was coined merely to ostensibly justify rampant speculation, gambling, or taking a flier. On the other hand, though, value investors will certainly buy the stocks of growth companies—if those companies and their stock prices meet a good number of the historically based margin-of-safety valuation metrics. Indeed, to distinguish themselves from the growth fanatics, value investors had to coin the phrase "growth at a *reasonable* price."

Do not fall for modern-day semantics that attempt to position value versus growth. When you buy stocks or real estate, you either get good value or you don't. Potential growth (or the lack thereof) represents a variable that all investors should factor into their value equations. Growth investors either invest with a value orientation or they are not investing at all.[40]

Consumer Spending

Along with heeding Graham's advice that investors adequately distinguish true investing from speculation, gambling, and taking a flier, today's value investors must also not confuse spending with investing. A friend of mine, for example, recently bought a new Mercedes. When telling me about the car, he exclaimed, "I think it will be a good investment. These cars really retain their value."

Rationalizing Spending

Increasingly, advertisers and individuals justify spending as investment. Value investors never think of cars, jewelry, antique furniture, or any type of collectible as investments—no matter how good their resale value. At best, one might refer to such items as speculations or taking a flier.

But more often than not they're merely consumer spending. To call such items investments—and most sellers will certainly encourage you to do so—merely rationalizes spending that you (deep down) know stands contrary to good economic sense.

The Danger

"Never mingle your speculative and investment operations in the same account, nor in any part of your thinking," said Graham.[41] Why? Because only through investment can you safely and surely build wealth over time. When you mix up your thinking—and your money—within your separate accounts, chances are that you will underinvest, overspeculate, and spend unwisely.

Easy Mistake

I confess, I have made this mistake on more than a few occasions. Perhaps some details can help you spot similar confusion in your own thinking and spending. This particular mistake concerns "investing" in antique furniture.

In the early 1980s, a friend had been trying for six months to sell her 150-year-old dining room set at a price of $6,000. Yet her sales efforts had not met with success. Because she was preparing to move and needed money, she offered the furniture to me for the mere sum of $3,000. She persuaded me to believe that at such a bargain price, this antique set would make a great investment.

Of course, value investors love acquiring assets at prices less than their fair or intrinsic value. I bought. But no matter what I told myself at the time, that furniture was not an investment. At best, it represented some combination of taking a flier and mere consumer spending for furniture I really didn't need (although it did look magnificent).

Where I Went Wrong

Value investing requires first, a thorough analysis of the asset; second, a margin of safety; and third, an attractive return (preferably in terms of annual yield). Yet, like most people who forget to consciously and explicitly apply value investing rules to their investments, I erred in the following ways:

1. *No real knowledge of the asset.* At the time, I knew nothing about antique furniture. I just *assumed* that 150 years old meant very valuable. Later, I learned that color (light or dark), construction techniques, style, condition, geographic origin, type of wood, and so forth can affect the value of antique furniture by a magnitude of 10 or more.
2. *Undue reliance on others.* Value investors never merely accept facts from others without follow-up confirmation or verification. Instead, I simply accepted my friend's estimate of fair value. I do not accuse her of intentional deception. But due to sentimental attachment and subjective valuation, she certainly did not qualify as a knowledgeable, disinterested appraiser.
3. *Ignored facts.* Had I truly been investing in this antique furniture, I would have paid more attention to the fact that after six months of efforts, my friend had not been able to sell it. So why should I reasonably conclude that my sales methods could work where hers had failed?
4. *No current yield.* This "investment" produced no annual income. To compensate for this loss, the furniture would have to yield a strong and near certain rate of appreciation over my holding period. Yet I made no such calculations and had no reasonable basis for doing so.

Opportunity Cost

Some readers may puzzle over the preceding example. What does buying antique furniture have to do with value investing, let alone value investing in real estate?

The answer is twofold. First, my mistakes are repeated by investors across a full spectrum of assets. Forewarned is forearmed. And second, unwise acquisitions (or consumer spending) don't just cost money out-of-pocket. More importantly, you will lose the gains you would have achieved had you value *invested* your money in the first place. Economists call these losses opportunity costs. You should not choose your investments (or your spending) without first taking a hard look at the question, "Can I locate a more productive use for this money?"

In this sense, "productive" means yielding a more attractive return while still maintaining an adequate margin of safety. Value investors don't look for just a positive return. They look for the best return they can get for any given level of risk.

Profit as Loss

After 15 years of on-and-off selling efforts, I finally sold that antique dining room set for $3,750. In one sense, I did enjoy a $750 profit. But when this investment is measured in terms of opportunity costs, my losses amounted to perhaps tens of thousands of dollars. Imagine the true investment opportunities that were available in 1982. The stock market offered a myriad of bargains. Government bonds were paying 13%. Or I could have put that $3,000 toward the down payment on a rental house or condo. Any of these alternatives would have provided a more productive use for those funds.

$3,000 Is Not the Point

Of course, I haven't detailed this mistake to bemoan the unproductive use and lost rewards of a mere $3,000. The point is that most Americans routinely embrace unproductive speculation, gambling, and consumer spending (not to mention massive unproductive borrowing). Sure, a few hundred dollars here, a few thousand there, when viewed as individual outlays, don't seem like much. But when viewed collectively in the full glory of passed-by opportunities, these amounts total a fortune. Properly planted, acorns do grow into oak trees.

Value Investing: The Triumph of Reason over Hope

To paraphrase the esteemed Dr. Johnson, value investing represents the triumph of reason over hope; the triumph of experience over illusion; and the triumph of winners over losers. Mathematical laws dictate that among the 60 to 80 million or so Americans now investing for family goals, financial security, retirement, and the ability to live a later life of comfort and adventure, a large majority must end up disappointed. At any realistic rate of growth, the economy will not (and cannot) yield anywhere near enough bounty to create comfortable wealth for all who are pursuing it.

The Wealthy Minority

If you really do want to join the wealthy minority of successful investors, you can't merely pursue the commonplace. Average won't do it. You must become a thinking investor, and that means becoming not only a value investor but also a value spender and a value borrower. All too often, Americans fail as investors not just because of bad investments per se. Rather it's because they fail to control their spending and their borrowing. Obviously, before you can invest successfully, you must have money to invest. Accordingly, value investors don't just spend and borrow, then invest whatever happens to be left over. They first decide how much money they will need to set aside to reach their long-term goals. Then, after securely placing that amount into their investments, they budget the remainder of their funds for consumer spending, speculation, or gambling.

As an example, Warren Buffet, the world's foremost value investor, with a net worth in excess of $40 billion, still lives with his wife of 50 years in the relatively modest home they bought in Omaha, Nebraska, back in 1958—a home bought for around $25,000 and now worth around $250,000. Throughout his life, Mr. Buffet has proved to be not only the consummate value investor, but also a consummate value spender and borrower.

Age-Old Question: Stocks, Bonds, or Real Estate?

In *Security Analysis*, Graham and Dodd emphasized, "It is unsound to think always of investment character as inhering in an issue *per se*. The price [i.e., potential yield] is frequently an essential element, so that a stock (and even a bond) may have an investment merit at one price level but not another."[42]

In other words, no specific class of investment always proves superior to any other. The value investor must always weigh price, yield, and risk to discover the relative merits of one investment vis à vis other possibilities.

Yet today, far too many stock enthusiasts—and far too many unknowing investors—continue to falsely believe that stocks always can be counted on to outperform all other types of investments. The notion is nonsense. All asset classes enjoy days in the sun as well as days rocked by storms and freezing winds.

Bad Outlook for Stocks?

In 1965, Graham warned people against loading their portfolios with stocks. After moving through some calculations, he concluded,

> The above arithmetic indicates a much lower rate of advance in the stock market than was realized between 1949 and 1964. That rate had averaged a good deal better than 10 percent and was quite generally regarded as a sort of guarantee that similarly satisfactory results could be counted on in the future.
>
> Few people were willing to consider seriously the possibility that the high rate of advance in the past [1949–1964] means that stock prices are now [1965] too high, and hence that, the wonderful results since 1949 would imply not *very good*, but *rather bad* results for the [foreseeable] future.[43]

Could not the same thing be said for our market today?[44] Do you wish to *bet* your future prosperity on the belief that the average annual returns of more than 15% experienced between 1982 and 2000 will on average continue for the next 10, 15, or 20 years? Do you confidently believe that you can achieve average annual stock market returns of even 10% or 12%?

Isn't there at least some nontrivial chance that we will see returns more similar to the period of 1964–1982—when, after accounting for taxes and inflation, stock market returns fell into negative territory?[45] (In other words, about the same level of miserable return that I realized on my antique dining room set?)

Opportunities in Real Estate

"The outright ownership of real estate has long been considered as a sound long-term investment, carrying with it a goodly amount of protection against inflation," wrote Graham in the last edition of *The Intelligent Investor*.[46] After these few words of praise, Graham then expressed the need for knowledge (i.e., thorough analysis) before buying. In the end, though, he excused himself from further discussion of the subject by noting, "This, too, is not our field."[47]

Yet the principles of value investing laid down in *Security Analysis*, *The Intelligent Investor*, and Graham's other writings clearly can be applied to real estate, just as they can be applied to stocks, bonds, or any other investment. Even better, once we cut through the contemporary hype surrounding "stocks for the long run," you will see that the principles of value investing dramatically favor real estate over stocks. In terms of current price, yield, and risk, real estate wins as a value investment—the safest and surest way to build wealth in today's investment climate.

Chapter 2

The Case Against Stocks for Retirement

Perhaps the most difficult challenge facing Americans is to realize—actually and consciously—that to assure their financial future, they must actively and intelligently begin to set and achieve financial objectives. Studies by life insurance companies, pension councils, universities, government agencies, and investment firms all point to the same universal conclusion: A majority of Americans (1) fail to invest enough, (2) fail to invest sensibly, and (3) fail to come to grips with the first two items in this list.[1]

The Dire Results

If Americans do not remedy these failures, as many as 7 out of 10 households will fall substantially short of their retirement income needs, wants, and expectations. Certainly, as a reader of this book, you stand a cut above the majority. Nevertheless, experience does show that for every person who reads a how-to book, 80% fail to act on what they've learned.

In many ways, I do not want to just alert and inform; I also want to inspire and motivate you to take action now. In just 20 years, the age wave will place almost 40% of the U.S. population into the 55-or-over category.[2] Though this spectacular growth of seniors may do wonders for membership in AARP, it also will create a degree of financial uncertainty that we have never had to deal with before.

Stocks for the Long Run: The Current Drug of Millions

As briefly explained in Chapter 1, even many Americans who believe that they are following a sure and safe path to financial security are bound to fail. These tens of millions of people are unthinkingly imbibing that intoxicating elixir called "stocks for the long run." In fact, this prescription for building wealth has been and continues to be dosed out in numbers exceeding those for the miracle drugs Prozac and Viagra.

Yet contrary to the claims of so-called financial experts, the efficacy of "stocks for the long run" is still open to serious doubt. Those who swallow this drug must understand that they are the guinea pigs in an experiment that may prove fatal. As I will show, "stocks for the long run" may likely prove hazardous to both your wealth and your well-being.

Old Prescription, New Container

Although many investors may not recognize his name, Jeremy Siegel, a Wharton School professor of finance, has dispensed for the masses a prescription that was previously issued in 1924. In Siegel's book, *Stocks for the Long Run*, this professor claims that "the total return on equities [common stocks] dominates [exceeds] all other assets."[3] Therefore, he unabashedly and enthusiastically tells the world, "It is within the grasp of *all* investors to avoid the pitfalls of investing [short-term trading, failure to diversify] and reap the *generous* rewards that are *only* available in equities" (italics added).[4]

If you've read any articles or books on investing, or even if you've only looked through the brochures and reports of your mutual fund, 401(k), or 403(b) account, you've undoubtedly been exposed to this popular idea. In fact, in the months after September 11, 2001, this advice became even more pressing as many financial planners and mutual funds tried to persuade their clients and customers to stay the course in stocks.[5] Now the question is: Do you believe it? You shouldn't. "But if it's not true," you may ask, "How did 'stocks for the long run' become the most accepted cliché of the day?"

A Huge Profit-Generating Idea Backed by Authority

Siegel's phrase "stocks for the long run" has become the most accepted cliché of the day for two related reasons (neither of which tests the soundness of his conclusion):

1. *High stature*. Siegel is a professor who holds high stature in the field of finance. *Business Week* has called him "America's No. 1 equities expert."[6]
2. *Conventional wisdom*. As a result of Siegel's status, his work has been cited favorably and authoritatively in literally thousands of books, articles, speeches, commentaries, promotional brochures, television shows, and other media outlets. Without a doubt, in the fields of investment, financial planning, and personal finance, his work has become *the* conventional wisdom. And why not? If you can rely on a prestigious professor to support your firm's quest for profits, go for it.[7]

As (presumably) an idea whose time has come, "stocks for the long run" now ranks as the sales promotion of choice for a plethora of mutual funds, stockbrokers, 401(k) advisors, and innumerable financial magazines and newsletters. This idea has generated more profits for the financial services and financial publications industry than any other idea in history. Even many of those in politics are using Siegel's conclusions to sell their political agenda (i.e., private stock accounts in lieu of Social Security).

In *The Intelligent Investor*, Ben Graham wrote, "There are no sure and easy paths to riches on Wall Street or anywhere else."[8] Siegel, as he has been popularly interpreted, argues just the opposite. Want to get rich? The answer is easy. Just continue to buy stocks. Hold through thick and thin. And in 20 years—at most 30—you will achieve wealth. In fact, more wealth than you could have achieved through any other way.[9]

With such a simple and appealing message, you can see why "stocks for the long run" has become far more popular than Graham's advocacy of value investing, which requires work. The Siegel approach demands no applied intelligence, no thinking, no real effort, and virtually no risk. Merely accept the prescription, take your medicine regularly (monthly deposits in a stock fund), and you will emerge rich.

But before you swallow this supposed sure and simple cure for financial need, take a close and critical look at Siegel's advocacy and, yes, also his caveats.[10] Before you pass up investing in real estate in favor of "the lazy man's way to riches," let's return to the 1920s. You may find it surprising to learn that this idea—as popularly interpreted and promoted by stock enthusiasts—helped create the 1929 stock market crash and the ensuing Great Depression.

Common Stocks as Long-Term Investments

Before Jeremy Siegel was born, Edgar Lawrence Smith wrote a highly influential book entitled *Common Stocks as Long-Term Investments*.[11] Smith, a prominent financier in that former period of prosperity, wanted to compare the relative risks and returns of stocks and bonds. In doing so, he asked two central questions:

1. Is it not possible that the association of speculation with common stocks has somewhat influenced a majority of investors against them, and has exaggerated in their minds the danger of possible loss to those who buy them for long-term investment?
2. Is it not possible that the definite weakness of otherwise perfectly safe bonds is overlooked—namely, that they cannot participate in the increasing [economic] activity of the country—that they are defenseless against a depreciating currency?[12]

As you might expect, Smith answered yes to both of these questions. Through a study of the stock and bond markets during various periods extending back to 1866, Smith told his readers,

> A well diversified investment in common stocks, held over a long period, may be counted on not only for a somewhat more than normal income return [dividend yield as compared to the then lower bond interest rates], but also for a definite increase in principal value. That this increase is not based upon speculative factors, but upon factors inherent in the nature of the security.[13]

Smith went on to explain that in formulating a principle of sound investment, even conservative investors and investment management companies should consider placing well-selected common stocks into their portfolios. Such stocks (although more volatile than bonds) would provide good protection against inflation over a term of years. "No one," Smith wrote, "may be regarded as having invested conservatively whose funds have suffered a permanent loss of real [inflation adjusted] as opposed to nominal value. This is the first requisite of conservatism."[14]

Dignified and Reasonable

In publishing his work, Smith maintained a dignified and reasonable approach. He simply wanted to modify the way most *professional* investors and investment managers then thought about stocks (speculative) and bonds (safe, conservative). Although one may quarrel with both his data and his methodology, overall Smith presented his argument effectively.[15] In sharp contrast to today's stock enthusiasts, Smith did not boldly promise wealth without risk. Nor did he in any way puff up the stock market to encourage millions of ordinary Americans to get rich in stocks.

Siegel Touts Smith (Unfairly)

In his effort to promote stocks, Siegel touts Smith unfairly. The gains from stocks "which accrue so assuredly to the long-term stockholder must be the center of most people's investment strategy," writes Siegel. "The doctrine that common stocks provide the best way to accumulate long-term wealth, first expounded by Edgar Lawrence Smith . . . has been reconfirmed in all [sic] subsequent research."[16]

Whenever favored ideas are pushed upon a generally uninformed and unknowledgeable public, advocates frequently enlist authorities of an earlier age to give them support. (Notice how many contemporary politicians of left and right claim that America's founding fathers would have endorsed a current pet political position.) When met with such an argument from history (especially when large sums of your money are at stake), never accept the contemporary advocate's version without checking the record for yourself. You will often find a distorted and unfair interpretation.

In the case at hand, here's what Edgar Lawrence Smith actually wrote:

> Bonds as a class have certain recognized attributes. A diversification of common stocks has its own attributes, which differ from those of bonds. Each class of investment has its useful purpose and its proper place in any investment plan.[17]

Smith was not expounding a doctrine. He did not tout stocks as the one best way to become wealthy. He was encouraging considered judgment. Stocks? Bonds? Don't jump to conclusions. Don't rely on conventional wisdom without a clear view of the actual facts. That was Smith's central message, and that is the message value investors should put into practice today.[18]

True, for the years Smith studied, and for the bonds and stocks he compared, stocks yielded higher returns. But in contrast to Siegel, Smith's writing was much more tentative and measured (i.e., dignified and reasonable). Smith did not even come close to Siegel's position that "stocks *must be* [italics added] the center of *most people's* [italics added] investment strategy."[19]

Nor did Smith write about the *best* way to accumulate long-term wealth. He studied only a narrow class of common stocks and bonds. Smith presented no "tests" (as he called his work) for real estate, collectibles, discounted bonds, discounted mortgages, business ownership, venture capital, or any other avenue that various wealth builders might travel.

Most importantly, perhaps, and unlike Siegel, Smith never claimed that *everyone* who follows his recommended investment program will most assuredly "reap generous rewards." For, as is befitting a reasonable man,

Smith never proposed any specific type of investment program that all investors should adopt.[20]

The Importance of Income and Inflation

In unfairly enlisting Smith to support his intemperate brand of stock advocacy, Siegel omits the two essential investment attributes that Smith stressed: (1) earn a good annual income and (2) protect capital against the ravages of inflation. Because real estate meets these two criteria far better than our current stock market, we will further discuss each of these criteria later. For now, just take notice of the enduring principles that Smith set forth. These two sober-minded Smithian principles go to the core of value investing.

1. Constancy of income
2. Safety of principal

Annual Income

"Constancy or regularity of income is placed first," writes Smith, "because it is the factor that is ordinarily considered to be most at hazard in common stocks as contrasted with bonds."[21] In specifying an income standard, Smith believed that over a period of years, "stocks may be relied upon to pay an annual income that averages more than the average [interest] rate available on commercial paper."[22]

In other words, Smith ranked stocks highly (relative to then prevailing opinion) because he discovered that dividend yields on stocks had significantly exceeded the rates of interest investors earned from corporate bonds. In fact, for all 12 of Smith's dividends versus interest tests, dividends proved to be the much larger sum.

Now compare those results to the present. The dividend yield on the S&P 500 has recently ranged between 1.20% and 1.40%. In contrast, investment-grade bonds currently pay interest of 5% to 7%.[23] The income standard that Smith applied has been obliterated. Few U.S. stocks today could pass Smith's income test.[24] Siegel never mentions this startling difference between Smith and his own advocacy of stock.

Safety of Principal

In addition to an attractive annual yield, recall that Smith argued, "No one may be regarded as having invested conservatively whose funds have suffered a permanent loss of real [inflation-adjusted] as opposed to nominal value."[25] Although in general, Smith's stocks showed nominal increases in values over the studied periods, their real inflation-adjusted values did not always keep pace. Unfortunately, his analysis (in contrast to his specified standard) tends to focus on nominal values. Thus, the careful reader is left in the dark on too many occasions.

Nevertheless, in terms of Smith's purposes, he does show that over all time periods that experienced inflation, a collection of well-selected stocks maintained (or increased) their market prices much better than bonds.

Relevance to Today

Although the future could prove me wrong, I would hazard to guess that *when compared to most bonds*, stocks will experience a greater rise in both their market prices and their inflation-adjusted prices—at least over a period of 10 to 20 years. Yet that does not mean you can count on stocks to meet the Smith standard. Since 1929, we have gone through several long periods when stock prices failed to keep up with inflation (e.g., 1929–1959, 1966–1992, and various other periods of somewhat shorter duration).

In addition, Smith's data showed that with regard to investing after an historically noteworthy rise, it can take quite an extended period (15 years or more) just to get even in nominal terms (e.g., 1929–1954). Thus, because we remain perched near the peak of the most astonishing stock price rise in U.S. history, should we not justifiably temper our expectations? Although Siegel raises that possibility, he nonetheless continues to urge stocks, stocks, and more stocks.

Relying on his distorted review of history and a distorted reading of Edgar Lawrence Smith, Siegel sticks to his guns: "My contacts with shareholders reveal a remarkable acceptance of the core thesis of my book: that stocks are the best and, in the long run, safest way to accumulate wealth. . . . It can easily be seen that the total return on equities dominates all other assets."[26]

Remarkable Indeed!

As noted earlier, it is necessary to critically evaluate Siegel's core thesis because as he justly remarks, that thesis has achieved a "remarkable acceptance." Remarkable indeed! In a span of less than a decade, Siegel (and his acolytes) have imprinted an idea into the minds of millions. And like most ideas that reflect conventional wisdom, most people blindly accept and recite Siegel's thesis as fact without even questioning its source, its factual foundation, its truth, or its applicability to current and expected economic and demographic conditions.

Recent Examples of Acceptance

To illustrate this point, here's just a brief sampling from among hundreds that I have recently read:

- "Based on the best available data and the opinions of experts I respect, I'll settle for 12 percent as the average annual return [on stocks]. . . . While the exact number may be in dispute, the point is conceded by all: No readily available asset—cash, real estate, bonds, or other asset classifications—has performed as well over the years as stocks."
- "Over the long term, stocks grow more and faster than other assets such as bonds, CDs, or real estate."
- "But let's not get carried away [about real estate]. All the mythology and all the statistics should not cloud the fact that, histori-

cally speaking, real estate hasn't appreciated nearly as quickly as large U.S. stocks. Even more significant, real estate—unlike stocks or bonds—demands an investment of not just money but time."

- "Over history, stocks have been the best place to grow your long-term savings [sic], returning on average 11 percent annually since 1926, as measured by the S&P 500" [sic] (The S&P 500 was not created until 1958. As to stocks as *savings*, my, how times and language have changed.)
- "It's time for stock investors to get used to normality. What's that? It means stocks will outperform all other assets over the long run—just not at the double-your-money rates of the late 1990s. . . . That's the view of America's No. 1 equities expert, University of Pennsylvania finance professor, Jeremy Siegel."[27]

And since September 11, 2001, the story remains the same:

- "The market since 1926 has returned an average of 11% per year and can serve as a pretty good forecast of what you can expect. . . . Hold stocks long enough and they become no more risky than bonds."[28]

I will discuss the termite-ridden foundation that supports the preceding quotations later. But for now, consider the strong implications for both stocks and real estate.

Self-Fulfilling Prophecy Becomes Self-Defeating

Without regard to truth, let's think about the consequences of the accepted belief that over the long-run, stocks will outperform all other assets. As this idea has taken hold, hundreds of billions of dollars have continued to flow into mutual funds. Even with the 2000–2001 slide, funds experienced a net outflow of money during just one month. Even after September 11,

2001, investors pulled very little money out of stocks. So for the time being, this belief is working as a self-fulfilling prophecy. The more it is accepted and recited by rote, the more it appears to create the result it is intending to predict.

Good News for Real Estate

That's good news for people who would like to begin investing in real estate. Why? First, because this relative lack of public attention makes good real estate values easier to find. Second, it almost guarantees that at some point, the stock market Ponzi scheme will falter. When that occurs, investors who have gained a strong base in real estate will see their properties' values shoot up as fleeing stock investors seek a safer haven for their money.[29] Not just a safer haven, though—a haven where they can earn a decent annual income for their investment dollars.

The Self-Defeating Prophecy

In 1924, when Edgar Lawrence Smith first published *Common Stocks as Long-Term Investments*, the book achieved moderate sales in the investment community, favorable reviews (including one by Keynes, no less), and scant attention from the general public. Later, though, as the stock market began to soar in the late 1920s, stock touters began to (mis)quote the book, using its findings to justify stocks for everyone. Eventually, however, the imagined possibility of everyone getting rich in stocks—especially on borrowed money—met hard reality. Stock prices collapsed. Outsized expectations dissolved. "Stocks for the long run" had become a self-defeating prophecy.

In (unfairly) blaming Smith, Graham and Dodd wrote,

> The self-deception of the mass speculator must, however, have its element of justification. . . . In the new-era bull market . . . [There is] a small and rather sketchy volume [which was used to encourage the masses]. The book is entitled *Common Stocks as Long Term Investments*.[30]

Another respected author also conducting postmortems on the 1929 crash wrote, "The 'boom psychology' was everywhere in evidence. No doubt the [Smithian] 'common stock theory' gave even the outright speculator the feeling that his actions were based upon the solid rock of scientific finding."[31]

One can only wonder: After some future wide-scale stock market disappointment, will Jeremy Siegel's book become the touchstone of postmortem critique? I don't know. But today's investors should remember the lessons of history. Not only can prophecies fulfill themselves; when followed mindlessly by tens of millions of people, they can also bring about their own defeat when those tens of millions realize that they will never reach the promised land.

The Total Return

Nearly every so-called expert in financial planning and personal investments accepts the Siegel thesis that over time stocks have earned (and can be expected to earn) a higher total return than all other assets—including real estate. Although the precise rate of return varies according to how long the stocks were held and the specific years studied, most writers quote a figure in the range of 11% to 12%.

Strangely, such figures dramatically misstate the real gains that actual stock investors have received. True, some astute (or lucky) speculators have earned far more. So too have professional value investors such as Ben Graham, Warren Buffet, John Neff, and John Templeton.[32] But the great majority of stock investors have undoubtedly pocketed far less.

Why Is the Rate of Return So Important?

Most people who buy and sell stocks do *not* keep tabs on the rate of return their monies are earning. Whether inside or outside a retirement plan, they mistakenly focus on how much their account balances are growing (or shrinking, as occurred during 2000–2001).

Yet this focus on year-to-year dollar balances instead of rate of return creates a big problem. Unless you know the annual stock market return you can reasonably expect to earn over time, you can't possibly know whether you will accumulate enough money. When accumulating stocks for retirement—or some other longer-term financial goal—your success or failure will relate directly to your rate of return.

Compare the Results

The figures in Table 2.1 show why rate of return can mean the difference between standing in line for food stamps and booking trips to Europe on the Concorde. In this table you can see the enormous differences between the lowest yearly rate of return (3%) and the highest rate (15%). To illustrate: Say you deposit $2,500 per year at 3% over a period of 20 years. You would accumulate $67,175 ($2,500 × 26.87). If instead you had earned 15% on your annual investments over 20 years, you would have accumulated $256,000 (2,500 × 102.4). Over an investment period of 30 years, the difference between accumulations at 3.0% and 15.0% rates of return grows far larger: $118,925 (3%) versus $1,086,750 (15%). As you can see from this simple example, the rate of return you earn on your annual stock investments will dramatically affect the amount of your total accumulations.

Now do your own calculations. How much do you plan to invest each year? What rate of return can you confidently earn? What sum do you wish to accumulate? Simply multiply the amount of your annual investments by the appropriate figure in Table 2.1. You will need at least $3 to $5 million in stocks to provide a comfortable (not luxurious) retirement income if you want to retire within the next 15 to 30 years. Remember, you must allow for both inflation and income taxes. Of course, if you plan to liquidate your capital, you may need less. But drawing down capital presents grave risks. You may outlive your money.[33]

What Rate Is Reasonable?

The stock enthusiasts want you to believe that over the long term, you can reasonably expect to earn at least 9% and possibly 12% on your yearly

Table 2.1 Retirement Accumulations at Selected Rates of Return

Years of Accumulation	*Rates of Return*				
	3%	*6%*	*9%*	*12%*	*15%*
15	18.59	23.27	29.36	37.28	47.58
20	26.87	36.79	51.16	72.05	102.4
25	36.46	54.86	84.7	133.3	212.7
30	47.57	79.06	136.3	241.3	434.7

Note: To discover estimated amounts of your accumulations, multiply the appropriate sums shown in the table by the amount of your annual contributions.

investments. (Most commonly, stock enthusiasts cite 11% as the near-guaranteed long-term return.) History, they say, supports this range. You can safely bank on it. Leaving aside the big difference in final results between the rates of 9% and 12% (especially over 30 years), you must decide whether you should really rely on such numbers. If the stock market will give you a safe and sure route to the financial future you want, why bother with owning real estate, wayward tenants, roof repairs, and stopped-up toilets?

Can You Really Count on 11%?

The great majority of financial planners and financial journalists agree that give or take a bit, over the long run the stock market has returned around 11% a year. Is it not amazing that a figure so tenuous should have gained such wide and unchallenged acceptance? But then again, maybe not. As the experience of the Beardstown Ladies proves, most people simply accept rate of return figures without question. You may recall the Beardstown Ladies—an investment club of "grandmas" from Beardstown, Illinois, who rose to celebrity status with their best-selling book (800,000 copies sold), *The Beardstown Ladies' Common Sense Investment Guide*.[34] The book's front jacket cover featured a group photo of these 60-ish-plus ladies, along with the bold caption,

**How We Beat the Stock Market—
and How You can, Too**

23.4% Annual Return

For the three years following their book's release, the Beardstown Ladies were engulfed in a whirlwind of activity and commendations: They generated hundreds of interviews, national television and radio appearances, and four or five publishing sequels and were the motivating force for thousands of new stock market investment clubs. They even signed a movie deal with Disney. Alas, though, the ladies had seriously erred.

Upon noticing a troubling inconsistency in the ladies' numbers, one enterprising reporter from *Chicago Magazine* asked a few embarrassing questions. Neither the ladies nor their publisher could satisfactorily answer. Price Waterhouse was brought in to redo the ladies' rate of return calculations. The verdict: Rather than masterfully beating the market, this celebrated investment club had underperformed miserably. During the great bull market of the 1980s and early 1990s, their investments had returned a mere 9.1%.[35]

Just imagine. For more than three years, these ladies attracted millions of readers, listeners, viewers, and followers. Major media kept on their heels. Yet only one person followed through to check their story. Now the next time someone throws a rate of return figure in your direction, remember the Beardstown Ladies. Ask, "How was the figure calculated? Does it make sense? Can I confidently rely on it?"

More often than not, you'll find that smart questions raise doubts. Questioning—even if you can't supply answers—forces you to think more clearly. That is certainly true of the 11% "stocks for the long run" number that, much like the Beardstown Ladies, has mischievously captivated Americans.

How Was the Figure Calculated?

That ubiquitous 11% stock market return figure assumes that, in 1926, you bought a portfolio of stocks with an original investment of, say, $1,000.

You then remained completely invested until 1999. During that period not only did you refuse to pull any money out of this account, but also you continued to reinvest all of your dividends. Furthermore, you never paid any brokerage fees, nor did you pay any taxes on your dividends or capital gains.

What specific stocks did you buy? Many experts claim that this stock portfolio is represented by the index for the S&P 500. Sounds good, except for two rather serious problems:

1. The S&P 500 wasn't created until 1958. Moreover, during the years since 1958, more than 1,300 companies have appeared in the index at one time or another.
2. For the years before 1958, researchers have chosen stocks or stock indexes according to the companies that you could have included in your portfolio had such a stock selection strategy been known to you.

In other words, researchers who perform stock rate of return calculations assume that you bought a large basket of diversified stocks in 1926 (or some other year such as 1802). Then, as some of your companies seemed to falter, and as other newer, more promising companies came to your attention, you sold some companies and bought others (yet you paid no income taxes or trading fees). After 1958, you simply sold and bought companies to match the composition of the S&P 500 (or other market proxy). In 1976, John Bogle created Vanguard, the first S&P 500 index fund. You then could have relieved yourself of personally following the market. You could have just turned over all of your money to his fund.[36]

Does This Method of Calculation Make Sense?

Of course, this method of calculation makes no sense. Such an investment program stretches even the most vivid imagination. Not only does it fail to reflect any type of meaningful investor "average," but I will pay $1,000 to anyone who can bring to my attention just one person in the entire world who has bought and sold stocks according to this fanciful investment program. (Undoubtedly, the IRS might also like to get this person's name.)

Real people pay taxes; they pay brokerage fees; they pay fund management fees; and they do not leave their money to accumulate through thick and thin for 75 to 200 years. Moreover, between 1926 and 1999, real people experienced a more than 500% increase in their cost of living. That 1926 five-cent loaf of bread now costs $1.89; that 1926 five-cent movie admission now costs $8; that 1926 $500 new Ford now costs $20,000; that 1926 $25-a-month apartment now costs $750 or more.[37]

Recent Perspective

The truly spectacular stock market advances of the 1980s and 1990s make a long-term rate of 11% sound reasonable. But as you think about your future, try to see more clearly. You might also note that the supposed annual returns of 14% to 16% that presumably apply to the past two decades are overstated in the same way as the 11% 1926–1999 rate. These recent quotes also ignore taxes, fees, costs, and inflation. And they do not apply to most individual investors.

Individuals versus Indexes

A realistic look at the returns investors have actually received would give you a more reasonable view of history's verdict on the wisdom of buying and selling stocks. Unfortunately, such studies are few in number. Even worse for the stock enthusiasts, the studies that have focused on the actual profits and losses of real people fall far short of 11%.[38]

Indeed, I would suspect that throughout the total history of the stock market, most investors have fared far worse than the Beardstown Ladies. Why? Buying high, selling low, failing to diversify, paying high costs and commissions, taking too many fliers on tips and hunches, being overconfident, fund switching, and tax-inefficient trading. More recently, such errors as failing to roll over tax-deferred 401(k) plans and getting hit with not only huge taxes but also big IRS penalties—push many investors into subpar performances.[39] Prior to 1934, when the SEC was created, of course, all types of stock scams, swindles, and manipulations also took their toll on investors.[40]

Human Nature

An old (and recently revitalized) field of study now called behavioral finance helps to explain this dismal performance by most people who buy stocks.[41] Even Peter Lynch—the star manager of the Fidelity Magellan fund during its growth and glory years—has admitted that the returns most of his fund's investors earned failed to match fund performance statistics. While taxes and costs ate up much of his investors' potential profits, buying into the fund at high prices and selling out at low prices also took a toll.

The Silence of Wall Street

If Wall Street brokerage firms and mutual funds had actually produced battalions of real investors who had achieved long-term rates of return of 11%, why their silence? Why don't these firms and funds publish reports showing the successes of their customers? Consider those real estate infomercials featuring Carleton Sheets: personal testimonials piled one atop another. Wouldn't a similar strategy work for Wall Street stock enthusiasts?

No. Such a promotion would raise too many questions. Somebody (maybe the Securities and Exchange Commission) would ask for a full disclosure on the performance of all of a firm's accounts. So why invite trouble? It's far safer and far more lucrative to legally mislead the public with irrelevant index (or fund) performance statistics. Actual individual customer returns? Better to keep those hidden. This omission explains why the delightful and perceptive 1940 book *Where Are the Customers' Yachts?* still continues to sell well today.[42]

Confidence?

Remember, all of this talk about rate of return isn't some mere quibble. Absent a financial windfall, the rate of return you earn on your stock investments will determine your future prosperity (or deprivation). The lower your return, the more you must put aside each year to build the sums you need and want. If you can't place much confidence in a stock return rate of 11%, what rate should you confidently use? I don't know, and neither does anyone else. As I show later, no matter what measures you adopt, the variance of historical returns jumps all over the map. As a beginning, though, you must deduct for expenses, taxes, and inflation.

Index Rate Minus Taxes, Fees, Costs, and Inflation

A few financial planners suggest the following formula:

Long-term rate (gross)	11.0%
minus	
Inflation	3.0%
Taxes	2.0%
Costs and commissions	1.0%
Effective rate	5.0%

If you are building your funds in a tax-deferred retirement account, you could omit the charge for taxes. But that's no free lunch. When you begin to withdraw those monies, you will lose the right to declare capital gains. Every dollar you eventually pocket will be taxed at the higher rates for ordinary income. Instead of losing, say, 20% to capital gains taxes, your income tax bill could claim up to 30% or 40% of your accumulations. (Of course, constantly changing tax laws add another element of uncertainty to your financial and investment planning.)

In any event, you can see that even when you assume that your stock investment will achieve a gross total return of 11%—that most familiar and fanciful long-term figure—you should not expect to net, after taxes, costs, and inflation, more than 5% or 6%. (This result also assumes that you conquer human nature and safely navigate around common investor mistakes.)

Past Performance No Guarantee of Future Results

Past performance no guarantee of future results: These are the seven most repeated words on Wall Street. They are displayed in nearly every mutual fund advertisement and included in every fund prospectus. And you should heed them. Upon review, at least eight reasons could create lower stock returns over the next several decades.

1. *Self-defeating prophecy*. The more people who adopt a specific system of investing (i.e., "stocks for the long run"), the lower the likelihood that it will succeed for the majority.
2. *Dividend yields*. Eventually people want their stocks to produce income. Absent enormous jumps in payout ratios, stock prices must fall. Yet if payouts increase, reinvestment decreases, and stock prices will still decline.
3. *Corporate earnings slowdown*. The mid- to late 1990s saw corporations report record levels of corporate earnings. The early 2000s revealed that these earnings growth rates were not only unsustainable but in many cases were also the work of fiction. "Creative accounting," "managed earnings," "earnings restatements," "pro forma" reporting, and massive write-offs have recently dominated the financial pages.[43]
4. *Lower price-to-earnings (P/E) ratios*. Once investors realize that the supposed new-era economy of high growth and low risk has disappeared for the foreseeable future, P/E ratios may retreat to historical norms.[44]
5. *Profit margins*. Heightened competition among domestic and global businesses will weaken corporate pricing power and squeeze profit margins.
6. *Lean and mean companies*. Quick boosts to profits by cutting costs and downsizing may offer less future potential. Most firms have already moved from fat and flabby to lean and mean.
7. *Replacement costs*. Stock market valuations dramatically exceed the actual replacement costs of most businesses' physical plant and equipment. In other words, theoretically, you can build cheaper than you can buy. (Historically, over time, asset values and business valuations have maintained a much closer relationship.[45])
8. *Superiority of real estate*. Within the not-too-distant future, stock buyers will learn that, in fact, real estate offers higher returns, more safety, and less volatility than stocks. We may witness a flight to income and quality.[46]

Indeed, even some stock enthusiasts are taking notice of these eight potential value-destroying factors. Recently, a *Kiplinger's Retirement Guide* told investors to expect a "regression to the mean."[47] Above-average returns in one period are likely to be offset with below-average returns in immediately succeeding periods. (Of course, as mentioned earlier, such results were discovered by Edgar Lawrence Smith in his 1924 study.)

Likewise, in the *Business Week* article cited earlier, Jeremy Siegel agrees. Although not backing away from his advocacy of stocks, Siegel says, "The inflation-adjusted returns on the stock market looking forward may not be as favorable as the long-run historical average, but stocks will return considerably more than the [real] 3.5% return you'd get from an inflation-indexed bond."[48]

The Real Issue

Maybe stocks will beat inflation-indexed bonds; maybe they won't. But Siegel misses the real point: Beating bonds can hardly be called financial success. Success comes when your investments steer you safely and surely to your financial goals. Unfortunately, Siegel—like most other stock enthusiasts—never raises the possibility that lower stock returns could impede the retirement plans of the tens of millions of people who are currently following his prescription.

The Dangers of Coming Up Short

In singing the praises of "stocks for the long run," few advocates give much thought to defining the "long run" over which investors can justly expect to earn that promised 11%. Most experts simply lead their readers to believe that sticking through thick and thin for 15, 20, or at most 30 years will do the trick. It might; it might not.

Historically, timing has mattered greatly. For example, Princeton professor Burton G. Malkeil shows that even since 1950, some 25-year periods have yielded stock returns of less than 8%. And not only was Malkeil's 8% calculated according to the fanciful index method discussed earlier, but it also failed to subtract for inflation, taxes, and costs.[49] In fact, even Siegel shows that on an after-tax, after-inflation basis, the 15-year period between 1966 and 1981 actually yielded negative returns for stocks.[50] So why is it that nearly every stock enthusiast fixates on 11%

when the numbers actually reveal a significant downside? In addition, you must realize that the real after-tax rate of return figures for nearly every "long run" time period since 1802 fall substantially below 11%.

A 75-Year Record

Indeed, the long-term figures that best provide perspective on the recent bull market are those that run from 1906 to 1981, a period of 75 years. This long span of history began with travel by horse and carriage and ended with college students jetting all over the country and the world. Surely, it was the greatest period of material progress in human history.

Yet over that astonishing period the Dow-Jones Industrial Average rose from 100 to just 800—a compound rate of increase of only 2.75% a year. In stark contrast stands the outsized performance of 1981 through mid-2001. During those years, the DJIA increased from 800 to 10,500—an annual compound rate of nearly 14%. So, as we look to future increases (decreases?) in the Dow (or other market proxies), what's the appropriate rate to use? How much confidence can you place in any particular rate? During the first three-quarters of this century, increases in the Dow barely matched the increases in consumer prices. Throughout history, investors earned most of their rewards from dividends, not stock price appreciation.

The Myth of the Long-Run Average

The stock enthusiasts have given us the long-run average rate of return of 11%. This figure now beckons like an airport searchlight to lure investors into a future that promises to replicate the past. But which past? For when viewed in its messy and distinct variations, the past fails to confirm any single rate of return figure and does not confirm any specific forecast. The best that can be said is this: You play the game, you take your chances.

So do you really want to risk your financial future on the misleading and historically overstated rate of return of 11%? Can you reach your financial goals with an after-tax, after costs, inflation-adjusted return of, say, 3% to 5% (or less)? Are you truly comfortable in taking these chances?

Chapter 3

The Case for Real Estate

If you read or listen to most stock enthusiasts, they will tell you to avoid investing in real estate. Yes, you might buy a home as a comfortable place to live, they say. But certainly don't think of it as a bank account with a white picket fence. Chiefly, they advise you to avoid real estate because, as they say, the historical record proves that stocks outperform all other types of investment. So why behave foolishly? If you can make more money in stocks, forget everything else.

In fact, some financial experts have even encouraged homeowners to borrow against their houses, then take the proceeds and use them to buy more stocks. In his book *Stocks for the Long Run*, second edition, Jeremy Siegel recommends that long-term "moderate" risk takers allocate 113% of their investments to stocks and "aggressive" investors up their ante in stocks to 131.5%.[1]

How can you invest more than 100%? Borrow the money. Take out a low-cost home equity loan. Pay the mortgage lender 8%, earn 11% in stocks, then pocket the difference.

What's the Evidence That Stocks Outperform Real Estate?

We've already seen in Chapter 2 that the stock market rate of return figure of 11% isn't quite the sure and precise fact that the stock market advocates would like you to believe. In fact, history shows that, except for over the past two decades, stock price appreciation rates as well as total returns normally fell well below this figure. If you deduct for taxes, costs, and inflation, the stock return figures sink to 5% or 6%—sometimes lower, sometimes even into negative territory. Nevertheless, maybe even this rate beats real estate. So let's see what the stock advocates have come up with.

Studies of Real Estate Returns

We're now going to review all of the studies that support the conclusion that stocks outperform all other assets, including real estate. . . . Okay, we're done. That's right, we're done.

You will never see such a study, because none has ever been conducted. So where did the stock enthusiasts get this false idea? Here are three sources: (1) from each other; (2) from reputed "studies" conducted by Roger Ibbotson; and (3) from recent stock price appreciation rates.

Stock Enthusiasts Parrot Each Other

As with much conventional wisdom, an advocate quotes (or more often misquotes) a so-called fact. Other interested parties (especially unthinking journalists) read or hear this "fact." Without bothering to check its original source or its validity, they repeat it over and over until the "knowledge" becomes so well accepted that few if any even think to question it (as occurred with Beardstown Ladies, discussed in Chapter 2). As the old saying tells us, "A falsehood can march halfway around the world before the truth is able to get its boots on."

In her thought-provoking book *Tainted Truth*, *Wall Street Journal* staffer Cynthia Crossen illustrates this tendency of the media to spread falsehoods—especially when doing so fits their firmly held interests or biases.[2] For example, in a review of the media, Crossen found hundreds of news articles citing these three statements as uncontested truths: (1) 150,000 girls die of anorexia every year; (2) America's streets are populated by 3.5 million homeless persons; and (3) on Super Bowl Sunday, domestic abuse (men beating women) skyrockets.

If you're not a news junkie, you may still recall these statements as substantive truth. As it turned out, each was manufactured by an advocacy group and put up for bid, and the media bought without even asking to see the warranty. The statement that "stocks outperform real estate" represents another of those media falsehoods that's been marching without opposition for quite some time.

Roger Ibbotson's Work

In many investment books and articles, you will see Roger Ibbotson's work cited to back up various rate of return claims.[3] Although Ibbotson chiefly studies the (hypothetical) returns on stocks, bonds, and U.S. Treasuries, he has also tried his hand at real estate.[4] However, this work has absolutely no relevance to individual investors. Ibbotson has studied only a series of appraised values for multimillion-dollar properties (regional shopping centers, Class A office buildings, 600-unit apartment complexes, etc.) that were owned by pension funds free and clear of mortgage financing.

Even here, his data suffer numerous methodological flaws (e.g., he ignores the potential effect of leverage.) If you happen to see Roger Ibbotson cited, realize that his work relates only—to the extent that it relates at all—to the types of billion-dollar pension funds and other mega-financial institutions that pay fees to Ibbotson's consulting firm. Let me again emphasize, then, that Ibbotson has never studied individual investors. Although often quoted, his published work does not—and never has—reported the actual *investment results* of specific individual (or institutional) investors in either real estate or stocks.

Appreciation Rates

Obviously, nearly everyone who cares to look can see that over the past two decades stock prices have jumped 10-fold—a compound annual growth rate of around 12%. No one would argue that most real estate has appreciated at rates anywhere near that pace. Thus, stocks win. It's as plain as the sun rising in the east and setting in the west.

Even a widely respected investment manager like Charles D. Ellis errs with this kind of thinking. In his acclaimed book *Winning the Loser's Game*, Ellis writes, "Owning residential real estate is not a great investment. Over the past 20 years, home prices have risen less than the consumer price index and have returned less than Treasury bills."[5]

We'll defer the debate on home price appreciation rates until later. That's not the critical source of the Ellis error. Rather, Ellis, like other unthinking observers, equates returns *solely* with the rate of appreciation.[6] Nonsense. Most people invest in real estate because it yields a large and growing stream of income (rent payments). You cannot reasonably conclude that stocks outperform real estate until you make a full accounting for price increases *and income*.

Impossibility of Studies

Not only have no studies demonstrated that stocks beat real estate over the long run, but in fact, such a study would prove impossible to conduct in any sensible way. Why? Because investor returns in real estate are localized and personal. Unlike stocks and bonds, which are traded in public national and international markets, real estate trades primarily in private, local transactions.

There's no comparable Dow Jones or S&P 500 index for rental houses, small apartment properties, neighborhood shopping centers, or low-rise office buildings. Indeed, any such national index or average would prove meaningless. Although most local governments do post some property transaction data, you can't judge rates of return or investor performance from public information for at least six reasons.

1. *Improvements*. Between the date of purchase and date of sale, some owners invest additional monies in property improvements. Others may never reinvest a nickel; they simply milk a property until it runs dry.
2. *Financing*. Your real estate returns will relate directly to the terms of your financing and refinancing.

3. *Rents.* Realty investors earn most, or much, of their returns through net rent collections. No one except the investor can access that information. (Of course, the IRS tries, but it admits that short of a full-blown audit and investigation, it can't know for sure.)
4. *Taxes.* Tax benefits (e.g., tax shelters, tax deferments, tax credits) may enhance a realty investor's returns.
5. *Management matters.* Investors who oversee their properties intelligently can earn far more than those who don't.
6. *Strategy counts.* Realty investors may combine many different strategies (e.g., buy and hold, fix and flip, conversion, rehab and rent) with one or more types of properties. Not only will the execution of each specific strategy yield different returns in different locales, but it is up to the intelligent (i.e., value) investor to fashion the best strategy for a given place and time.

As in the stock market, timing will influence an individual realty investor's actual returns. And unlike in the stock market, in real estate you can use fundamental analysis to anticipate market moves.

Conventional Wisdom Strikes Out

Once again, you see that value investors must always question conventional wisdom. Here we have a widely accepted investment maxim—stocks outperform all other assets—that's been repeated thousands of times. Yet not one well-known journalist, author, or financial expert (prior to this book) has ever exposed the fallacies inherent within such a claim (as eventually occurred with *Chicago Magazine* and the Beardstown Ladies).[7]

As a result, millions of average Americans falsely believe that the stock market gives them a near certain and far superior opportunity for financial independence, security, and long-term wealth.[8] Yet one can easily disprove the "stocks beat real estate" maxim through some very simple calculations.

A Simple Example

Naturally, home prices and rent levels vary greatly throughout the country. Figures in this example may not match those in your area. But don't get fixated on the specific numbers. Instead, focus on the basic rent-price ratios.[9] Nevertheless, I visit at least 30 states every year, and the price and rent figures below do represent the rent-price levels widely available outside of our notorious high cost areas. Moreover, as a value investor, you typically should not buy properties whose rent-price ratios fall significantly below those shown here.

Income Property Returns (3% Example)

Perhaps you can best see the potential superiority of real estate over stocks by looking at expected dollars rather than abstract *rates* of return. Table 3.1, for example, shows total dollar returns for a rental house over a 20-year period. The assumptions for this example are as follows:

1. You buy today at a price of $100,000.
2. You place $20,000 down.
3. You finance $80,000 with a 30-year 8% mortgage. Your payment runs $587 per month for a total of $7,044 per year.
4. The house rents for $800 a month for a total of $9,600 per year.
5. Upkeep expenses, property taxes, and insurance cost $2,500 per year.
6. At the end of each year, rents, expenses, and the property value all increase by 3% per year.

Reading down the table, Table 3.1 shows where you stand financially with the property after years 1, 5, 10, 15, and 20. You can see that just in terms of owner's equity (market value less outstanding mortgage balance), your original stake of $20,000 has doubled by year five. After 20 years, your equity has multiplied 6.5 times (to $132,301). After accounting for all yearly before-tax cash flows (BTCF) that total around $40,000, your compound annual rate of return over 20 years would fall just under 14%.

Conservative Assumptions

Do you know of a well-kept single-family home that over the past 20 years has appreciated at a rate of less than 3%? I don't. Yet even using this low rate of growth yields a rate of return that beats the much-ballyhooed long-run return from stocks of 11% by 3 percentage points.

Table 3.1 Income Property @ 3% Price Increases Pro Forma*

3% Increases (Rents, Expenses, Market Value)							
Year	*Rents*	*Expenses*	*Mtg. Pymt*	*BTCF*	*Market Value*	*Mortgage Balance*	*Equity*
1	$ 9,600	2,500	7,044	**56**	103,000	79,194	**23,806**
5	10,804	2,898	7,044	**862**	115,900	75,924	**39,976**
10	12,525	3,358	7,044	**2,123**	134,300	70,058	**64,242**
15	14,516	3,892	7,044	**3,580**	155,700	61,319	**94,381**
20	16,824	4,511	7,044	**5,269**	180,600	48,299	**132,301**

*Original investment equals $20,000.

Moreover, as we'll discuss later, the owner of this property could have significantly boosted that 14% return by any number of moves, such as buying at a bargain price (below market value), profitable property improvement, making a lower down payment, or financing or refinancing at an interest rate of less than 8%. To see the effect of moderately more optimistic (and realistic) returns, see Tables 3.2 and 3.3.

Moderate Optimist (Realist)

In Tables 3.2 and 3.3, you can see the enormous power of compound interest. By nudging the growth rate from 3% to 4% and 5%, respectively, cash flows and owner's equity both jump up. With a 4% appreciation rate over

Table 3.2 Income Property @ 4% Price Increases Pro Forma*

4% Increases (Rents, Expenses, Market Value)							
Year	*Rents*	*Expenses*	*Mtg. Pymt*	*BTCF*	*Market Value*	*Mortgage Balance*	*Equity*
1	$ 9,600	2,500	7,044	**56**	104,000	79,194	**24,806**
5	11,673	3,040	7,044	**1,589**	121,600	75,924	**45,676**
10	14,208	3,696	7,044	**3,468**	148,000	70,058	**77,942**
15	17,280	4,495	7,044	**5,741**	180,000	61,319	**118,681**
20	21,033	5,466	7,044	**8,523**	219,000	48,299	**170,701**

*Original investment equals $20,000.

Table 3.3 **Income Property @ 5% Price Increases Pro Forma***

5% Increases (Rents, Expenses, Market Value)							
Year	*Rents*	*Expenses*	*Mtg. Pymt*	*BTCF*	*Market Value*	*Mortgage Balance*	*Equity*
1	$ 9,600	2,500	7,044	**56**	105,000	79,194	**25,806**
5	12,249	3,190	7,044	**2,015**	127,600	75,924	**51,676**
10	15,630	4,070	7,044	**4,516**	162,800	70,058	**92,742**
15	19,944	5,194	7,044	**7,706**	207,800	61,319	**146,481**
20	25,499	6,627	7,044	**11,828**	265,300	48,299	**217,001**

*Original investment equals $20,000.

20 years, the owner's beginning investment of $20,000 multiplies 8.5-fold; at 5%, nearly 11-fold. Add in cash flows and you would have earned a mind-boggling compound annual rate of return of around 18% or 20%, respectively.

Without any heroic assumptions that violate the historic record, without any unusual creativity, without any value-enhancing activities (other than normal maintenance and replacement), the owners of this property would have outperformed Professors Ibbotson's and Siegel's stock market averages hands down.

Stocks versus Income Property

For a head-to-head comparison of stocks versus real estate, look at Tables 3.4 and 3.5. Table 3.4 merely brings forth the cash flow and owner equity results from Tables 3.1, 3.2, and 3.3. You can now conveniently judge the performance of stocks versus that of income property for yourself.

Table 3.5 shows the dollar returns an investor might expect to receive from stocks. We calculate the figures according to the following assumptions:

1. At the beginning of year 1, the investor pays $20,000 for a widely diversified portfolio of stocks.
2. The beginning dividend yield on that portfolio equals 1.5%. (Currently, the dividend yield for the S&P 500 is around 1.3%.)

Table **3.4 Income Property versus Stocks Pro Forma***

Income Property (Summary Tables 3.1, 3.2, 3.3)								
3%			*4%*			*5%*		
Year	*BTCF*	*Equity*	*Year*	*BTCF*	*Equity*	*Year*	*BTCF*	*Equity*
1	$ 56	$ 23,806	1	$ 56	$ 24,806	1	$ 56	$ 25,806
5	862	39,976	5	1,589	45,676	5	2,105	51,676
10	2,123	64,242	10	3,468	77,942	10	4,516	92,742
15	3,580	94,381	15	5,741	110,681	15	7,706	146,481
20	5,269	132,301	20	8,523	170,701	20	11,828	217,001

*Original investment equals $20,000.

3. Dividends grow at the annual rate of either 6% or 7%. (Over the long term, the corporate dividend growth rate has averaged 6%.)
4. The value of the total stock portfolio grows by either 6.0%, 9.5%, or 12%. (During the past 40 years, stock prices have appreciated at a compound rate of around 7% per year. As noted earlier, between 1906 and 1981, the DJIA grew at a compound annual rate of 2.75%.)[10]

No matter how you mix and match these results, one point consistently becomes clear. With only one exception, the income property outperforms stocks. If you bought stocks and they gained 12% a year for 20 years, at that

Table **3.5 Stock Returns***

Dividend Growth			*Stock Portfolio Appreciation*			
Year	*6%*	*7%*	*Year*	*6%*	*9.5%*	*12%*
1	$300	$ 300	1	$21,200	$ 21,900	$ 22,400
5	401	420	5	26,760	31,480	35,240
10	537	590	10	35,805	49,549	62,093
15	718	827	15	47,907	77,990	109,408
20	961	1,159	20	64,099	122,758	192,776

*Original investment equals $20,000 and earns a beginning annual dividend yield of 1.5%.

time you would surpass the buy-and-hold property owner who by year 20 had experienced a 3% annual increase in rents and property appreciation.

Although it looks like year 15 stocks (12%) also beat year 15 income property (3%), such is not the case. In addition to $94,381 in equity, during these 15 years the (3%) property owner would have pocketed significantly higher annual cash flows.

The Proof Is in the Numbers

Most people, it seems, would rather get their teeth pulled than work through numbers. But if you're going to invest safely and intelligently, you've got to crank out some figures and create likely or reasonable outcomes, then compare possibilities. Just as important, put the numbers down and carry them into the future to make sure your investment plan will actually yield enough money. It's a lot easier to correct for errors and wishful thinking at age 45 than at age 58.

What the Numbers Show

When you closely compare the figures in Tables 3.4 and 3.5, you should be struck by two facts:

1. *Cash flows*. If you want to count on your investments to generate inflation-protected retirement income, you'll choose real estate. At current yields, stocks produce paltry cash flows.
2. *Wealth building*. Conventional wisdom says that you can build wealth faster in stocks than through any other type of investment. Yet at the reputedly dismal property appreciation rates of 3%, 4%, and 5%, you can more than double your money in five years (even with a 20% down payment). Over 20 years you can watch it grow by multiples of 6, 8, 10, or greater.

No one who closely and fairly evaluates these performance numbers could ever again agree with the conventional wisdom that stocks beat real estate.

Risk of Nonperformance

Certainly, no one can guarantee the future. But which of the following two statements seems most likely to prove true?

1. Over the next 20 years, home prices and rents will grow at an average rate of 3% to 5% a year.
2. Over the next 20 years, stock prices will rise far above all *long-term* historical norms; they will appreciate at an average rate of 9% to 12% a year.

Of course, before you can confidently agree with statement 2, you will have to seriously consider answers to these two questions:

1. Who in the future could buy your stocks at such inflated prices?
2. Who would want to buy your stocks at such inflated prices?

In 15 to 20 years, as the age wave flows to high tide, the people who want money will become stock sellers. They might easily flood the smaller number of baby bust–generation buyers (i.e., those who will then be entering their prime wealth-building years of, say, ages 40 to 55).[11] But just as important, where's the economic rationale to buy? Here's what those future stock dividend yields would look like—even if dividends grew by 7% a year:

Year 20 Dividend Yields

6% Stock Appreciation	*9.5% Stock Appreciation*	*12% Stock Appreciation*
$\frac{\$1,159}{\$64,099} = 1.8\%$	$\frac{\$1,159}{\$122,758} = .94\%$	$\frac{\$1,159}{\$192,776} = .60\%$

Why would anyone be willing to buy a portfolio of stocks at $64,099, $122,758, or $192,776 for the right to receive such piddling cash-on-cash rates of return? Would these future buyers also figure that the stocks they purchase will continue to appreciate at rates of 6% to 12% a year? That's surely a Ponzi scheme: Profits continue for present investors only as long as a perpetual stream of new buyers enters the market.

Yet the longer the system operates, the lower the cash yield. The more stock prices inflate, the more they become "castles in the air."[12] When will it end? How will it end? No true value investors should stake their future on stocks until they can satisfactorily resolve each of these quite likely dilemmas.

The End of Income?

Since the late 1940s, the dividend yield on stocks has fallen from a peak of over 7% to today's 1.31%. Even as recently as 1990, the dividend yield averaged 3.61%. Such a vast change has no historical precedent. It seems now that most stock buyers have come to believe that income no longer matters—only appreciation counts.[13] But such a belief slaps the face of investment theory. The true *investor*—the value investor—knows that without a strong foundation of income, castles in the air come crashing down from the clouds.

Because, dollar for dollar, *income* properties yield far more income than stocks (at today's prices and yields), income properties provide the far better investment value.[14] Consider these excerpts from what is perhaps rightly regarded as the most influential investment book ever written. In the opening pages of *The Theory of Investment Value*, John Burr Williams affirms the original work of Graham and Dodd and then elaborates,

> Every thoughtful investor knows that he should not confuse the real worth [intrinsic value] of an investment with its market price. No buyer considers all investments equally attractive. . . . On the contrary, he seeks "the best at the price." He picks and chooses among all possibilities. Even then, he may not buy at all, for fear that everything is priced too high and nothing will give him his money's worth.
>
> If he does buy, and buys as an investor, he holds for income; if as a speculator, for profit at sale. But [over the long run] speculators can profit *only by selling to investors* [i.e., those who value income]; therefore in the end, all investment values depend on

> someone's estimate of future income. [Of course] investors differ in their estimates . . . [Thus], our problem is twofold: (1) to explain the market price as it is, and (2) to show how to calculate the investment value as it should be.[15]

Up to this point, Williams sticks pretty close to major points made by Graham and Dodd: Speculators buy with the hope (illusion?) that they can sell what they've bought at a substantively higher price. Speculators try to anticipate or ride momentum.[16] Although investors often gain from appreciation, they pay for only the value of income (or assets) they can reasonably count on receiving. In following these Graham and Dodd insights, Williams added the following definition:

> We shall see fit to define Investment Value, as the present worth of future dividends. . . .[17]

In other words, Williams was the first to develop mathematically the technique of specifically calculating investment value. Today, that technique is known as discounted cash flow (DCF). It is now taught to nearly every business school student in the world. All Fortune 500 corporations use this technique to help them decide when to build a new plant, develop a new line of products, or buy another company. Recent *Business Week* articles even champion DCF and its compatriot, net present value (NPV), to calculate the value of brands and to assist in making effective sales presentations.[18]

Yet in valuing stocks, the chief purpose for which J. B. Williams developed DCF, investors have decided to bury this otherwise universally accepted technique in the academic graveyard. Why? Because it's the familiar story of killing the messenger who brings bad news.

The News Is Bad for Stocks

In the stock portfolio shown in Table 3.5, you can see the puny cash flows now generated by stocks. But we didn't actually show how these flows of dividends should be converted into a fair investment value figure. To do that, we can use this shortcut formula:

$$V_I = \frac{d}{r - g}$$

where: V_I = investment value
r = desired rate of return
d = current dividend amount
g = rate at which you expect dividends to grow

If we assume (1) your \$20,000 portfolio currently pays \$300 a year in dividends, (2) you expect the dividends to grow by 7% a year,[19] and (3) you want to earn (pretax) an 11% rate of return, then you should value your current portfolio at just \$7,500:

$$\$7{,}500 = \frac{\$300}{.11 - .07} = \frac{\$300}{.04}$$

This doesn't look good, does it? Your \$20,000 portfolio (Table 3.5) is worth only \$7,500 as an investment. Why are investors now willing to pay \$20,000 for no more than \$7,500 worth of value? Take your pick: (1) speculation, (2) gambling, (3) taking a flier, or (4) greater optimism about future growth in dividends. For instance, maybe you expect your portfolio's dividends to grow by 10% a year. Then you could pay up to \$30,000:

$$V_I = \frac{d}{r - g} = \frac{300}{.11 - .10} = \frac{300}{.01}$$

$$V_I = \$30{,}000$$

Yet, if you really do expect a much higher than average growth in dividends (i.e., really "betting" on speculative company success), you would wisely seek a higher rate of return on your investment, say 15 percent. Then your investment value for this portfolio would equal:

$$V_I = \frac{300}{.15 - .10} = \frac{300}{.05}$$

$$V_I = \$6{,}000$$

Of course, you can make your discounted cash flow models as complex as you want. You can vary the amount of cash flows. You can try various discount rates and growth rates. But you must see that, as Ben Graham and John Burr Williams emphasized, the *price* of a stock and the *investment value* of a stock are separate and distinct things not to be confused.

Buying stocks and *investing* in stocks truly reflect separate and distinct things. Intelligent investors work hard to ferret out value and avoid the many risks of speculation, gambling, or taking a flier. Yet at the prices and dividend yields recently prevailing, the stock market incorporates too little investment value and too much betting on a highly optimistic (and historically unsupported) future performance.

What About Earnings as Cash Flows?

As dividend yields have fallen, price to earnings (P/E) ratios have climbed far above their historical norms.[20] Nevertheless, if you discount earnings (as some investors do), you can come closer to justifying today's market valuations and yields. In other words, instead of using dividends as the numerator of our V_I formula, plug in the figure for earnings. With a market P/E of 25 (earnings yield of 4%—1 ÷ 25 = .04), the total dollar earnings on our $20,000 portfolio (at market averages) would equal $800 (.04 x 20,000). Thus, investment value of the portfolio would equal $20,000:

$$V_I = \frac{\text{earnings}}{.11 - g} = \frac{\$800}{.11 - .07} = \frac{800}{.04}$$

$$V_I = \$20,000$$

You can now justify paying $20,000 for this portfolio.

Unfortunately, though, this sleight-of-hand change in the DCF calculation is manifestly wrong. John Burr Williams effectively anticipates and rebuts such a method. "Earnings," he correctly asserts, "are only a means to an end, and the means should not be mistaken for the end."[21]

What might seem surprising, given his perpetual advocacy of stocks, Jeremy Siegel strongly endorses the Williams viewpoint:

> The [investment value] of a stock is always equal to the present value of all future *dividends* [italics in original] and not the present value of future earnings. . . . Valuing stock as the present discounted value of future earnings is manifestly wrong and greatly overstates the value of a firm, unless all of its earnings are always paid out as dividends.[22]

Still, just because you pay more than investment value for a stock (or any other type of investment) doesn't mean you won't make money. It does mean, though, that—whether you realize it or not—you are exposing your investment dollars to a substantial and likely chance of loss.

Ben Graham's Shortcuts (More Bad News for Stocks)

Revised editions of *Security Analysis* accepted discounted cash flow (sometimes called dividend discount model, or DDM).[23] However, Ben Graham originally developed several other reasonable indicators of investment, which include the following:

1. Multiply earnings per share by 50 and divide by the AAA bond yield.
2. Multiply dividends per share by 150 and divide by the AAA bond yield.

If we continue with our running example, let's value the $20,000 stock portfolio using these two Graham techniques:

$$1.\ V_I = \frac{50 \times 800 \text{ (earnings)}}{6.5 \text{ (AAA bond yields)}} = \frac{40{,}000}{6.5}$$

$$V_I = \$6{,}154$$

$$2.\ V_I = \frac{150 \times 300 \text{ (dividends)}}{6.5} = \frac{45{,}000}{6.5}$$

$$V_I = \$6{,}923$$

Clearly, Ben Graham would not pay $20,000 for a market basket of stocks with such feeble earnings and dividends. Should you?

What's Your Exit Strategy?

"The way you pay yourself in retirement can make a world of difference," advises a recent *Business Week* article on investing and retirement. You've got to be able to open your nest egg without breaking it.[24]

Even before the baby boomers reach retirement age, many retirement-ready longtime stock market investors already are finding that a million-dollar-plus portfolio of stocks won't feed their retirement needs and wants without taking large bites out of their nest eggs. For many, this dilemma creates surprise, disappointment, and anxiety. *Business Week* points out, "As Americans approach retirement, they, too, will have to grapple with the problem facing the Nelsons [a couple featured in the article]: how to parlay retirement savings and other assets into the income and assets that will support the lifestyle they desire during the next 30 years or so. . . . Most [potential retirees] wait until retirement is only a few years off before plotting a financial exit strategy. But ideally, you should start pinning down [this] crucial decision at least 10 years before you retire."[25]

Excellent advice! And it's further evidence that the end of income (i.e., dividends) could also spell the end of stocks. Without a substantive flow of dividends, stocks can't provide income security, much less retirement adventure.

Good News for Real Estate Investors

Tables 3.1, 3.2, and 3.3 reveal that leveraged income property outperforms stocks—even under quite elementary and conservative assumptions. Yet the stock advocates may shout foul; you can't fairly compare the returns from leveraged real estate to unleveraged stock buying.

Later, I will show why—fair or unfair—such a comparison makes sense from the standpoint of investing. But to appease the critics, let's go ahead and calculate the investment value for real estate when paid 100% in cash, relying on the purchase, rent, and expense figures used earlier:

1. Purchase price = $100,000
2. Rents = $800 per month ($9,600 per year)
3. Expenses begin at $2,500
4. First year BTCF (no mortgage) = $7,100 ($9,600 – $2,500)
5. Rents and expenses each increase by 3% per year; thus, BTCF increases by 3% per year.
6. You insist on a gross rate of return of 11%.

When held for the long term, the investment value (V_I) of this rental house would equal:

$$V_I = \frac{BTCF}{r - g} = \frac{\$7{,}100}{.11 - .03} = \frac{\$7{,}100}{.08}$$

$$V_I = \$88{,}750$$

As you can see, the investment value of this house falls about 12% shy of its $100,000 market value. Nevertheless, even under these conservative assumptions (all-cash purchase, 3% rent increases), this investment trumps stocks. Under less constrained assumptions, similar calculations for stocks produced investment values of just one-third of our stock portfolio's market price.

But we might also think about this comparison from a different perspective. Because rental properties offer lower risk of major decline in value and more protection against inflation (points proved later), maybe you might accept a 10% (unleveraged) return.[26] If so, then

$$V_I = \frac{\text{BTCF}}{r - g} = \frac{\$7{,}100}{.07(.10 - .03)}$$

$$V_I = \$101{,}428$$

Thus, without adding in any return from property appreciation, you can expect the income flows alone to justify an investment value of more than this property's $100,000 market price. As always, you can play with the numbers in a dozen different ways. As long as you stay within the realm of history and reason, though, you can find rental properties widely available—though not always single-family homes—that match or exceed the income/yield performance of this example.

Before we leave this unleveraged return analysis, you might wonder how much the slightly higher rental increases of 4% and 5% (Tables 3.2 and 3.3) would lift this property's investment value (without factoring in appreciation). Here are the answers: 4% and 5%.

$$1.\ V_I = \frac{\text{BTCF}}{r - g} = \frac{\$7{,}100}{.11 - .04} = \frac{\$7{,}100}{.07}$$

$$V_I = \$101{,}428$$

$$2.\ V_I = \frac{\$7{,}100}{.11 - .05} = \frac{\$7{,}100}{.06}$$

$$V_I = \$118{,}333$$

Even when you reset your required rate of return at 11%, this property's investment value exceeds its market price. In other words, without any allowance for property appreciation, modest increases in rent alone will assure you of a return in excess of 11%. When you can get income returns at this level, why choose stocks? How can any true investor prefer the feeble income and questionable appreciation of stocks to a near certain stream of property rent collections (with asset appreciation to boot)?

"Well," the stock advocates might say, "you could be right about stock returns trailing real estate over the next decade. But real estate lacks other advantages when compared to stocks." Again, the stock advocates argue with their biases, not their intellect.

Round Up the Usual Suspects

Whenever stock advocates want to downplay the investment qualities of real estate, they go out and round up the usual suspects: (1) illiquidity, (2) management headaches, (3) up-and-down cycles, (4) lack of diversification, and (5) low appreciation. As you will soon see, the accused remains innocent of all charges.

Illiquidity

Sticking to the party line, financial planners and stock enthusiasts routinely write down real estate because, as they say, it's illiquid. "Homes, in general, are illiquid investments—meaning they can be tough to turn into cash during stressful times," writes Patrick Barta. "Stocks by contrast, can be sold instantly."[27]

How about an echo from *Business Week:* "There's no liquidity in property," says financial planner Thomas Grzymala, in giving advice to retirees. "You can't take that unused bedroom to the supermarket to buy groceries."[28]

Illiquidity: A Disadvantage?

In the first place, of course, if you're trying to invest for retirement, why would you, or should you, desire liquidity? Without a doubt liquidity can be hazardous to your wealth. Here's how David Schumacher responds to the supposed disadvantage of illiquidity:

> When I was teaching real estate courses at UCLA Extension and Los Angeles City College, I used to invite a stockbroker as a guest speaker to tell the class how fabulous it is to own stocks and bonds because they can be sold in two minutes. Then, after he would leave, I would emphasize to the students how it is even more fabulous to own real estate precisely because you *can't* sell it in two minutes. You can't sell real estate to solve your immediate financial problems because real estate is not easy to sell. You have to find another way to solve your problems. Some financial advisers think that is a disadvantage.
>
> But I think it is a terrific advantage because it compels you to think things over before you make the decision. Suppose you have a diversified investment portfolio and own both stocks and real estate. Suddenly, a crisis occurs and you need $50,000. The first thing you would sell is the stock. If you didn't have any stock you would figure out another way to solve your dilemma. You might borrow some money on your real estate or you might figure out another way to obtain a loan, but you aren't going to get rid of your real estate because it usually takes a period of time—weeks, months, or even years—to sell.
>
> So you think of other ways to solve the problem. To me, that is a tremendous, built-in advantage of investing in real estate. It forces you to hold on to the property and, rather than receive a small profit, gives it time to appreciate. Maybe your dire financial situation or problem will pass. Once you get over that hurdle, you'll still be left with the property. If you hold it and keep it for the long pull, you'll be much better off.[29]

All we hear is "stocks for the long run" as the best way to wealth. Yet as Schumacher so capably points out, the ability to sell stocks instantly simply means that you probably won't hold for the long run. In fact, even with horrendous taxes and IRS penalties, one-third of employees who leave their jobs cash out their 401(k) funds. How can "stocks for the long run" compete with both human nature and that spiffy-looking new ski-boat or SUV?

"Stocks Sold Instantly"—At What Price?

It's laughable to talk of selling stocks instantly without mentioning price. Of course you can instantly sell stocks, but only at the price the highest bidder is willing to pay. What if stressful times arrive during a period when your stocks are down? Such as, say, when Apple Computer fell from 73 to 12 in less than a year? Or how about Xerox, Nortel, Motorola, Enron, and dozens of other companies whose stock prices have crashed?

If that's what the stock enthusiasts mean by an instant sale, then you can certainly sell real estate just as quickly. Simply take out a large ad in the real estate section of your local paper:

AUCTION
Sunday, June 15, 2:00 P.M.
Fourplex—Perfect Condition
Absolute to Highest Bidder
Details—555–7777

For an instant sale, merely hold a property auction. That's the way stocks are sold every day. Stock sellers are guaranteed a sale—not a price.

Need Money Fast? Don't Sell; Borrow

With stocks you must sell to raise cash. Unless you want to play the high-risk game of margin borrowing, no one will give you a long-term loan against your stock portfolio. Not so with real estate. If you own real estate and want to prepare for a cash emergency, prearrange an equity line of credit. Just write a check when you need the money. Better yet, manage your finances to avoid a cash crunch.

Bedrooms (Houses) Can *Buy Groceries*

It's time for financial planners to learn a little bit about real estate. Any retired couple who owns a home can convert the home to cash (equity credit line) or, with far more safety, a reverse annuity mortgage (RAM). With a RAM, you are entitled to a large lump-sum payment or a regular monthly income. For as long as you live in your house, you need never repay the RAM.[30]

As to that unused bedroom, hasn't this planner ever heard of mother-in-law suites or efficiency apartments? Or those whom, in an earlier era, we used to call boarders? (To cite just a few of the many books on using bedrooms to buy groceries, see *Creating an Accessory Apartment*, *Living with Tenants*, *Squeeze Your Home for Cash*, and *How to Open and Operate a Bed and Breakfast*.)[31] House rich, cash poor? Not possible, unless you choose it.

Management Headaches?

The party line continues: If you're going to own rental properties, get prepared for trashed houses; midnight telephone calls; and weeks, even months, of worry over finding tenants. Nonsense. Any owner plagued by such annoyances needs a quick course (or a good book) on property management. Property owners get the types of tenants and problems they ask for (deserve).

Times Have Changed

Twenty or 30 years ago, individual landlords typically accepted any tenants who showed up to rent a property. They would look the people over, ask a few personal questions, and maybe call the tenants' current landlord. The property owner's supposed margin of safety was a strong lease, the threat of eviction, and maybe a month's rent as deposit. Credit checks were rare.

In a similar vein, individual property owners frequently adopted a hard-line "I'm the owner—You're the tenant—Do what I say or else"—attitude. Needless to say, such an approach created more enemies than friends, and more complaints than customer satisfaction. Accordingly, destructive parting shots fired by tenants as they moved out were not uncommon.

Today, intelligent investors have adopted a much more professional and consumer-friendly approach. The old language and attitude of landlord versus tenant has been pushed aside in favor of property owner and property resident, or even service provider and resident. Together, careful tenant selection, better property maintenance and presentation, and owner professionalism can eliminate (or at least severely alleviate) managerial headaches.

In the past, owners demanded compliance but often bought trouble instead. Today, consumer-friendly property management benefits both property owners and residents. (See, for example, Chapter 11 of my book *Investing in Real Estate*.[32])

Delegate

If you don't want to manage your own properties, delegate the job to a professional property-management firm or a "handyman" type of supervisor and caretaker. Yes, professional property managers charge for their services. But they don't cut into your rate of return anywhere near as much as do most stock asset managers or mutual funds.

On that point, it is amazing how loudly the critics rail against the high fees that most financial advisors and fund managers charge, yet how little the public seems to care. Maybe it's like the situation with ex-Teamster boss Jimmy Hoffa and his union members. When first faced with the allegations that Hoffa was siphoning off millions of dollars from the union treasury, members yawned and remarked, "Who cares? As long as he gets me my ten dollars an hour, I'm not complaining."

The mutual fund industry is charging its customers billions of dollars. But as long as customers were making their 15% a year, they paid little attention. Time will tell. In a world of shrinking returns (and shrinking asset values), maybe stock buyers will come to understand that the huge fees charged by fund managers and investment managers make real estate property managers look like the bargain of the century.[33]

Real Estate Cycles

"The [1980s] boom in real estate went bust, and my friends went bust, too," writes Jonathan Clements, the widely read *Wall Street Journal* columnist.[34] Like most stock enthusiasts, Clements uses the experience of his friends to warn potential investors away from real estate because it's too cyclical: You get sucked into a whirlwind of appreciation and are lifted into the sky; then when the flurry ebbs, you fall back hard to the ground. Clements, though, like most others who parrot this type of horror story, omits a few critical points: (1) stock cycles, (2) investment versus speculation—or worse, and (3) rents versus property prices.

Stock Cycles

Is it not the height of folly for Clements to urge people into stocks because *real estate* prices run in cycles? I would urge any stock enthusiast to compare the relatively moderate ups and downs of property prices to those wild gyrations found in the stock market. Has he, or any other stock advocate, ever seen the price of a decent property fall 50%, 60%, 70%, or more within a period of 12 months or less, as did stock in Nortel, Xerox, IBM, Sunbeam, Kodak, and Motorola? I hardly think so. Have the stock advocates ever seen home or apartment prices across the nation fall by over 20% in a period of 12 months or less—as have both the Dow and the S&P 500? (I shall remain kind and not cite figures for the crashes of the NASDAQ [2000–2001] or for the Dow circa 1987, 1973 to 1974, or 1929 to 1932.)

Is it not amazing that the stock enthusiasts want to push people into stocks because property markets sometimes hit the skids? Even more amazing, to the extent that they acknowledge the wild swings in stock prices and protracted bear markets, they say, "Great; now's your opportunity to buy more stocks at bargain prices. Remember, you're in this for the long run. And in the long run, stocks (at least the market indexes, that is) always bounce back. Just hang tight; you'll come out okay."

Shouldn't the same principle of hanging tight and using low prices to pick up bargains also apply to real estate investors? Do the stock enthusiasts know of any substantive housing market in the United States that displays lower prices today than in 1990?[35] Is there any 10-year period since 1900 over which homes have not increased in price? United States history shows that home prices appreciate with far more dependability than stock prices.[36] (Plus, of course, a far higher and more dependable annual yield.)

Investment versus Speculation—Or Worse

The vast majority of property buyers who have crashed to the ground after a whirlwind of appreciation weren't truly investing in real estate; they were speculating—or worse. They usually bought properties with low down payments, high loan-to-price ratios, and low (or negative) cash yields. In the steaming California market of the late 1980s, homebuyers and would-be investors were buying $400,000 houses with 10% down and $4,000-a-month payments. Yet rents for such homes typically fell in the range of $1,500 to $2,000 a month.

How could these people *reasonably* expect to make money on their investments? Of course they couldn't. Nevertheless, here's how their minds worked:

Purchase price @	$400,000
Property appreciation (assumed) @ 12%	.12
Profit from appreciation	48,000
Negative cash flow (12 × $2,000)	24,000
Total gain	$ 24,000

These buyers forgot (or had never learned) a prime rule of investing: When you can't justify the asset price by the income you can reasonably expect it to produce, you're not investing—you're speculating (or maybe taking a flier) on future appreciation. In addition, most buyers in such situations are usually sucked in only after multiple rounds of price increases have occurred. As Clements said of his unfortunate (foolish?) friends, they arrived at the party just as the music stopped. Lesson: If you wish to attend an appreciation party, don't wait until late in the evening. Get there early.

Rents, Housing Starts, and Property Prices

Although I'll show you how to anticipate building and price cycles in a later chapter, for now, here's just one more point: Realty market ups and downs primarily affect homebuilders and late-to-the-party investors and homebuyers. Except in isolated instances of massive overbuilding or serious recession, residential rent levels seldom fall substantially (especially rents for single-family homes).[37]

In other words, in most communities, long-term individual investors in rental properties will experience stable flows of rental income. Unlike large corporations whose earnings often swing wildly between billion-dollar profits and billion-dollar losses, owners of rental properties need not fear the curse of volatility.

Lack of Diversification

Today, with the exception of "stocks for the long run," no gospel is preached more loudly than that of diversification. "Never put all of your eggs into one basket," the stock advocates say. No doubt, this advice has merit. But it doesn't apply to real estate in the way the stock enthusiasts think it does.

Own Your Own Home? That's Enough

"Most experts argue—correctly, in my view," writes Jonathan Clements of the *Wall Street Journal*, "that if you own your own home, you already have plenty of real estate exposure."[38] And from *Barron's Guide to Making Investment Decisions*, the same party line: "We will argue that one's own home [if that!] is probably enough exposure to the real estate market for the average individual investor. If you're thinking about buying [a home], please, at least consider the alternatives."[39]

Why this hostility to real estate? According to this critique, real estate fails the test of diversity. If you maintain your job, your home, and your investments in the same community, then you're placing too many eggs in one basket. If your employer, your industry, and your community slide into recession, your wealth portfolio could take a triple hit.

Clearly you do need to weigh the possibility of this risk. But for most people, this triple-threat risk to job, home, and property investment remains slight. In any event, no general rules apply. Intelligent investors coolly evaluate their personal risks and the long-term stability of property prices in their communities.

Own Property Elsewhere

Unlike many real estate advisors, I encourage you to consider owning rentals in towns other than where you live. Not just for reasons of diversification per se; rather, because you might find better investment opportunities in other locations. This advice especially holds for people who live in areas where rent collections—even after the owner makes a large down payment—won't cover monthly mortgage payments and property expenses.

If not done right, owning property elsewhere may create some difficulties. But the benefits of higher returns as well as diversification can more than compensate you for this potential drawback.

I can testify from experience that long-distance landlording can prove easy and profitable. At one time, I lived in the San Francisco Bay area, yet owned rental houses—previous residences I'd retained—in Dallas, Texas, and Winter Park, Florida. At another time, I owned a dozen houses and another 18 apartment units in a city a thousand miles from where I lived. In that instance, I employed a "handyman" manager to rent and maintain the properties. For the Dallas and Winter Park houses, though, no local management was necessary because I had taken care to select perfectly responsible long-term tenants.

Low Appreciation?

I've already addressed the fallacy of the low-appreciation complaint elsewhere. But to recap: Over the real long term, say, 1906 to the present, stocks and homes have appreciated at about the same rate. Between 1906 and 1981, home price appreciation beat that of stocks. Between 1960 and 1982, home price appreciation beat that of stocks. Between 1982 and 1999, stock price appreciation beat home prices. During 2000 to 2002, home prices beat stocks. So no one can rightly name a universal winner in the contest for appreciation. But that's not true for income.

In every year since 1900 (and earlier), the rental revenues from housing have produced superior amounts of annual income as compared to stocks. Thus, when you measure long-term total returns, most homes have probably outperformed the great majority of stocks. (I say probably only because enormous variance can arise depending on the assumed dates and amounts of investment, reinvestment, financing costs, and withdrawal.) Nevertheless, on an after-tax cash-in-pocket basis of computing returns, real estate wins by a country mile.

Don't Accept "Market" Returns

Due to the enormous differences among individuals, it is absurd to say—as financial planners and writers invariably do say—that over the past *X* years, "stocks have returned . . . " or "real estate has returned . . . " some stated amount. A hypothetically constructed market average does not and cannot produce reliable measures for individual performance or individual decision making.

Nevertheless, we do know, with a relatively high degree of certainty, three facts: (1) Most professional stock market investors have failed to outperform market indexes, (2) most individual stock market investors have failed to outperform market indexes, and (3) nearly all real estate value investors outperform the stock market.

Why? Because smart real estate investors don't just passively accept market rates of return or appreciation. Instead, they create value through profit-enhancing improvements, they enhance rental revenues through superb management, they buy at bargain prices, and they choose to buy in locations that show the most promise for gain.

Gains in Equity

Remember, too, most property investors employ leverage (financing) to boost their rate of wealth building. Even when the prices of stocks do appreciate faster than a specific property, the realty investor can still outperform stocks (compare Tables 3.4 and 3.5).

Anyone who argues that (on average) stock investors outearn long-term owners of income properties needs to get acquainted with the facts. While 80% of professional fund managers (and, of course, their clients) have not consistently beat the S&P 500, value investors in real estate routinely earn rates of return that even Warren Buffet might envy.

Chapter 4

Real Estate Risks and Returns

No idea ranks higher in the world of modern finance than the maxim "The higher the risk, the greater the reward." Or, as it is often stated, "You can increase your potential rewards only when you increase your risk."[1] To value investors, though, this widely preached maxim seems completely wrongheaded. It not only confuses the meaning of risk, it also denies the importance of applied intelligence. As a result, the finance and investment experts who worship at the altar of efficient markets completely miss the extraordinary profit potential available with income properties and other realty investments.

By assuming that risk and return are linked together like love and marriage—you can't have one without the other—modern finance continues to err in its comparison of stocks and real estate. Even worse, most practitioners of modern finance (such as Siegel) do not accurately contrast realty returns to stock returns even within the constricted view of their so-called efficient markets. They so want to promote stocks that they ignore their own teachings.

A Quick Trip through Modern Finance

If you're new to the field of investing, you may think that debates over esoteric terms like risk and return, modern finance, and efficient markets hold no practical implications. Yet whether you realize it or not, these ideas will influence the financial advice you receive and the investment strategy you choose to pursue.

If you accept the tenets of modern finance, you will never again try to pick individual stocks. You can tune out the "Money Honey" (CNBC's Maria Bartiromo) and "Wall Street Week," cancel your *Barron's* and *Kiplinger's*, and fire your stockbroker. If you want to reach for above-market returns, there's only one way to get them: Build yourself a portfolio of high-risk stocks.

Forget Value Investing in Stocks

Modern finance is called modern because it directly challenges the so-called naive, old-fashioned investing principles that Ben Graham expounded in *Security Analysis* and *The Intelligent Investor*. Whereas Graham and other value investors believed that you could win the investment game through fundamental analysis (stock picking derived from extensive research), modern finance holds just the opposite. Followers of modern finance believe that picking stocks makes for a loser's game. "If you want to make money in stocks," they say, "put your cash into a diversified portfolio." Forget market timing, fundamental analysis, or any stock-picking technique that you may have read about. Once you choose a diversified portfolio of stocks, just hang tight and ride the market wherever it takes you—which, over the long run, is sure to be up.[2]

Efficient Markets

The modern finance school of investment believes that stock picking fails because financial markets respond immediately to new economic information. By the time value investors have figured out whether the news is good or bad, the stock price has already adjusted up or down. Research becomes futile. Market efficiency rules.

Because no one can accurately predict the news, no one can accurately predict the movement of stock prices. All that can be said is this: In the short run, stock prices move up and down randomly. Over the long run, stock prices move up and down randomly with an upward drift.[3]

Risk, Reward, and Efficient Markets

If you believe that stocks merely walk randomly up Wall Street, how can you beat the market? You can't. You can only boost your returns by buying stocks in companies that move up and down more erratically than the stocks of other companies. To achieve a greater return, look for a wilder roller coaster. Put together a portfolio of high beta stocks—stocks that historically have shown more volatility. You can't earn a higher return by individual stock picking. Instead, you must climb aboard the Millennium. To advocates of efficient markets, risk equals volatility. Nothing else matters.

At first glance, you may think that modern finance sounds nutty. Most people do.[4] But in fact, the developers of this school of thought have won several Nobel prizes in economics; nearly all business schools in the United States and Canada teach modern finance (only a few teach Graham and Dodd); and a growing body of financial planners, investment advisors, and fund managers now promote this theory to their clients and customers.[5]

What's the Evidence?

To support their theories of risk and efficient markets, thousands of finance professors have cranked out tens of thousands of research studies. In the main, these studies tend to show that the following statements are true:

1. *Professionals lose*. Seventy percent to 80% of all professional money managers fail to consistently beat the market.
2. *Individuals lose*. Very few individual investors consistently beat the market.
3. *Pundits lose*. Investment newsletters, financial magazines, and media commentators are wrong more often than they are right.
4. *Costs rule*. Fund fees, trading commissions, costs, and taxes tend to offset the so-called superior performance of even the best active (stock picking) professionals and individuals.

In his easily readable book *What Wall Street Doesn't Want You to Know*, Larry Swedroe summarizes much of this "efficient market" research.[6]

Accordingly, he encourages stock investors to discard their illusions of beating the market and simply join the growing ranks of investors who buy a portfolio of low-cost, tax-efficient index funds. Even the renowned value investor Warren Buffet has now endorsed the index approach to stock buying for most individual investors.

Has Buffet Rejected Value Investing?

Buffet has not abandoned value investing in stocks. Nor has he accepted the basic tenets of modern finance. He rejects the notion that the market always prices stocks correctly. He rejects absolutely the idea that risk equals volatility. Nevertheless, Buffet recognizes that in their efforts to beat the market, stock investors face several tough obstacles:

1. *Lack of knowledge*. Value investing in stocks (in its various forms) requires sophisticated knowledge of balance sheets, income statements, competitive markets, industry outlook, and other value fundamentals.[7]
2. *Lack of discipline*. Even when investors develop expertise in stock (company) valuation, they need to overcome their all-too-human behavioral tendencies that lead to losses.[8]
3. *Costs*. Without knowledge and discipline, investors tend to get their returns eaten up by trading costs, fees, ill-conceived market timing, and tax inefficiencies.[9]

In other words, Buffet still believes that value investing stands superior to the tenets and implications of modern finance. Realistically, though, history does show that few investors can (or will) pursue it successfully.

Ben Graham Agrees

In *The Intelligent Investor* Graham divides investors into two classes: passive and enterprising. The passive investor wishes to avoid mistakes (large losses) and remain free from "effort, annoyance, and the need for making frequent decisions." On the other hand, the enterprising investor—what we now call the value investor—seeks a superior reward for an additional investment of skill and effort in analyzing and selecting securities.[10]

In concluding his thoughts on passive versus enterprising investors, Graham expressed serious doubts about whether (active) value investing could still deliver superior profits.[11] Because our stock market today stands far more competitive and far more overvalued than when Graham last wrote (1973), his doubts remain valid.

Implications for Stocks

You can either accept or reject the efficient market view of stock pricing and risk.[12] But regardless, one of its basic premises holds true: As an individual or professional investor, you stand little chance of beating the stock market.[13] From the modern finance view, you can't beat the market because the market can't be beaten. You can possibly achieve higher returns—but only by accepting a wilder ride of ups and downs with a portfolio of high-beta, volatile stocks.[14]

To make matters worse, even hopeful value investors who reject modern finance can't expect to perform much better. Lack of knowledge, lack of discipline, and high costs conspire to force most stock pickers into the loser's game.[15] So what's a true value investor to do? Stick to the principles, but change the medium.

Value Investors Should Choose Real Estate

If you want to outperform the stock market, you've really only two choices:

1. *Gamble*. The research evidence overwhelmingly shows that among all investors, the great majority have failed to match the hypothetical returns of a broad-based market index such as the S&P 500. That's why playing the market to win has become known as the loser's game. (Note, too, that because most individuals *and* professionals have failed to match the S&P 500, it makes no sense for stock enthusiasts to use the S&P 500 benchmark as a proxy to represent actual investor returns.)
2. *Invest in real estate*. True believer or not, no one seriously believes that the risk-reward, efficient market tenets of modern finance apply

to real estate investors. Within the field of real estate, enterprising investors routinely beat the returns of the S&P 500 while incurring *less* risk.

Notwithstanding the preceding facts, the stock enthusiasts never compare point by point the relative risks and returns of stocks and real estate. In other words, to legitimately claim that stocks outperform real estate not only requires a measure of real estate *market* returns (which is irrelevant and impossible), but also stock advocates must adjust these real estate returns for risk—which they never do.

In other words, even if you accept some fanciful market real estate return figure, that figure remains aloof until it is hooked up with an appropriate measure of risk. Have you ever seen such a measure used when the stock advocates say that stocks outperform all other assets? No? Well, neither have I. For it would not serve their biases.

Volatility: Stocks versus Real Estate

Modern finance chiefly defines risk as price swings up and down.[16] But as we've already discussed, downward price swings in real estate occur far less frequently and with far less severity than in stocks. Moreover, unlike corporate earnings and dividends, cash flows from rental properties generally show stability.

Indeed, for proof positive that real estate experiences fewer and less severe price slides than stocks, try this experiment. Call several mortgage lenders. Ask them if you can borrow 80% of a property's purchase price for a period of 15 to 30 years at a fixed rate of interest. Of course you can. Now, ask those same lenders—or even your stock-touting brokerage firm—if they will make you a similar deal on a portfolio of stocks. "What? Are you crazy?" they'd respond. (Or, just as likely, they'd tell you to pay cash for your stocks with money borrowed with a *low-interest-rate home equity loan*.)

This simple, commonsense approach to risk assessment speaks volumes. If stocks are less risky than real estate, why won't lenders grant stock portfolio loans for the same duration, terms, and cost that are widely available with mortgage loans? (Remember, too, property loans never include a margin call.)

Lower Risk Typically Ignored

In other words, even if it were true that returns on stocks beat those typically available in real estate, that's not the end of the story. Performance must include measures of both risk and return.

The next time financial planners or stock enthusiasts tell you that stocks outperform real estate, put those experts on the hot seat. Ask them not only what measure of return they're using, but also what measure of risk. Then wait for a long silence, or, more amusing, a stuttered makeshift explanation that can't withstand even a breeze of reason.

Risk: A Broader View

Although the prices of income properties and homes have proven more stable and far less risky (volatile) than stocks, no sensible investor can accept such a constricted definition of risk. As Ben Graham wrote in critique, "We find this use of the word 'risk' more harmful than helpful for sound investment decisions—because it places too much emphasis on market fluctuations."[17]

As a minimum of risk assessment, we should also consider the investment risks presented by changes in the overall price level (such as the Consumer Price Index, or CPI). These risks include (1) inflation, (2) disinflation, and (3) deflation.

Inflation

In today's world of ever-higher prices, no one should weigh the merits of an investment without thinking through the possible effects of inflation. As you plan to accumulate wealth to meet your long-term spending needs, you must think in real (inflation-adjusted) dollars, not nominal dollars.

A cool million bucks may seem like a comfortable amount right now. But what will it buy in 20, 30, or 40 years? Relatively few people explicitly consider the effects of inflation on their need for retirement income or other future spending.

Time Shrivels Money

To make sure you truly comprehend this point, consider an investor who hopes to accumulate that million dollars in 20 years. With a 2.5% average annual rise in prices, that $1,000,000 will then buy only $606,000 of goods and services in today's prices. At 3.5% inflation, the investor's buying power falls to $497,000; and at an average annual 5.0% inflation rate (such as that experienced between 1960 and 1985), that $1,000,000 nest egg would hatch a very small chick—just $368,600. Even though this investor has built up a $1,000,000 account, in terms of purchasing power, that sum falls far short of appearances.

The Worst Is Yet to Come

To illustrate: Say this investor retires with his accumulated $1,000,000 and can somehow manage to conservatively preserve capital and still pull out 7% ($70,000) a year in income on which to live. Again, this $70,000 figure may today seem like a decent amount to many people. But if you assume a 30% tax rate, that leaves only $49,000—and 20 years from now (at 2.5%, 3.5%, or 5.0% inflation) that $49,000 would be the equivalent of, respectively, $29,735, $24,357, or $18,063 in today's dollars.

Our investor, though, doesn't die just one year after receiving his gold watch. He plans to stay healthy and live another 25 years. If he still wishes to live on his posttax $49,000 of income, the buying power of that income will continue to erode. Even after just 10 years of inflation (say, 3.5% a year), that investor's buying power, in today's prices, will have dropped to a mere $17,172, and after 20 years, a piddling $12,107.[18]

Protect Your Investment and Income

Naturally, we could rework the preceding figures under all kinds of inflationary assumptions. But any outcome within the realm of history and reason will show similar results.

Even moderate rates of inflation will seriously diminish the buying power of your future wealth and future income. Investors (or savers) who don't protect themselves against the ravages of inflation must prepare for ever-smaller grocery baskets; fewer visits to the doctor; shorter, less frequent vacations; a cramped apartment; and financial help from the kids (if, of course, the parents can sacrifice their pride and the kids are willing and able to sacrifice their money).

Stocks versus Inflation

In *Stocks for the Long Run*, Jeremy Siegel, like most other stock enthusiasts, claims that "stocks are excellent long-term hedges against inflation." By hedge against inflation Siegel says that he means, "Stocks will increase in value sufficiently to compensate investors for any erosion in purchasing power of money."[19]

Yet, a few pages later in this book, Siegel remarks, "By the end of 1974 real [inflation-adjusted] stock prices, measured by the Dow Jones Industrial Average, had fallen 65 percent from their January 1966 high—the largest decline since the crash of 1929."[20] Elsewhere, Siegel displays a long-term inflation-adjusted rendition of the DJIA.[21] For example, consider the contrasts I've reconstructed in Table 4.1. Even a quick glance at those figures show wildly erratic stock price fluctuations as well as decades over which no permanent increase in *inflation-adjusted* stock prices occurred. Siegel's own data prove the folly of his contention that over long periods stock *prices* keep investors ahead of inflation.

Table 4.1 **Selected Year-to-Year Comparisons for an Inflation-Adjusted Dow Jones Industrial Average in Terms of 1996 Prices**

Year	1885	1889	1921	1932
Dow Jones Index	466	408	556	485
Year	1906	1916	1942	1982
Dow Jones Index	1,404	874	925	1,272
Year	1929	1940	1987	1992
Dow Jones Index	3,529	2,188	2,415	2,800
Year	1966	1982	1987	1994
Dow Jones Index	4,869	1,272	2,415	4,500

The data in Table 4.1 do clearly show that if you pick the right time to buy and sell, you can make a bonanza. If you pick the wrong time to buy and sell, you can lose big. Think of those unfortunate souls who plunged into the stock market near those peak years of 1885, 1906, 1929, and 1966 (or 1999?). If they merely bought and held, they would have had to suffer through many periods when they could not have sold profitably—in real, inflation-adjusted dollars.

The Reinvestment Assumption

To recover their argument that stock prices compensate for inflation, the stock enthusiasts pull a neat trick and hope no one notices (few have). They assume that through thick and thin investors continue to reinvest their dividend payments in more stocks. As a result, over most (but not all) periods of 10 years or more, the investor has earned a positive real rate of return—even though stock prices themselves may have stagnated or fallen.

Before 1982—and going back as far as the mid-1800s—this dividend kicker typically averaged between 4% and 6%. With stock price increases averaging less than 3% a year (1850–1960), dividends alone could usually keep stock investors ahead of inflation. Of course, given a current dividend yield of around 1.2% to 1.4%, that's no longer true.[22]

Implications for the Future

As far as the future goes, all bets are off. With annual dividend yields now dropping to record lows, stock prices must increase significantly to win the battle against rising prices. Yet today's level of stock prices sits dramatically above the long-term trend line. If, as in the past, stock prices simply move sideways until the trend line catches up, we could wait at least 5 or 10 years, possibly longer. Will this occur? Who knows? Who is brash enough to forecast? But because the present differs so markedly from the historical past (distant or recent), any intelligent investor must question whether the past can dependably assure us that future stock prices will protect (and enhance) our purchasing power.

Two Types of Inflation

In talking about inflation, far too many investment advisors fail to distinguish expected from unexpected inflation. If you could simply plug a single inflation figure into your financial planning, life would prove far simpler. But you can't. Given our current relatively low rates of 2.0% to 3.0%, it would seem that the risk of an upward burst is certainly possible.

With rising rates of unexpected inflation, stock prices undoubtedly would fall—especially from their now-lofty P/E ratios. Today's new-era valuations assume no increases in the rate of inflation. That's why the markets tend to worship Federal Reserve chairman Allan Greenspan. With such a dedicated inflation fighter at the helm of monetary policy, all seems to be well. But history shows one permanent feature—times change.

Greenspan won't always be with us. Government fiscal responsibility won't always rank as the top priority. If we should again live through a period similar to that between 1965 and 1982, stock prices and total stock returns could easily head into negative territory. During that total period, inflation-adjusted stock prices fell by more than 65%. And even dividends weren't enough to push total returns into positive territory.

The Preretirement Risk

Because no one can know when periods of unexpected inflation might arise—otherwise it wouldn't count as unexpected, would it?—stock investing becomes riskier as you get within sight of retirement. Imagine a 35-year-old investor in 1950 who decided to put his retirement savings into stocks. Until reaching age 50 (circa 1965), this investor was well on his way to a comfortable and prosperous retirement. Annual returns of 8% to 12% percent were racked up in (more or less) dependable fashion.

Then the market stalled. Inflation warmed, then overheated. For the next 15 years, the real value of his first 15 years of accumulations steadily shrank. Just as bad, his new contributions showed only negative returns. By 1980, this investor had accumulated only 30% of the amount he had anticipated. Fortunately, with a much larger than expected Social Security check, a generous Medicare program, and a company pension, this retiree did okay.

But what about you? Can you expect expanded Social Security benefits, more generous Medicare, and a company pension to bail you out of the dire investment results created by unexpected inflation? Not likely.

Postretirement

It's bad enough to get hit with a stalled market during the later years of your wealth building. But what would have happened to our investor's buying power had he retired in 1965? Absent ever-increasing Social Security benefits and an inflation-adjusted pension, this investor would have faced financial disaster.

Between 1965 and 1982, the CPI rose from 94.5 to 294, an increase of more than 200%. Yet during this same period, the DJIA basically bounced up and down between 600 and 1,000. The 1982 DJIA high of 1,070 was only 10% higher (nominally) than its high of 969 attained in 1965. And during those 17 years, the Dow fell to as low as 577. No one should ever argue that stock prices adequately protect preretirees or retirees against a serious loss of buying power.

History shows that stock market investors can get whipsawed by an updraft in consumer prices and a simultaneous downdraft of stock returns. This financial ship will likely right itself and again sail profitably after some unknown number of years. But along the way, many of the travelers on board may not make it safely through the storm.

Summing Up

Too many investors falsely believe that stocks reliably return 10% to 12% a year—year in and year out. Granted, they must suffer a few stops and starts, zigs and zags along the way, but that's merely the cross they must bear for a near-certain fantastic long-run reward. As Keynes reminds us, however, "In the long run, we're all dead." For preretirees and retirees, a short run of 10 to 20 years can slice their wealth building and spendable income by 30%, 40%, 50%, or more.

Unless you love tempting fate, you cannot assume that "stocks for retirement" will keep you financially fit. Even Siegel warns, "The message of this chapter ["Inflation and Stocks"] is that stocks are not good hedges against inflation in the short run. . . ."[23] What he omits emphasizing, however, is that as we age, the short run becomes much more important to us.

Real Estate versus Inflation

Unlike stocks, real estate offers dependable increases in price and income. Although no national index perfectly captures the often wide variations among local housing markets, commonsense experience tells most of us that home prices seldom sink like stocks and that rents continue their persistent upward march. If not every year, most certainly every few years home prices and rents tend to ratchet up.

At What Rate?

Though no one knows for sure, my best guess as to the annual rate of rent increases is around 4% to 6%. Usually, rents and home prices go up by the rate of inflation plus the annual increase in national productivity (typically between 1% and 3%). Another widely held view figures that home prices and rent levels tend to track the annual increases in nominal incomes.

However, many cities and neighborhoods do much better, whereas others lag behind. It depends largely on population, jobs, incomes, new construction, building regulations, and environmental restrictions. So by studying these factors (discussed in later chapters), you can identify geographic areas of promise.

The Rule of 72

To check the historical rate of appreciation and rent increases in your area, you could go to your public or college library. Get the microfiche for your local newspaper. Then check the real estate classifieds for sale prices and typical rents of 10, 20, 30, and 40 years ago. Of course, a helpful real estate agent may be able to dig this information out of office files or multiple listing records.

Once you've put together some price (rent) figures, you can easily compute how long it has taken for prices to double. If 10 years, then appreciation has run about 7.2% a year (72 ÷ 10); if 18 years, then the rate of increase has averaged 4.0% annually (72 ÷ 18); if 24 years, the appreciation rate drops to 3% (72 ÷ 24). Take any number of years you choose; divide it into 72, and you'll find the appreciation rate over which prices (rents) double.

Simplified Rate of Return

As noted, the magic of real estate doesn't lie in the rate of appreciation per se. As Tables 3.1, 3.2, and 3.3 illustrate clearly, you can easily double your money within five years—even at a low rate of appreciation. To a significant degree, returns depend on the amount of leverage (financing) you use. Here's a simplified illustration:

Purchase price	$100,000
Appreciation rate	3.0%
Down payment	$25,000
Amount financed @ 30 years/8%	$75,000
Rent collections ($900/mo.) × 12	$10,800
Mortgage payment ($550/mo.) × 12	$6,603
Expenses	$2,500
BTCF	$1,697

$$\text{ROR (Rate of Return)} = \frac{\text{BTCF + Appreciation + Mortgage Reduction}}{\text{original investment}}$$

$$= \frac{1{,}697 + 3{,}000 + 725}{25{,}000}$$

$$21.68\% = \frac{5{,}422}{25{,}000}$$

Note. BTCF = before-tax cash flows.

If instead of a 75% loan, you financed 85%, your figures would look like this:

$$\text{ROR} = \frac{817 + 3{,}000 + 718}{15{,}000}$$

$$30.23\% = \frac{4{,}535}{15{,}000}$$

Most stock investors would drool over these rates of return. Yet they're nothing out of the ordinary for value investors in real estate. As to CPI inflation-adjustments to returns, subtract 3% to 6%. Would *real* rates of return of, say, 15% to 25% satisfy you?

True Inflation Fighter

To really see the power of leveraged real estate to fight inflation and protect your buying power, think of this unlikely scenario: You buy the aforementioned $100,000 property using the $75,000 loan ($25,000 down). Assume that your rent collections merely cover property expenses and monthly mortgage payments. Over the 30 years of loan repayments, the property fails to appreciate, yet the CPI advances steadily at a rate of 3% a year. Nevertheless, measured in terms of today's buying power, your original $25,000 down payment still would have grown to $41,986 ($100,000 x .41986).

Try that experiment with stocks and you'll end up eating dog food for dinner. Your money will evaporate. You can't achieve these results with stocks because (1) you can't finance stocks; they're too risky, and (2) even if you could finance stocks, the dividends wouldn't come close to covering your required annual repayments of debt. You would consistently have to come up with money out-of-pocket.

Unexpected Inflation

As proved by the 1960s and 1970s, unexpected inflation can kill stock returns and stock appreciation. Squeezed corporate profit margins due to operating expenses that outpace profits, higher replacement costs for plants and equipment, and investor demand for increased nominal yields can all conspire to pull stock prices into Filene's basement. Fortunately, realty investors enjoy quite opposite results. As even Siegel admits, "Only real assets, such as . . . real estate, were able to outperform inflation during the 1970s."[24] Why does real estate perform so well? Here are three important reasons:

1. *Fixed costs*. Realty investors fix their largest cost, mortgage interest, for a period of 15 to 30 years. Even investors who use adjustable-rate mortgages (ARMs) gain because their interest-rate increases are typically capped. Most ARMs include maximum limits for both year-to-year and lifetime rates. Naturally, ARMs go down as well as up, too. In sum, real estate investors can shift all or much of the inflation risk to their long-term lenders.
2. *New supply falls short of needs*. During periods of sharp, unexpected inflation, new construction will lag behind household formations. Higher interest rates and higher construction costs drive developers and builders into retreat. Thereafter, the resulting decline in newly built housing leads to higher rents for existing tenants and to higher profits for property owners.
3. *Rising incomes*. Absent new construction, inflationary wage increases add to the pressure for higher rents.

Think back to the earlier example on page 109. Imagine a burst of 10%-a-year inflation. Yet our investor sees his property operating expenses shoot up to, say, $2,875 (a 15% increase). On the other hand, to maintain high occupancy and tenant loyalty, he boosts rents by only 8%. Look at the strong positive effect on cash flow (pretax):

Rent collections	$11,664
Operating expenses	$2,875
Mortgage payments	$6,603
BTCF	$2,186

Even with rent increases that lag the CPI, this investor gains a 29% increase in cash flow ($1,697 to $2,186) in an environment of 10% increases in the CPI. Now, let's say this general level of inflation, rent, and expense increases continues for five years. Here's how rents and expenses would look in year 5:

Rent collections @ 8% increases	$17,138
Operating expenses @ 15% increases	$5,782
Mortgage payments	$6,603
BTCF	$4,753

In a period where the CPI advances by a cumulative total of 61%, this investor's cash flows nearly triple (i.e., a gain of 188%). Whereas stock-dependent preretirees and retirees must constantly fear unexpected inflation, owners of income properties will welcome it as they enjoy a great boost to their incomes and buying power.

Price Increases

Unlike with stocks, periods of unexpected inflation will eventually send property prices up—although in the short run investors may suffer some temporary declines in value. If mortgage rates jump up in response to inflation, potential new buyers of properties would face much higher mortgage payments than existing property owners. Many investors and homebuyers will postpone their purchase plans until higher rent levels once again make ownership (for new buyers) look economically sensible (or until interest rates fall).

The 1970s Exception

Due to interest-rate regulations and the prevalence of assumable mortgages, property investors in the 1970s got a free ride on the backs of mortgage lenders. Lenders were stuck with below-market lending. Alas, those days are probably gone forever. That's why—unlike in the 1970s—a future burst of unexpected inflation will stall property price increases.

Nevertheless, even today few lenders can call their existing mortgages due or immediately adjust rates to market. Existing property owners will still gain substantially from inflationary rent increases. This free bonus, though, won't benefit passengers who haven't yet bought their ticket.

Never Wait for Inflation to Rise

Quite wrongly, some financial planners and writers still urge investors to consider buying properties after they spot inflation creeping (shooting?) up. In an era of regulated low-interest mortgage rates (like the 1970s), such advice may have held some merit. But in our current era, even a whiff of coming inflation will send mortgage rates skyward.

The moral: Don't wait until you see inflation advancing to buy properties. Buy when people think our wise policy makers have subdued inflation forever. Lock in a low-interest-rate mortgage.[25] Then enjoy your free ride the next time—and you can count on there being a next time—the CPI starts climbing.

The Benefits of Disinflation

Nearly everyone agrees that a falling rate of inflation (disinflation) typically helps boost the prices of stocks and bonds. Nearly everyone agrees that during periods of rising inflation, property owners gain. Yet surprisingly—and especially with the experience of the 1990s in recent view—few financial experts point out that property owners profit not only during periods when the CPI is rising, but also when the CPI slows its upward drift.

In other words, whether the CPI moves up quickly or slowly, property owners stand to receive a windfall. Income properties offer the ultimate protection against an ever-shifting rate of inflation.

Cash Flows Up

To illustrate how property owners gain increased cash flows during disinflation, return to our earlier example (page 109). For that property, the owner financed his purchase with a 30-year mortgage for $75,000 at 8% interest. These terms called for mortgage payments of $6,603. The numbers originally looked like this:

Rent collections	$11,664
Operating expenses	$2,500
Mortgage payments	$6,603
BTCF	$1,697

But with a lower inflation, our investor could refinance his mortgage. So five years into ownership, let's say mortgage rates fall to 6.5%. With cumulative 3% annual increases in rents and expenses, here's how this investor's cash flows would improve:

Rent collections @ 3% p.a.	$13,518
Operating expenses @ 3% p.a.	$2,898
New mortgage @ 6.5% for 30 years on current balance of $71,260	$5,404
Year 5 BTCF	$5,216

With disinflation, our investor is able to reduce his yearly mortgage payments by $1,200. When coupled with previously modest rent boosts, his cash flows from this property jump from $1,697 (year 1) to $5,216 (year 5). In an era of falling inflation (not falling prices, which is called deflation), this investor saw his cash flow grow by an average compound rate of around 25% per year.

Real estate offers the ultimate hedge: During inflation, rents go up, yet mortgage payments remain stable. During disinflation, rents stabilize, yet owners can refinance at lower interest rates. Either way—whatever happens—property owners enjoy income growth that far outpaces the climb of the CPI.

Property Values Up

In contrast to how most people think, a fall in the rate of inflation nearly always puts upward pressure on property prices. Lower mortgage interest rates not only make properties more profitable to own, they also improve their affordability for homebuyers. As more investors and renters try to buy, their heightened competition pushes property prices up.

During the low-inflation 1990s, most investors watched in awe as their stock accounts multiplied. Far more quietly, though, run-of-the-mill property investors during this same period earned rates of return on equity that surpassed the best-performing mutual funds. In a decade that surprised us with historically astonishing gains for stocks, property investors more than held their own. Even better for property owners, their gains (unlike those of stock investors) did not evaporate. Most property owners continued to profit from rent increases, equity build-up, and refinancings through 2001.

The Risks and Rewards of Deflation

It seems to be ingrained in people's minds that realty owners stand to gain only during periods of inflation. But as we've seen, a quiet refinance may add just as much to profits as a heralded boom in property prices that must be financed with higher-rate mortgages. Thus, just as disinflation can bring higher yields through lower interest rates to property investors, so too can deflation (falling consumer prices). It all depends on the nature and source of the price fall.

General Prosperity

Property prices and rents generally benefit from deflation—if the deflation results from outstanding advances in technology and productivity. Throughout the 1800s, for example, the general price level fell as real estate investors like Vanderbilt, Carnegie, Flagler, Crocker, and Stanford made millions from property speculations. Such "unearned" wealth motivated the 1800s socialist-progressive Henry George to write his famous tract, *Progress and Poverty*.

In that tract, George proposed a large tax on all unearned property appreciation. George, however, failed to realize that most Americans valued their opportunity to get rich in real estate far more than they wanted a political scheme to redistribute wealth. As a result, *Progress and Poverty* failed to gain political traction. Nevertheless, as an offset to today's popular view, George reminds us that progress—not inflation—stands firm as the ultimate cause of increasing rents and property prices.

If we should ever truly enter a new era of progress, prosperity, and a downward-sliding CPI, realty investors will surely gain. Rising real incomes, low mortgage rates, and environmental limits will make real estate a favored investment. As to stocks, the outlook is more mixed. For stock prices to gain during deflation, competition must not evolve into ruinous competition and overcapacity. That result could produce—as it has in the past—profitless prosperity. Consumers, workers, and property owners reap the lion's share of the productivity rewards.

Economic Crisis

Americans have not lived through a serious and persistent decline in the CPI since the 1930s. Even in periods of relatively high unemployment—such as the 1970s and early 1980s—the consumer price level went up. As to the future, the post-1930s trend of inflation will almost surely continue. That is because our country, like most others, has abandoned hard currency.

Since the government no longer backs U.S. paper money with gold or silver, the Federal Reserve now creates money at will. Any sign of deflation will almost surely bring about an increase in the supply of money. With huge volumes of outstanding government and consumer debt, the politicians could not permit a serious and persistent decline in prices. Debtors not only want cheap money, they *demand* cheap money.

Remember Shay's Rebellion and, later, William Jennings Bryan's famous "cross of gold" speech? Unlike in Bryan's day, though, the politics of debt has turned 180 degrees. In our credit card–I.O.U.–Social Security "trust fund"–mortgage-driven economy, voters (debtors) and government policy makers (debtors) would not tolerate a sharp, sustained deflation such as occurred from 1929 through 1932.

What If?

Reason, history, and six decades of post-1930s experience combine to minimize the outlook for serious deflation.[26] Nevertheless, as a prudent investor, you still may want to incorporate the possibility of economic depression into your portfolio planning. What might happen to your investments in stocks? What would likely happen to your investments in real estate?

Economic Crisis (Deflation) and Stocks

Whether it's inflation or deflation that creates economic crisis, stocks suffer. Between September 1929 and January 1932, stock prices fell by almost 90%. Although throughout the 1930s the Dow bounced up and down, it never surpassed its high of 1927. Even after the United States was well into World War II, the Dow of 1943 was still off its 1927 high by around 35%. Even worse, it still sat below its 1929 high by 60% to 70%. Deflation during economic crisis typically sends stock prices plummeting.

Economic Crisis (Deflation) and Real Estate

Deflation brings bad news to owners of highly leveraged real estate. In a general collapse of prices and economic crisis, overleveraged, financially weak real estate investors typically sink and drown. A severe decline of property prices can bring wide-scale mortgage defaults. Defaults bring foreclosures that in turn dramatically increase the number of properties for sale. Hence, a vicious cycle: More downward pressure on prices, more defaults, and more foreclosures. Not a pretty picture.

But it does have a possible bright side. Financially strong investors can pick up bargains—often without putting up any cash. Because wide-scale foreclosures create a domino effect of even more foreclosures, lenders become amenable to workouts and restructurings. Absent loan workouts, lenders risk their own solvency. Those lenders who pile up a portfolio of foreclosed properties (REOs) can quickly exhaust their lender's reserves.

Moreover, because most residential mortgages today are backed directly or indirectly by the federal government (Fannie Mae, Freddy Mac, Ginny Mae, FHA, VA, USDA), Congress, or possibly activist courts, would more than likely step in with foreclosure moratoriums or other bailout assistance. Obviously, the exact play of this scenario would depend on the politics of the moment. But you can reasonably bet that a nation of debtors would not permit millions of homeowners and real estate investors to lose their properties.

Regional Deflation in Real Estate

In the 1980s and early 1990s, several regional real estate markets suffered price deflation due to localized economic distress. Although these downturns did not adversely affect most long-term property owners, they did punish speculators and highly leveraged, financially insecure recent buyers.

In later chapters, we'll go over how you can measure and mitigate this type of potential localized risk. For now, realize that these regional and local realty deflations did not upset the finances of value investors. Rent levels for established properties did not fall in any significant way—and many rents continued to rise, albeit slowly. (I speak here from experience as I owned interests in properties during these times in both Texas and California.)

So as you assess risk, don't confuse investment risk with speculative risk. If you pay highly today for expected future gains previously unknown to reason or experience, you are speculating (or worse). If you mortgage heavily without strong reserves of cash or credit, you are speculating (or worse). Value investors don't throw their nest eggs into the air and then hope they land safely.

Risk: Volatility and Price Declines

During economic good times, people tend to forget that all types of investments can languish. Prices never move up steadily without intermittent stalls; slides; and, yes, sometimes collapse. Overall, though, history shows that residential real estate has proven far more reliable than stocks.[27] Even in those relatively few times and places when property prices have seriously slipped or fallen, rents for established properties have not dropped precipitously—as have corporate earnings.

Anticipating Unexpected Inflation

Moreover, in looking to the future, we will surely encounter periods of unexpected inflation. Nobody knows when or for how long. But we do know that upward spurts in the CPI will add to the profits of real estate investors. In contrast, during past periods of unexpected rising inflation, stocks have suffered. Higher interest rates on certificates of deposit (CDs) and bonds lure money out of stocks. Why settle for risky dividend yields of, say, 1% to 3% when you can get, say, a guaranteed 8% to 12% on safe CDs or bonds? (The post–September 11, 2001, flight to quality and yield further supports this point.)[28] At least that's the way most reasonable investors think and behave.

Unexpected Disinflation

Contrary to the understanding of many financial planners and journalists, real estate not only outperforms stocks during periods of unexpected inflation, but it can also match or exceed the returns from stocks when CPI increases slow their upward march. During these times, real estate investors may not see big jumps in rent levels or property values (although they might), but they can easily and significantly boost their cash flows with a refinance at lower interest rates.

You must obliterate the wrongheaded idea that real estate investors require inflation to do well.[29] A growing, prosperous, and stable economy with falling mortgage rates can ratchet up cash flows, rents, and property values. The period 1993 through (at least) 2001 provides Exhibit 1 in affirmation of this often overlooked advantage for real estate.

Overall Risk Comparison: Stocks versus Real Estate

No matter what your age, you must consider your inflation-adjusted rates of return. You must weigh the uncertainties of unexpected changes in consumer prices. You want strong, dependable returns regardless of whether the CPI crawls or gallops. Yet history shows that only real estate performs well under any general price level assumptions you can make—except, of course, deflation created by economic crisis.

If you wish to prepare for economic crisis, then load up on U.S. government bonds. Otherwise, you will find that relative to stocks or bonds, residential real estate offers long-term value investors both lower risks and higher rewards—a combination that modern finance declares quite impossible, yet history proves quite true.

Chapter 5

The Enterprising Investor

Conventional wisdom and modern finance both hold dear the notion that low risks make for low rewards. Ben Graham's view is different. Rather than simplistically relating return to risk, Graham argues, investors should expect rewards proportionate to the amount of intelligent and enterprising effort they can bring into their investment decisions.[1]

As we've just seen in Chapters 3 and 4, Graham's view wins. Real estate investors can outperform stocks with lower risk and greater returns. It is conventional wisdom and modern finance that err. Moreover, even when judged according to the risk-equals-volatility criterion (with either nominal or inflation-adjusted returns), the efficient market view fails. Over the long or short run, well-selected residential real estate has offered even passive investors outsized rewards with relatively slight downdrafts.

But when we factor in the intelligence quotient, enterprising realty investors can pile up extraordinary profits while still minimizing the possibility of loss. How can they achieve this ostensibly miraculous result? By understanding the inefficiency of real estate markets.

Market Efficiency: Stocks versus Real Estate

As you'll recall, modern finance claims that every stock is always priced exactly right. Perfect information makes for perfect pricing. Think you've found a stock market bargain? Think again. You just don't realize the pitiful prospects that company actually faces. Think you've found a great stock to short? Don't believe it. You just don't see that company's truly awesome potential. Want evidence of stock market efficiency? Just look at the dismal performance records of amateurs and professionals alike.[2] Very few consistently beat benchmark indexes.[3]

Mr. Market's Manic Depression

Long before any investor had ever heard of modern finance or efficient markets, Ben Graham explained why beating the market has proved so difficult. In contrast to today's academics, Graham rejected super-rationality. Instead, he focused on irrationality—the ever-present push and pull of those human emotions greed and fear.

Graham playfully described the parable of "Mr. Market," the unpredictable manic-depressive business owner who swings back and forth between liquidation and accumulation: sell low, buy high. Mr. Market's mood, more than any file folder stuffed with economic reports and financial analyses, determines the direction of stock prices.[4]

Thus, the value investor in stocks faces three problems: (1) finding a company whose current stock price sits below its investment (intrinsic) value, (2) predicting when Mr. Market's mood might change, and (3) hoping Mr. Market's positive mood hits before that company's fortunes change for the worse. "To achieve *satisfactory* investment results," Graham writes, "is easier than most people realize; to achieve *superior* results is harder than it looks."[5]

Take Your Pick

You can reject efficient markets and accept Graham's Mr. Market. Or you might reject Graham and accept the efficient market theory. Either way the conclusion remains the same: You won't easily beat the stock market. Whether you believe in chaos or market perfection (i.e., manic depression or random walk), for most investors, trying to pick winners remains the loser's game.[6]

You Can Win in Real Estate

It is so odd that the stock enthusiasts seldom notice that whatever merit it holds for stocks, the theory of efficient markets could not possibly apply to real estate. Consequently, they fail to realize the superior prospects that value investors enjoy in real estate as contrasted to stocks. In real estate, using intelligence to pick properties has proved to be a winner's game for at least six reasons:

1. No single market price rules; real estate appraisers and realty agents speak of value ranges, not perfect prices.
2. Each property stands unique. Not only must you learn the selling (or asking) price for a property, but you also must discover its detailed features—its advantages and disadvantages.
3. Buyers and sellers can uniquely structure financing to meet their needs and return requirements.
4. All terms of a property transaction are subject to negotiation.
5. No one central source lists all properties that are available for sale; many properties available for sale aren't listed anywhere. Some owners don't even realize they're potential sellers until they receive an offer.
6. Relevant property, economic, and financial information isn't widely available. No analysts follow specific properties, as they do stocks. Selling prices, terms of sale, and property earnings reports never get published in a financial newspaper, or anywhere else. If buyers want this information (as they should), they've got to dig it up and piece it together for themselves.

As a result of these so-called inefficiencies, enterprising realty investors can most certainly use their intelligence, talents, skills, know-how, and superior information to secure large returns with low risk. Yet stock enthusiasts persistently refer to real estate "market" returns. What nonsense. In real estate, "markets" don't merely give returns; investors earn them—just as Ben Graham earned his market-beating rewards in stocks.

Chaos versus Optimal Inefficiency

All value investors agree with Ben Graham: Mr. Market rules stock prices. The studies of behavioral economics (what Charles Mackay called the madness of crowds) defeat the perfect pricing theories of modern finance.[7] Rather than efficiency or inefficiency, stock markets give rise to various shades of chaos. Robert Shiller has convincingly shown that stock price levels jump around far more than underlying economic data warrant.[8] So, even if you find a bargain-priced stock, you're never sure whether you can make any money on it. At the base of chaos lies unpredictability.

No such chaos reigns in in real estate. Realty markets price properties inefficiently only in the sense that you can find bargains; you can negotiate bargains; and you can dramatically and safely enhance profits through terms of financing, property improvement, and property management. Yet the realty market typically maintains enough rationality to stay within the bounds of reason and experience.[9] Perfect pricing, no. Reliable analysis and predictability, yes.

We might say that residential real estate provides investors with optimal inefficiency. Learn the market. Develop the necessary skills. You will gain outsized rewards.

Degrees of Time and Expertise

Understandably, if you're pursuing a career, you may believe that real estate investing will require too much time, effort, and attention. In fact, real estate requires only as much time as you wish to give it. After you develop your time, effort, and financial constraints, you can delegate as much or as little as you choose.

In their perpetual critique of real estate, the stock enthusiasts always frame real estate as management intensive. This is true only in a limited sense. You do need a well-thought-out management strategy. As to everything else, from rent collections to repairs, you can structure an investment program that routinely operates on automatic pilot.

Case in Point

In addition to my own experiences, which I mentioned earlier, here's another case in point: Since the mid-1980s a friend of mine who works as a pharmacist has owned three rental houses. She possesses no talent or inclination for hands-on property management. Her properties are located in two different cities, each located more than 150 miles from her hometown. She employs no local management. When a property does need attention, she either asks the tenants to take care of it, or she phones a reliable service provider from a list she has put together.

Because she seeks out quality long-term tenants, this investor has averaged less than one vacancy a year. When a vacancy does occur, she asks her current tenants for referrals. If this effort fails to yield good results, she will spend a weekend in the town where the property is located, run an open-house ad, and invariably find a good tenant from the 10 or 15 people who show up to view the unit.

Because she has friends and family in the towns where she owns her rental properties, my friend always combines her property trips (tax-deductible) with personal visits. Ten years from now, when my friend expects to take early retirement, she will own her properties mortgage free. They will have been paid for completely by her tenants. At historical rates of price and rent appreciation, these properties then will be worth over $500,000 and produce rents of $4,500 a month. All of this gain for a total cash investment of $25,000 and a time commitment averaging less than 30 hours a year.

More Difficult Today?

Granted, you may find similar outsized returns more difficult to come by today. The great home price run-up since 1995 has pushed down cash-on-cash returns in many areas. But the situation is only going to get worse—or better, depending on your perspective. As preretirement boomers scramble to make up for lost time, they will continue to drive down cash yields on all types of investments, and income properties will prove no exception. Obviously, low dividend yields on stocks both reflect and foreshadow this trend.

Stand Out from the Crowd

Fortunately, in real estate, you can outperform the crowd. Unlike stocks—where most investors must passively accept returns that will surely fall below both real estate and historical stock market norms—most real estate investors can still rely on their intelligence and enterprise to secure safe, sure, and attractive returns. Even though many real estate markets now show relatively high gross rent multipliers and relatively low cash flows, numerous property submarkets, geographic areas, financial techniques, turnaround situations, and other types of opportunities still spell high return and low risk.

So, "stand out from the crowd" incorporates two meanings:

1. *The passive.* Relatively passive property investors (such as my pharmacist friend) still can reasonably expect to outperform the large and growing crowd of stock buyers.
2. *The active.* Enterprising (though not necessarily management-intensive) real estate investors still can reasonably expect to profit handsomely through the application of enterprise and intelligence.

The Magic of Leverage

As noted earlier, stock enthusiasts cry foul when real estate investors praise the magic of leverage as a way to boost returns on investment properties. Stock enthusiasts claim that stock investors, too, can use leverage. Therefore, to fairly compare the two investments, you must compare leveraged stocks (margin buying) to leveraged real estate. This idea proves false for five reasons:

1. *Corporate debt.* Stock returns already include the benefits of leverage. Nearly all companies use debt in their capital structure. Using leverage to buy stocks really involves double borrowing—at the corporate level, and at the individual level.

2. *Risk*. Due to high volatility, borrowing to buy stocks is as foolish as it is foolhardy.
3. *Capital market void*. Because lenders recognize the high risks of financing stock purchases, no lender offers long-term permanent financing. You can finance stocks only with short-term loans that are callable if the collateral stock falls in price.
4. *Mismatch of maturities*. Never borrow short to invest long. The S&Ls learned that lesson in the inflationary 1970s. To increase returns, S&L savers demanded higher market yields. Yet the S&Ls were locked into long-term lower interest rate mortgages. They had borrowed short from their depositors and had loaned long to mortgage borrowers (not unlike Japanese insurers today who find themselves similarly squeezed).
5. *Yields too low*. Even if you could finance your long-term stock investments with long-term capital, you wouldn't want to. Your monthly interest payments could exceed your cash returns by a factor of three, five, or more. Over the short term, iffy appreciation and unstable dividends could easily put you into a cash squeeze. Stock market alligators prey with far more ferocity than those gators that real estate investors meet up with in the swamplands of negative cash flow.

Although leverage may boost your possible returns from stocks, the high offsetting risks typically negate any financial advantage in making the attempt. If you wish to speculate, gamble, or take a flier, then borrow to buy stocks. If you want to invest, pay cash.

Real Estate: Caution First

Investors can safely borrow to invest in real estate under the following conditions:

1. *Maintain cash reserves*. Even the best of properties can suffer an unexpected market downturn or vacancy. Make sure your cash reserves or steady income will permit you to go at least three months without a rent collection. As you build up a portfolio of rental units,

you can safely reduce this amount to one month of rent for each unit you own.

2. *Never overfinance.* In their eagerness to leverage out, novice investors sometimes borrow more than a property is worth. For example, a seller may offer very liberal owner financing to entice a hopeful but naive buyer into overpaying. Avoid this trap.[10]
3. *Avoid negative cash flows.* Value investors do not accept negative cash flows. If your rent collections won't cover routine property expenses and monthly mortgage payments, either (1) renegotiate or restructure the deal, (2) put more money down, or (3) look elsewhere. As Warren Buffet reminds us, value investors don't need to swing until they see the near-perfect pitch. Buffet might also have added that value investors must exercise the necessary discipline and patience to wait for that near-perfect pitch.
4. *Beware of pro formas.* Value investors pay for the here and now. They expect to get a rosy future for free (or at least quite cheap). Be wary of buying with the idea that you can quickly boost rents to cover a negative cash flow. Absent a carefully calculated property-improvement program, rent increases tend to provoke vacancies and turnovers as well as attract lower-quality tenants. Too often, pro forma cash flows fail to materialize.

The preceding caveats apply only to *value* investors. The warnings do not necessarily apply to truly professional investors who knowingly seek higher returns as compensation for their superior expertise, intellect, and skill. In my own investing, I have profitably (as it turned out) violated every one of these rules. Of course, I was then young, inexperienced, and lucky. Nevertheless, if you *really* know what you're doing, at times you might make an exception. Just realize, though, it's those "sure bets" that frequently come back to haunt those who place them.

Leverage and Appreciation

Most often high leverage works its magic best when your property appreciates quickly. You can achieve this type of gain by (1) choosing locations that are situated for boom times, (2) creating value through improvements, or (3) some combination of the two. For ease of exposition, we'll continue to illustrate points with a property purchased at $100,000:

Purchase price	$100,000
Mortgage @ 8%, 30 years	$75,000
Down payment	$25,000
Appreciation rate (annual, 5 years)	.05
Selling price @ 5 years	$127,600
Mortgage balance outstanding	$71,295
Net proceeds	$56,305
Annual growth in equity	18%

Although an 18% equity growth rate looks very good, imagine the rate of growth if you had put only 10% down:

Purchase price	$100,000
Mortgage @ 8%, 30 years	$90,000
Down payment	$10,000
Appreciation rate	.05
Selling price	$127,600
Mortgage balance	$85,555
Net proceeds	$42,045
Annual growth in equity	33%

Now, let's say that through bargain hunting, you find a very similar, yet cosmetically disadvantaged property that you buy for $85,000. You place $5,000 down and put $5,000 into improvements. Your return on equity after five years (same assumptions) looks like this:

Purchase price	$90,000
Mortgage @ 8%, 30 years	$80,000
Original investment	$10,000
Appreciation rate	.05

Selling price	$127,600
Mortgage balance	$72,631
Net proceeds	$54,969
Annual growth in equity	40%

You can easily see from these examples that high loan-to-value ratios (i.e., leverage) when linked to strong appreciation significantly boost your rate of return on equity. Obviously, for shorter periods, the rate of return jumps much higher. For example:

$100,000 property—3-year holding @ 5% per annum appreciation

	75% loan ($25,000 down)	*90% loan ($10,000 down)*
Sales price @ 3 years	$115,700	$115,700
Mortgage balance	$72,953	$87,551
Net proceeds	$42,747	$28,149
Annual growth in equity	21%	40%

Naturally, leverage can create a downside. If you finance a larger percentage of your purchase price, you will increase your monthly mortgage payments. Larger mortgage payments may create negative cash flows. On the other hand, enterprising investors can sometimes overcome a pro forma negative cash flow by one of several methods:

- Arranging for a lower interest rate (mortgage assumption, owner financing)
- Using some type of balloon mortgage
- Using improvements to cut costs and boost rents
- Buying at a bargain price
- Increasing the intensity of use (e.g., adding or creating more rentable space)

In other words, enterprising investors never accept any property or its projected cash flow as offered. Rather, they always look for ways to make supposedly unworkable deals work. They know—other things being equal—the less of their own cash they put into a property, the greater their rate of return. In real estate, leverage can help you safely build wealth much faster than with any other investment medium.

Loss of Investment

What about a loss of value? With 10% down and a 10% slide in prices, you're wiped out. This is true if you're forced to sell when prices are down. But as Ben Graham always pointed out, value investors pick their moments.[11]

That's why he so adamantly rejected the definition of risk as preached by modern finance. Permanent loss results only when you overpay based on long-term investment value. It is foolish to label sound income-producing investments as risky merely because their prices may temporarily fall. Even with high leverage, your margin of safety comprises three basic elements: (1) positive cash flow, (2) cash reserves, and (3) your ability to wait out the storm.

Opportunities Abound

Indeed, the enterprising investor almost hopes for a storm every now and then, because that's a perfect time for strong investors to profit from troubled property owners and lenders. During a "perfect storm," work-outs, bargain prices, and unbelievable deals abound. From a purely economic perspective, I would welcome another Texas–Resolution Trust (RTC) fiasco.

In Dallas, I attended an RTC auction where properties were selling for less than 50 cents on the dollar. For the value investor, these bargains represented asset plays—as well as strong returns from income. Although I don't foresee any housing downturns as severe as the oil bust or defense bust, you can certainly expect a noticeable uptick in foreclosures during the next several years.[12]

Since 1996, too many low-down-payment loans have been shoveled out to less-than-creditworthy borrowers. The next severe housing recession will undoubtedly create a shakeout for many of these property owners. Value investors should stay closely tuned. During storms, even small amounts of ready cash can command great buys. (Of course, large amounts of ready cash can do even better.)

Leverage and Low Appreciation

As we saw in Chapter 3, over time, even small amounts of appreciation can create oak trees out of acorns. An annual property growth rate of 2% will immediately add 10% to an investor's beginning equity of 20% down. If the investor puts 15% down, at a 2% appreciation rate the investor gains a first-year 13% rate of return on equity. Over a period of 10 years, a 2% appreciation rate will grow a 20% down payment by more than 150%. Always remember that through leverage, you need not experience large rates of appreciation to gain outsized rewards. (Of course, don't forget that rental income will add to the total returns that a property will yield.)

Don't Wait Passively

Yet enterprising investors also realize that they need not wait for the market to rise. They can boost their rates of appreciation through selective value-creating improvements (see Chapter 10), as well as through buying at a bargain price. With stocks, buying at a bargain price means paying market value and trusting Mr. Market to change his mood. In real estate, you can certainly anticipate market moves (far easier than with stocks), but you've also got another possibility. Use your resourcefulness to discover a property owner who is willing to sell to you for less than a property is worth—not just in terms of its investment (intrinsic) value, but also in terms of its current market price.

Buy Below Market

Property owners may agree to sell their properties at a below-market price for any one (or more) of the following reasons: (1) ignorance, (2) duress, (3) opportunity, (4) convenience, and (5) negotiating weaknesses. Although value investors must always judge the intrinsic worth of each property, they also can profit by learning as much as possible about the people with whom they will be negotiating.

Ignorance

Every real property stands unique in terms of its exact location and specific features. In addition, most sellers lack detailed and accurate information about other similar properties that have recently sold, or those that are currently available for sale. Moreover, even when potential sellers hold close-to-perfect knowledge about their property and market activity, they still may not interpret or apply that knowledge correctly.

Lack of Imagination

Surprisingly, perhaps, many sellers can't even recognize the potential inherent in their own properties. I once located (and bought) an expensive lakefront home that offered good lake views from only two rooms. When I looked at the house, I immediately realized that at minimal expense (less than $10,000), the main living area and kitchen could be opened up, thus permitting a spectacular panorama.

After the remodeling, the home's market value increased by $35,000 to $50,000. In a "perfect" market, such value creation would not be possible. The market would discount the home's price only by the amount of money it would require to bring it up to its highest and best use. But, in fact, due to market ignorance and lack of imagination, many sellers miss these golden opportunities.

When the previous owners subsequently stopped by for a visit and to see how I had changed their home of 25 years, they couldn't believe the vast improvements whose possibilities had escaped their notice. "If we had thought of these changes," Mrs. Seller exclaimed, "we probably wouldn't have moved."

Markets Learn

At the time I bought that house, younger, professional baby boomers were just beginning to create demand for upscale houses currently owned by an older generation. As a result, these longtime property owners failed to recognize both the growing buying power of young buyers as well as their much different tastes and preferences (high ceilings, natural light, views, large master bedrooms, open floor plans, etc.). Bargains abounded.

But markets do learn. As sellers began to see the untapped renovation potential of their homes, they either upgraded the properties themselves—or simply priced them much closer to their (potential) renovated market value. Thus, new buyers eventually found it more difficult to create value in excess of their costs to remodel.

Stay in Front of the Market

To buy below market in the fashion just described, position yourself near the front of trends. As most other buyers and sellers recognize a particular opportunity, the once-sure-profit advantage gets bid away. Of course, that doesn't mean *all* opportunities fade; new potential always emerges. It does mean, though, that value investors must never relax their powers of insight, observation, and adaptation.

Other Gaps in Knowledge

Lack of creativity and imagination represents just one type of seller ignorance. Here are four other reasons property owners unknowingly underprice their properties:

1. *Bad advice*. Many sellers depend on less-than-competent realty agents or appraisers. Others may rely on friends, family, neighbors, or other ill-informed advisors.
2. *Ignorance of regulations*. The *legal* highest and best use of property depends on zoning laws, building regulations, and other government controls. Few property owners (or realty agents) know these laws in detail. Yet understanding such regulations precisely may uncover hidden value.
3. *Lack of awareness*. Some owners lose touch with a market. They may live out of town, they may cost base (i.e., price according to what they paid) rather than market base their value estimate, or they may

fail to seek out pertinent market information due to their own know-it-all egos and overconfidence.

4. *Special-buyer potential.* Some properties are perfectly suited for a particular buyer or type of buyer, yet the owners (or their agents) don't think of it—for example, a home located next to a business that may want room to expand or add extra parking. I once owned a property perfectly suited (and legally zoned) for use as a "share-a-home"—a type of assisted-living senior housing. But when I sought to list this property for sale, no realty agent I talked to was familiar with such a use, nor did any of them understand the property features such operators were looking for.

In many neighborhoods, an oversized four-bedroom, four-bath house would languish on the market. Yet an investor who owned rentals directed to college students may find this home's price a true bargain.

In the stock market, every stock trades at its then market price. Market ignorance proves no disadvantage to sellers; superior knowledge serves no benefit to buyers. In contrast, realty investors who ferret out full information about a property's location, its features, and its market of potential buyers (renters) can immediately earn premium rewards for their efforts.

Of course, ignorance doesn't cause sellers to always underprice their properties relative to a currently justified market value. Even more frequently, sellers err with an upward bias. So, in a manner similar to that of the stock market, value investors in real estate must sort through piles of offerings before they find gold mispriced as lead.

Duress and Distress

Like people everywhere, property owners can hit difficult times. They may lack cash, time, or competency. Their businesses may be failing; their careers may have skidded into a rut; they may have suffered personal or financial tragedy. Whatever the reason, they may need a quick sale of their property. If you are willing to bring sure relief to them (even if it's not the ultimate source of their trouble), they may very well be willing to accept your offer at a bargain price.

Antennae Up

On occasion, owners in distress will admit their troubles. They will tell you straight out: If you close in the next 7 to 10 days, we'll give you a great deal. More often, though, such sellers will not be forthcoming. You must keep your antennae up. Listen attentively for signals of desperation and confusion. Then, upon further inquiry or discussion, make your offer of quick relief in exchange for seller concessions on price (or other terms of value such as carryback financing or inclusion of certain personal property).

Tact, Not Ultimatums

When dealing with sellers in distress, never use the cliché "Take it or leave it." Apart from proving you to be a tactless amateur, such a ploy seldom works. In most cases, even property owners under duress would sooner part with their money than with their ego and self-esteem. The same negativity attaches to out-of-the-blue lowball offers that blast out untethered by reason, empathy, or understanding. To work best with a troubled owner, work together, not against each other. With these types of sellers (as well as nearly all others), mutual problem solving outperforms one-upmanship. Don't conquer; conciliate.

Opportunity Knocks

Some property owners may be willing to sell at a bargain price if they are planning to redirect their sales proceeds to opportunities they find more promising. Rather than relief per se, these sellers are looking to future gains. For them, delay means lost time and money. The more you can keep this type of seller focused on the bright prospects of their next endeavor, the less they will find it necessary to extract every dollar of potential from this current sale.

Builder Closeouts

Sometimes home builders or developers make for a special case of the opportunity seller. As a given building project or development nears completion, building pros often get antsy to close out and move on. Keeping a sales office open and a sales staff on call costs money. Getting these resources shifted to the next building site frequently offers far better payback potential.

In negotiating with builders, though, note that they may be willing to deal, but not so much on price. Previous home buyers in the development would not be pleased to learn that the builder was cutting prices. People expect appreciation, not depreciation. So instead of price cuts, ask for concessions on financing costs, upgrades, landscaping, warranties, or any other item that may add value.

Stage-of-Life Sellers

Potential profit opportunities don't exhaust the list of opportunity sellers. Some people are eager to move into the next stage of their lives. Such sellers can include up-and-coming professionals who face a move for job-related reasons, retirees eager to relocate, or long-term owners of rental properties who now wish to liquidate their holdings—often offering favorable terms of seller financing.

In Florida, the "move-backs" and "get-out-of-the-heat" sellers frequently fit the stage-of-life profile. These are people who, with little planning, retired to Florida only to find themselves homesick. When they decide to move back home, they want to go now—not in three to six months.

Convenience (FSBOs)

Why do people sell FSBO (for sale by owner)? To avoid paying a real estate commission? Yes, sometimes. But also, a fair number detest the whole cumbersome and often unpleasant process of dealing with Realtors. So to avoid a protracted hassle, they price their properties at the low end of the market, put out a sign, run an ad, and go for a quick and easy sale. I have elected this approach on more than a few occasions. From a buyer's perspective, I also much prefer it. In my experience, dealing direct yields many advantages of both convenience and lower cost.

Although going without an agent—as either buyer or seller—is not recommended for everyone, at the least, you should sample this approach. When looking to buy, I always closely review the FSBO ads.

Negotiating Weaknesses (Strengths)

Unlike with stocks, the price you pay for a property will depend on your negotiation skills relative to those of the sellers. Enterprising investors in real estate should read the great books on negotiation by Herb Cohen, Roger Dawson, and Bob Woolf.[13] In the meantime, here are pointers that nearly all negotiation experts agree on.

Know Your Sellers

Before you begin to negotiate, learn as much as you can about the sellers. Why are they selling? How much do they owe on the property? What's their financial status? What's their personality? Discover everything you can. Such knowledge will help you determine their needs, wants, must-haves, or even their idiosyncrasies. Always remember, never insult, offend, belittle, or underestimate the sellers. Work to understand and anticipate their actions and reactions. To negotiate well, don't compete; cooperate for mutual advantage.

Negotiate an Agreement, Not a Price

In contrast to buying stocks, where most all transactions take place according to a market price and essentially fixed terms, in real estate everything's negotiable. If the sellers seem inflexible on price, look for other value-added concessions. Or, if they require a quick close or sure sale, oblige their demands with requests of your own.

For purposes of bragging rights, some sellers insist on a high price. Give them what they want. Then take back more in terms of favorable financing, closing costs, closing date, warranties, inspections, repairs, personal property, title insurance, or other terms and conditions of value. Remember, in real estate you can negotiate a valuable agreement without directly negotiating a bargain price.

Establish Favorable Benchmarks

Sellers often entertain some strange ideas about why their property warrants a particular price. If you encounter such a situation, don't argue. Seek information. Ask the sellers (or their agent) how they arrived at such a value. Frequently, you will find their benchmark either inaccurate or irrelevant. For example:

1. *Add-in-costs*. "We paid $25,000 for that kitchen remodel," the sellers might say.
2. *The Joneses' house*. "The Joneses down the street just got $245,000 for their house, and it's four hundred square feet smaller than ours" is a frequently heard rationale.
3. *The appraisal*. "$185,000 is a great price for this house. Look, here's an appraisal; the appraiser says it's worth $205,000."
4. *Their past purchase price*. "We paid $425,000 a year and a half ago. At $445,000 you're getting a steal. Homes in this neighborhood are going up ten to fifteen percent a year."

To negotiate successfully with owners who use these and other familiar types of benchmarks, subtly undermine their accuracy or relevance. Don't make direct challenges that put them on the spot, but instead use tactfully phrased investigative questioning. Lead the sellers to doubt the applicability of their benchmark "facts." Then amend their value estimates or supply your own more appropriate (and more favorable) benchmarks. (See Chapter 6, "The Ins and Outs of Market Value.")

When you can get the sellers to recognize and accept your benchmarks, you go a long way toward getting them to accept your price (or other terms and conditions). When you merely try to pull down the seller's price while leaving them to hold tightly to their benchmarks, you'll usually find it tough to break their grip.

Tit for Tat

Never concede without asking for a return concession: "If I can meet your need on this point, would you be willing to accept a need of mine?" To concede without making a corresponding request invites continued "nibbling." In addition, agreement without request gives the seller second thoughts. "Why is the buyer jumping at this? Am I selling too low?" Do the sellers a favor: Each time they receive, ask them also to give.

Get Concessions Early

In their eagerness to entice a buyer, many sellers will begin making concessions well before you formally open negotiations. During your initial casual discussions, test the waters: "Have you thought about carrying back financing? I know you're asking $415,000, but what kind of price would you be happy with? Which of the appliances are you willing to leave? How much of the closing costs had you planned to pay?"

By casually asking these types of questions, you lower the floor on which later negotiations will stand. Once negotiations begin, sellers tend to play their cards in a more calculated manner.

Come Ready to Buy

Know the sellers. Know the property. Know the neighborhood. Know the market. Know values. Know your finances. Know what you're looking for. Then, when you see it, move, move, move. The "Well, let me think it over" buyer won't score nearly as many bargain buys as someone who comes into the game ready to play. You can't expect good buys to remain unrecognized for long. During the past year, I've looked at around a dozen properties that I considered good to great buys. More than half of these sold within four weeks (or less) of hitting the market.

The Intelligent Investor

The value investor in real estate thinks the idea of market returns quite a joke. Operating in a market of optimal inefficiencies, real estate investors learn how to turn knowledge, talent, and skill into superior rewards. Value investors know that property markets are guided by reason yet lack easily obtainable information. Those who are willing to work for data and apply their intelligence will outperform their peers by a wide margin.

As to those proponents of modern finance, let them continue to believe that only greater risk can generate greater returns. Value investors in real estate know otherwise. But these investors do enjoy the relatively subdued level of competition that such beliefs generate. Indeed, real estate investors should thank the stock enthusiasts for their loud and persistent drumbeat that stocks outperform all other investments. Should the media and their Rolodex commentators again begin to promote real estate over stocks, competition for good buys will definitely become more intense.

Chapter 6

The Ins and Outs of Market Value

Traditionally, most real estate investors have focused on two basic buying techniques: (1) financing properties with little or nothing down (high leverage), and (2) buying properties for less than their market value. Though each of these techniques has worked well for hundreds of thousands of people, true value investors must go further. By understanding both the strengths and weaknesses of the market value concept, you can avoid common pitfalls, spot opportunities, and achieve even higher returns.

The Specific Conditions of Market Value

Except in unusual circumstances, a trader in the stock market always buys or sells at a price equal to a stock's current market value.[1] In such a situation, it's easy for the modern finance folks to claim price equals value—end of story. However, when real estate pros use the term market value, they refer only to property sales prices that meet certain specified conditions. Why is this fact critically important? Because whenever you (or an appraiser) seek to estimate one property's value, you will look to the prices at which other similar properties have recently sold. Yet if you don't look beyond the sales price itself, you may find that a "comparable" sale does not conform to the conditions of a "fair" sale. That transaction may fail to meet one or more of the following conditions:[2]

1. *Duress*. Neither buyer nor seller has been significantly motivated by duress or other emotional motives (fear, greed, love, charity, pride, compulsion).
2. *Knowledge and competence*. Buyers and sellers both possess full, current information about comparable properties, recent selling prices, market trends, and property features.
3. *Time*. Neither buyer nor seller has felt undue pressure to buy or sell in a hurry.
4. *Financing*. The sales transaction did not involve especially favorable terms or below-market-cost, owner-arranged financing.
5. *Sales concessions*. The transaction did not include any extraordinary concessions by either party (e.g., large quantity of personal property, postclosing, rent-free occupancy by sellers until their new home is constructed, large seller escrows for repairs or renovations).

Naturally, as a buyer, you would like your purchase price to violate in your favor any or all of the just-mentioned conditions of a fair sale. But when you put on your valuation hat, you must closely check the details of the other comparable transactions you bring into your comparative analysis.

In other words, say that you discover a property that recently sold at a recorded price of $165,000. You then locate a similar property nearby. The seller of that property is asking $155,000. Should you conclude that you've found a bargain? Not necessarily. As a first step, you want to contact the realty agents (or principals) involved in this comp sale. What were the details of that transaction? Does that $165,000 sales price truly reflect the conditions of a fair sale? Or was it influenced by, for example, any of the following?

1. The sellers carried back a 5% down, 6% interest rate mortgage.
2. The sellers included in the sales price a large amount of their furniture and appliances. (These types of sales are common in some areas.)

3. The out-of-town buyers of this house had been quickly relocated from a high-priced housing market (e.g., Boston) to a lower-priced market (e.g., Orlando). They lacked time and adequate local market knowledge of prices and properties.

Most property buyers don't pay much attention to the transaction details that may have influenced the selling price of a comp sale. Value investors, though, accept nothing at face value. They try to discover all they can about the transacting parties' motivations, emotions, knowledge, and terms of sale. They know that little details often can create big insights and the equivalent of insider knowledge.[3]

Comparing Comp Properties (Stocks)

In valuing stocks, most value investors today look at relative stock prices. They try to find a company with a low market valuation—not low in an absolute (naive) sense, but low as compared to other benchmark companies (or groups of companies). Value investors love to find companies with strong, stable earnings (or assets), yet priced well below their peer group companies.[4]

Value investors approach real estate with a similar perspective. As you probably know from your own experiences with home buying, you compare 5, 10, or maybe even 50 homes. Then you choose the one that best fits your criteria for price, features, and location. When buying property for investment, you will follow a similar process. However, buying for investment differs from buying a home in three important ways:

1. *Personal likes and dislikes.* When buying for personal use, you can quickly reject many homes because they're not the kind of house you want to live in. When buying for investment, you must develop a new set of criteria. You can't let your personal biases influence your economic valuations. A profitable rental need not be a place where you would want to move into.

2. *Complexity*. Value investors develop very detailed checklists. The more you know about a property and its location, the better you can size up the potential risks and rewards of owning that property.
3. *Multiple valuation metrics*. Just as value investors in stocks use multiple measures of value (e.g., price-to-earnings ratio, market-to-book value, net-net value, liquidation value, break-up value, takeover value, growth rate, dividend yield), so too must value investors in real estate.[5]

Admittedly, for those who believe they can get rich in stocks by plugging $500 a month into an S&P 500 index fund, valuing real estate may seem like too much work. But you will receive more than adequate reward for your efforts. Granted, you may have to trek up a steep 45-degree learning curve. But once you develop a sound buying and operating strategy, you can essentially coast—if you choose to.

Location, Location, Location

Without a doubt, location, location, location has become one of the most overused clichés in real estate. Yet if you ask people what they mean by location, you might get a dozen or more different answers. That's because location encompasses a dozen or more key elements. In practice, though, many of these elements aren't obvious—or even when they are, people fail to notice them. As a minimum, then, to estimate a property's market value, see how your comp houses (or apartment units) compare on the following items:

- Aesthetics
- Zoning
- School district
- Property taxes
- Highways, roads, bridges
- Public transportation

- Neighborhood residents (existing and newcomers)
- Appreciation potential

In an ideal world, all of your comp properties would perfectly match your subject property on every possible measure of location. Regrettably, you'll seldom find such a perfect match. More than likely you will discover significant locational differences (both favorable and unfavorable). When you do, you must adjust your estimate of the subject property's market value either up or down accordingly. You must carefully weigh "like for like." Otherwise you can easily miss a major piece of the value puzzle.

Aesthetics

As with all other elements of location, your first defense lies with a close personal inspection. Don't just look at the written description of a comp property; drive by it. Walk the neighborhood. Focus your attention on the neighborhood's overall attractiveness and appeal. Talk with residents. What do they like or dislike? Search for answers to questions such as these:

1. *Noise*. Does the neighborhood suffer from any undue traffic noise, airport flight paths, industrial sounds, or other disturbances (loud barking dogs, nearby construction, etc.)?
2. *Upkeep*. Do residents maintain their properties? Do homes and lawns sparkle with pride of ownership? Or do homes need paint and yard maintenance?
3. *Parking*. Are the streets relatively free of cars? Or does the neighborhood lack sufficient off-street driveways and garages? Or, worse, do you see cars parked in yards (neighborhoods heavy with student rentals sometimes display this type of eyesore)?
4. *Bad mix*. Does the neighborhood abut or merge into any commercial, industrial, or otherwise incompatible land uses? Do you notice unsightly vacant lots or boarded-up properties?
5. *Views*. Do neighborhood residents enjoy pleasant views of lakes, parks, woods, bays, or mountains?

6. *Overall feel.* What's your overall feel of the neighborhood? Does it seem to be moving up, stable, or moving down?

Zoning

In one sense, zoning can add to the value of properties in several ways. First, zoning can keep people from junking up the neighborhood with converted garages, home workshops, houses cut up into apartments, and other bastardized uses. Second, through restrictive zoning, the law can prop up values by limiting new construction.[6]

On the downside, restrictive zoning also can prevent property owners from adapting their properties to more profitable uses. No universal conclusion applies: Sometimes zoning boosts values; sometimes it stamps out the opportunity to change. Whatever the case in any specific situation, you must do the judging. Just realize that differences in zoning (or other types of land-use and building regulations) can materially affect the values of otherwise apparently comparable properties.

School Districts

If you have kids, you know how school district quality can boost or retard property values. Make sure the properties you compare lie within the same school district—at all levels (elementary, middle school, high school). Of course, unlike your own home, you need not buy your investment properties in the best—or even a good—school district. It all depends on their relative prices, rent levels, and the types of tenants you hope to attract to your property.

I have frequently found that it's wise to avoid homes in top school districts because home buyers with kids bid prices up too high. I am quite willing to sacrifice an unknown amount of future appreciation in favor of more rental income in my pocket today. Of course, you have to work the numbers for yourself. What is true in one city (or neighborhood) might not stand true elsewhere. Nevertheless, don't mistakenly overlook the poorer school districts. In most cities, fewer than 20% percent of rental households include school-age children.

Property Taxes and Services

In too many towns and cities, high taxes on property eat into rent receipts. Before you avoid high taxes per se, though, compare services. High property taxes undermine values only when area residents fail to receive a commensurate high level of government benefits. In addition to schools, government services can include parks; recreation areas; golf courses; community colleges; trash collection; water; sewers; and police, fire, and other emergency services.

Thus, should you find that two similar properties are taxed at different amounts, look further. Discover whether they also differ in the quality or quantity of their municipal and county services. In some instances, you may even discover that lower-rate taxing districts offer a higher level of services. Lower welfare spending and greater efficiency, for example, can account for such favorable types of disparities.

Crime Rates

Naturally, people wish to feel safe in their homes and on their neighborhood streets. Low crime makes for higher property values. But it's not just the quantity of crime that counts. More important is the type of crime. Drug dealing, gang shootouts, and house break-ins weigh much differently than occasional car thefts or domestic quarrels.

Often, too, perceptions don't match reality. Check facts with the police. Also, recognize that statistical reporting areas may not accurately apply to various submarket neighborhoods. Beware of broad-sweeping generalizations. Pinpoint as closely as possible the actual street boundaries that delineate high-crime areas. Note, too, the relative differences among reputed high-crime and low-crime areas. These differences may not range as far apart as many people think.

Highways, Roads, and Bridges

How quickly and surely can you travel from a neighborhood to job centers, shopping, professional services, recreation areas, schools, and cultural facilities? Are streets often congested? Must most to-and-from traffic flow through a nightmare-type interchange (e.g., Atlanta's famous spaghetti junction, perhaps more aptly named malfunction junction)? Do frequent auto accidents leave traffic stalled? What about tolls? They can mount up. Is the neighborhood served by just one bridge, or numerous ways in and out?

Public Transportation

In some cities, homes within convenient walking distance of a commuter train (or subway) station sell for as much as 5% to 10% more than quite comparable homes located slightly farther away. Homes near bus stops don't typically command the price premium they used to. But for some property buyers or tenants, this feature still proves to be an advantage worth paying for. As for other types of public transportation (taxis, airports, ferries, limousine service), easy availability may or may not affect a property's value. You must learn the tenant and home buyer market to tell for sure.

Who Are the Residents and New Buyers (Tenants)?

Whenever you compare locations (neighborhoods), learn who lives there now and who's moving in. What are their professions, educations, ages, incomes, lifestyles, races, religions, family sizes? Though it's true that open-housing laws bar discrimination, it's obvious that few neighborhoods in the United States perfectly reflect the Rainbow Coalition. More importantly, today we find considerable voluntary congregation of blacks, Latinos, Jews, Asians, seniors, and various other demographic mixes.

Today, neighborhood racial and ethnic changes can push values up—not down, as many stereotypical beliefs hold. For our brief purposes here, though, note that people influence property values. And although various laws and regulations forbid real estate agents from taking notice of the racial, ethnic, and religious characteristics of neighborhoods, investors need not avert their eyes and ignore reality.

Apart from demographics, notice whether neighborhood properties are primarily occupied by owners or renters. Like race, ethnicity, religion, and other personal characteristics, you can't judge owners or renters as better or worse, per se. Instead, you must weigh and consider. What are the implications for a property's market value? On occasion, in neighborhoods experiencing gentrification, for example, you may find younger, upscale renters displacing moderate-income home owners.

Appreciation Potential

Just as with stocks, expected appreciation (growth) potential gets reflected in the current market value of every property. Higher expectations (all other things being equal), create higher value. Yet, just as with stocks, sometimes property values in certain neighborhoods ride a crest of momentum. Higher rates of appreciation beget ever higher market values.

Foolishly, people then begin to say, "Buy in Expensive Acres; that area's experiencing the fastest rate of appreciation." But the real question is, can you *reasonably* expect such high appreciation to continue? Probably not. Just as it's nearly impossible for any given company to maintain a continuing rapid rate of growth, so it is for any given neighborhood. Consider the figures in Table 6.1. As the numbers show, when two neighborhoods appreciate at different rates over longer periods of time, their price differences become quite exaggerated. What begins as a $50,000 price gap over 10 years grows to a $129,500 gap. Unless the relative desirability of the neighborhoods also changes, at some point, the price momentum will shift.

Many homebuyers would get priced out of Expensive Acres. Others would simply decide that Modest Manor offers more value for the money. Within a period of several years, Modest Manor appreciation rates would begin to jump. Appreciation rates in Expensive Acres would slow. Obvi-

***Table* 6.1 Home Price Appreciation**

	Today	*3 Years*	*5 Years*	*10 Years*
Expensive Acres @ 7%	$100,000	$122,500	$140,200	$196,700
Modest Manor @ 3%	$ 50,000	51,500	57,950	67,150

ously, most value investors would like to find ways to spot those emerging Modest Manors before they hit their stride—or maybe, too, identify those Expensive Acres during periods when they've stopped to catch their breath, yet remain strategically positioned for another rapid run. It is toward this end that we devote Chapter 9.

Location: Summing Up

In real estate, everybody talks about location as if they know what they are talking about. But as with many other words in common use—democracy, equality, civil rights, wealth, capitalism, property rights—you can define location in many different ways. Routinely, though, residential real estate appraisals give short shrift to this topic. A standard residential appraisal form, for example, includes only one small box for price adjustments based on differences in location.

That's because, theoretically, appraisers and realty agents draw their comp sales from the same neighborhood as the property they are trying to value. Location essentially drops out of the value equation. If all properties are situated pretty much equally, then appraisers must explain sales price differences by other factors (e.g., property size, condition, lot size, and other features discussed later in this chapter).

All of this sounds good in theory. In practice, though, the location assumption often fails. Even properties that sit right next to each other can materially differ in their "locations." For example, my previous home at 73 Roble Road, Berkeley, California, was *not* located in Berkeley. The house sat too far back from the street. It therefore slipped into Oakland territory for purposes of regulatory controls. Given that Oakland's building regulations were less severe than those of (the people's republic of) Berkeley, this locational difference proved to be a substantial value advantage for my home. Yet, my neighbors' homes located along that same stretch of Roble Road were situated in Berkeley and thus fell under Berkeley's onerous (and value-diminishing) ordinances.

Although even this specific type of quirk in location occurs more often than you might expect, quirks of all types reflect the norm. In recognizing this fact, value investors never accept the same location assumption without first looking for those differences (quirky or otherwise) that may spell either profit or pitfall.

Comparing Properties and Their Features

As with location, value investors need to detail each feature of their comps. Then they compare these features point by point to the specific property (or properties) they are evaluating. Just as important, don't let personal biases (likes and dislikes) overwhelm your ability to value a property as an investment. At the right price, nearly any property can yield a strong financial return.

Especially avoid wandering through various houses or apartments and commenting randomly with remarks more suitable for home buyers intent on personal use, such as the following:

1. "Wow, look at this great master bedroom."
2. "This house will never do, the kitchen's too small."
3. "Skip this one. It doesn't have a two-car garage."
4. "Come over here. Did you see this beautiful grandfather clock?"
5. "Can you believe this knockout view? This is a great house."

To get around this personal "I like; I don't like" approach to comparing homes, evaluate each house or apartment unit you look at according to a consistent checklist of features. Compare homes systematically, not randomly piecemeal. You then can see how well the various properties rate when matched against your investment and operating strategy.

Although no checklist can anticipate every feature you might want to evaluate, here's one you can use for starters:

I. **Site description**
   A. Site value
   B. Size and configuration
   C. Buildable extra lot

D. Zoning and other site regulations
E. Site quality
F. Sidewalks, driveways, and other site improvements

II. **Exterior of the home**
A. Appearance
B. Condition
C. Maintenance and materials
D. Site placement

III. **Interior of the home**
A. Square footage and value
B. Aesthetics
C. Floor plan, room count, and layout
D. Condition

Site Value

When buying properties, you pay for the house and the lot. If in the suburbs, the lot value may range between 10% to 25% of the total price. In desirable city neighborhoods, site value may account for 50% to 75% of total property value. And in neighborhoods that are moving upscale, lot values can represent 75% to 100% of the property's value. In other words, the property is ready for tear-down or major renovation. (Ferreting out the next tear-down neighborhood ahead of the crowd can often yield superior returns.)

Site Features

As you shop for properties, evaluate each site as carefully as you do the buildings. The features of the site will influence the property's market value, appreciation potential, opportunities for creating value, and tenant enjoyment. For instance, if you were to buy an older home in a neighborhood that's moving upscale, you might be throwing money away by investing in improvements. If the buyers you sell to later plan to bring in the bulldozers, they won't be willing to pay you much for a beautifully remodeled kitchen and bath. With these types of properties, your tenants are merely covering your holding costs while you wait for the land value to reflect the higher status and desirability of the area.

Site Size and Configuration

To evaluate a site, first step off and measure its boundaries. Take this precaution and you'll get a better idea of what you're actually buying. Surprising as it may seem, site size and configuration aren't always as they appear. Friends of mine who bought a home loved their big backyard that ran from the house 200 feet back toward a row of trees. In fact, though, the property's rear lot line didn't correspond with the tree row as they had assumed. It actually lay 112 feet closer in. Their backyard was less than half the size they had originally believed it was.

Especially when a site adjoins a vacant lot, vacant land, wooded areas, or perhaps a creek or a lake, appearances can easily deceive. You can't tell just by looking where the property ends and another begins. Indeed, law books are filled with legal cases where buyers thought they were getting more land than they actually received.

To further verify a site's boundaries, look at a copy of the plat plan for the neighborhood.[7] You can confirm the dimensions you've stepped off against those shown on the plat. If a previous site survey is available, you might check whether it conforms to the seller's description of the site. You definitely don't want to wait until after you've bought a property to learn the true size and boundaries of the lot.

Does the Site Give You an Extra Buildable Lot?

"Where else but in Santa Fe," Realtor Dee Treadwell asks, "could you buy a home for $285,000, later subdivide the property, sell the house for $550,000, and still have a lot to sell?" Now, that's the kind of deal every value investor wants to find. Yet although this Realtor may not realize it, you can actually find similar transactions in every city throughout North America. Granted, Santa Fe's prices rank toward the high end. But whenever a house sits on two lots, you may be able to split one lot from the site and then sell the house or extra lot separately. Or, if an existing house sits across two or more lots, you can tear the house down and sell the vacant lots individually. This means that if you buy a house that sits on several buildable lots, you might be looking at big future profits.

The key word here, though, is buildable. Just because a house sits on a lot that's large enough to accommodate two or more newly constructed houses doesn't mean you can actually realize the site's profit potential. To reap the rewards, government building regulations must permit additional development. If zoning or other laws restrict new construction, then all you've got is a house with a large lot. So, to detect hidden value, you might search for homes situated on two or more buildable lots.

Other Zoning and Building Regulations

When you plan to build onto an existing house (either up or out), you'll need to check the site's zoning and building regulations. Most properties are regulated by floor area ratios, setback and side yard distances, and other restrictions. Floor area ratios (FARs), for example, limit the maximum square footage of a house. If your 10,000-square-foot lot is governed by a FAR of .20, the size of the house can't exceed 2,000 square feet (.20 x 10,000 = 2,000).

Note, though, that FARs are written technically. By this I mean that the law will specify which square footages count toward the maximum and which don't. Besides its livable floor area, a house may have decks, a basement, porches, patios, a garage, loft space, and storage buildings. FAR limits will apply to some of these areas but not to others. It all depends on the local governing regulations.

To get around FAR restrictions and make his condominium units larger, Vancouver architect and builder Andre Molnar built his units with unfinished loft space. According to technical specifications, this loft space did not count in the FAR limits. Theoretically, the loft space could be used only for storage. But as soon as Molnar's buyers moved into their apartments, they finished the space and used their loft areas as dens, studies, or extra bedrooms. By using this loft space strategy, Molnar created value for himself and his buyers. His condo units were among the most popular in the city.

As Andre Molnar's success shows, you must develop any plans for improvements in ways that comply with site and building codes. But sometimes you can creatively interpret these laws to yield profit opportunities that others have overlooked.

Site Quality

In addition to site size, configuration, and legal restrictions, pay attention to site quality. To the naive, dirt is dirt. You might think that all half-acre lots are created equal. But this is not true. Site quality in terms of topography, soil conditions, and landscaping can add (or subtract) thousands of dollars of value.

1. *Topography*. Is the lot flat? Or does the site slope toward (or away from) the buildings? Where will water run off? Are residents able to pull into and out of the driveway after a snow or ice storm?
2. *Soil conditions*. Is the site subject to earthquakes, sinkholes, or mudslides? Is there any well water contamination, radon, or underground storage tank leakage, or are there other harmful environmental exposures? Is the soil good for growing flowers, vegetables, or the most durable and easy-care type of grass?
3. *Landscaping*. Is there a good variety of well-kept shrubs, flowers, or trees? Is the grass healthy and well maintained? Does the landscaping add to or detract from the property's appearance? Can you think of any good ideas to improve the yard's appearance?

Sidewalks, Driveway, Fences, and Other Site Improvements

As you continue to note the features of a site, itemize all the improvements such as driveway, fences, sidewalks, paddleball court, swimming pool, landscape timers, and any other humanmade amenities that enhance the site's desirability. A concrete, double-car-wide driveway, for example, could be worth $3,000 to $6,000 more than a single-car driveway of crushed rock. Fences can cost anywhere from $500 to $5,000 or more—depending on size, quality, and condition. Sometimes a swimming pool might add $5,000 to $25,000 to a home's value. In other cases, a swimming pool can reduce a property's value.

No absolutes apply. Consider local market data and the advice of a Realtor. Like other features of a property, pay attention to site improvements so you know exactly what you're getting, how these site features compare to those of other comp houses or apartment buildings, and how much extra these features are worth.

The Exterior of the Property

After noting a site's features, next direct your attention to the exterior of the buildings: (1) appearance, (2) condition, (3) building materials and expense of maintenance, and (4) site placement (how the house is situated on the site).

Appearance

As you begin to inspect the exterior of a house or apartment building, stand back at least 50 to 100 feet. Place the building(s) in perspective with the site and with other properties in the neighborhood. Does it fit in? Is it too large or too small? Does the architectural style give the house an appealing uniqueness? Or is it a simple box design with no windows on either side? Have a half-dozen other houses in the neighborhood been built with the same design?

Can you imagine ways to enhance the property's value with shutters, flower boxes, a dramatic front door and entryway, new or additional windows, fresh paint, a contrasting color for trim, or accenting the design with architectural details? How well does (or could) the property's exterior distinguish it from other comparably priced properties? Do you rate its appeal as great, so-so, or awful? List possibilities for profitable improvements.

Condition

To evaluate the condition of a home's exterior (as well as its interior and major systems such as plumbing, electrical, heating, and cooling), hire a professional home inspector. Before making a purchase offer, though, develop a general idea about how much fix-up work the home might require. In addition, a home's state of disrepair may make it look much worse than it really is. As a result, through thoughtful review of condition, you might be able to find a diamond in the rough that other potential buyers have rejected too quickly.

Perhaps more than any other common problem, dirt turns buyers (and tenants) off. Dirty windows; accumulated dirt and debris on porches, patios, and entryways; and even old and dirty doormats seem to build a wall of emotional resistance. Dirt signals that a house has not been well cared for. Most buyers (and renters) steer clear of dirty houses.

But that decision could prove to be a costly mistake. Instead, imagine the home's appeal if it were given a top-to-bottom cleaning. Because houses with dirty exteriors frequently have unkempt yards, you may have to picture the home as if the grass were neatly cut, the shrubs trimmed, and the flowers blooming. Close your eyes. Now what does the house look like? If you could buy the house at a discount, would you be interested? Value investors view a home not just as it looks today, but as they could make it look tomorrow.

Materials and Maintenance

Each area of the country has its own types of construction materials that are popular and effective for that locale. Wood, brick, brick veneer, adobe, concrete block, stucco, and steel are possibilities. In addition, some houses are built on a pier-and-beam foundation; others sit on concrete slabs. Windows and roofs differ, too. Crank-style aluminum awning windows are popular in some warmer climates but seldom found up north. In California, you see tile roofs; in Maine, that type of roof is rare.

Evaluate the Quality of Construction and Building Materials

Regardless of the specific types of construction materials used in your area, you can bet that they vary widely in costs, function, and desirability. So before buying, talk to knowledgeable builders, contractors, or building-supply companies to learn the differences between high-end, midrange, and low-cost building materials. Talk with anyone you know who has recently built a new house. They've probably spent months shopping for materials. To compare homes effectively, you've got to move beyond appearance. You can't judge the quality of a house by its paint job.

Maintenance: Time, Effort, and Costs

Apart from the quality of construction materials, consider how much time, effort, and money it's going to cost to maintain the house. Growing up, I recall that every three or four years we had to scrape peeling paint with a wire brush to prepare our home for its next coat of paint. Now, with many of today's durable paints, stains, and materials, the time elapsing between major exterior maintenance work could be 10 years or more. This is certainly a feature to look for. If you don't want to own rental homes or apartments because you think they will require too much work, that need not be the case. For investors who prefer to hike, bike, fish, or golf rather than scrape paint or clean leaves out of gutters, low-maintenance properties are the only way to go. They also can dramatically reduce property operating costs.

Site Placement

In looking at a house from the outside, note how the building is situated on the site. Are the windows positioned to bring in beacons of natural light? How about privacy from neighbors? Can tenants sunbathe in the backyard without prying eyes invading their privacy? Are the sleeping areas of the house protected from street noise? How will prevailing winter winds (or summer breezes) strike the house? How will these affect resident comfort and energy bills? Does the site placement conform to the standards of feng shui?

The Interior of the Property

For most tenants, the interior of a home is the main event. With emphasis today on cocooning, make sure your rental properties will live as well as they look.[8] With my last house, I was so taken with its wooded views, expansive windows, beamed ceilings, hardwood floors, skylights, and Jacuzzi in the master bedroom, I didn't think carefully about floor plan, internal traffic patterns, and functional efficiency. After moving in, though, I came to recognize many serious flaws in the home's design and function. For example, the master bedroom was located directly above the den, and sounds from the television came right up; the hot water heater didn't have enough capacity to fill the Jacuzzi; and access to the kitchen from the garage was quite cumbersome for carrying in bags of groceries. (I might add that this house was only three years old!) Don't judge only the appearance of a property. Study how well it will live functionally for your tenants.

Square Footage and Property Values

Nearly everyone knows that size matters. But many beginning investors overlook the fact that measures of size vary greatly. Before accepting the square footage figure for a property, interpret it with caution. To avoid mistakes, use these guidelines to check the figures:

1. *Watch for measurement errors*. One of my previous homes was listed on the property tax rolls as 2,460 square feet. In fact, it was closer to 3,200 square feet. Errors happen.
2. *Take note of inferior-quality space*. The square footage of an attic that's been converted into a spare bedroom isn't worth as much as the square footage of the main house. A finished basement of 800 square feet isn't the equivalent of an 800-square-foot second story that's fully integrated into the home. Don't compare houses or apartment units only in size; also compare the quality and livability of the finished space.
3. *Be wary of inconsistent size comparisons*. The sellers of one house may describe it as 1,980 square feet and include in the square-footage figure a converted garage that's now a den. An owner of a similar home may describe it as 1,600 square feet and simply footnote the makeshift den as an extra but not include its size in the quoted square footage of the house.

Used carefully, square footage comparisons can give you a good idea of relative home or apartment values in a neighborhood. Used naively, they can mislead you into believing you're getting a bargain when you're actually overpaying. Watch out for measurement errors. Watch out for those converted garages, finished attics, enclosed porches, and basement dens. Figure them as nice extras. But keep in mind, they're often not worth as much as many sellers think they are.

Aesthetics: How Does the House Look, Feel, and Sound?

"I was once in a house," recalls real estate appraiser Dodge Woodson, "that made me feel as if there should have been a coffin sitting in the living room. The drapes were dark and heavy—a ghastly green that gave me an eerie feeling. I don't spook easily, and I'm used to seeing a lot of houses in a lot of different conditions, but this house made me uncomfortable. If I had been a prospective buyer, I would not have been able to focus on anything but the drapes."[9]

Woodson's reaction to this house with the eerie dark green drapes wouldn't have surprised Professor Mary Jasmosli of George Washington University. Jasmosli has developed an expertise she calls environmental sensitivity. Through her research she has found that people react emotionally to the interiors (and exteriors) of homes in ways that they themselves can neither explain nor understand. "Home features such as number of windows, window treatments, color schemes, views, placement of walls and doorways, room size, ceiling height, and amount of light all hold special meaning," reports Jasmosli.

Now, we'll return to Dodge Woodson. "The next time I entered that house, I couldn't believe the difference," he remarks. "The owners had replaced the dark green drapes with flowing white window treatments. . . . Not only was the house pretty, it appeared much larger. . . . I noticed features that I had never seen before. The house was alive with light. This experience convinced me of the power that window treatments have."[10]

Of course, it's not just window treatments that can change the emotional appeal of a home. You can dramatically improve the look and feel of any home by changing, replacing, or removing any of its negatives. If you are looking at a house that doesn't generate the warmth, brightness, or romance you think your tenants would pay extra for, don't rush out and get back in your car. Linger awhile. Isolate the source of your discomfort. Mull over ideas. How would the house (or apartment units) look, feel, sound, or smell if you . . .

- Put in skylights
- Removed a wall
- Eliminated the litterbox and pet odors
- Replaced the worn, ugly carpeting
- Increased the size or number of windows or added brighter, more modern window treatments
- Painted and wallpapered with different colors or textures
- Installed new cabinets or appliances
- Pulled out that dropped-ceiling acoustical tile and created a vaulted ceiling
- Soundproofed the home with insulated windows, shrubs, or an earth berm

Remember, little things can mean a lot. Put your imagination to work. With good ideas you can transform any property, making it more comfortable, appealing, and valuable.

Floor Plan: Does the Layout of the House Work?

Once you have moved beyond the aesthetics of a house, next evaluate its floor plan. Does the layout of the house offer convenience and privacy, and does it work efficiently?

When you first approach the main entry of the house, do you have to climb steep steps? Is there a covered area so visitors can avoid standing in the rain or snow while waiting for someone in the house to answer their knock? If the main entrance lies below grade, does it appear that water may build up in the entrance area? As you walk in the front door, notice whether you're dropped immediately into a living area or if the house has a foyer. Is there an adequate-sized coat closet nearby? Relative to the main entrance, where is the kitchen located? Can you walk from the entry door to other rooms of the house without passing through a third room? How are the locations and sizes of bedrooms, baths, and closets?

Now, imagine tenants living in the house. Where will their kids play—both indoors and outdoors? Will the parents be able to keep an eye on them? Does the house have a "Grand Central Station" living room? Or is it pleasantly isolated from other house activity areas?

Go into the kitchen. How long does it take the faucet to draw hot water? For purposes of work efficiency, can someone step conveniently between the refrigerator, oven, stovetop, and sink? Do you see adequate counter and cabinet space? How much natural and artificial light is there? Is there an eat-in kitchen area that separates the family members who are eating from those who are working (preparing meals, cleaning up)? Is there easy access to the kitchen from the garage or carport? Can someone conveniently enter the kitchen from the parking area while carrying several bags of groceries?

On this tour to evaluate floor plan, make back-and-forth trips throughout the house as if you were living there. Perhaps the long walk from the kitchen to the master bedroom wouldn't faze an investor on a quick walk-through. But how would you like to make that trip a dozen times a day or more? Would it then get tiresome?

Noise is a potential problem within households. Will sound from a television or stereo carry into other rooms? You might even bring along a portable radio on your house inspections. Place it in various rooms. Turn the volume up. Do the walls give you enough soundproofing? Roommate-type tenants want privacy and quiet. If your property fails to offer these essentials, you will lose tenants and rents.

Just as important, will tenants be able to hear neighbors or neighborhood noise from inside the house? Again, tenants pay for quiet. They discount heavily for noise.

Although potential neighbors and neighborhood noise are especially important to note in townhouses and condominiums, single-family developments are no strangers to loud stereos, barking dogs, and Indy 500 engine revving. Don't just assume that a neighborhood will offer peace and quiet.

Check it out with the sellers and talk to people who live in the neighborhood.

Condition: How Much Time, Effort, and Money Will the Property Require?

Before buying a house or apartment building, hire a professional to inspect it. Typically, you'll place an inspection contingency in your written offer to the sellers. Then, depending on what the inspector turns up, you can either go ahead with your purchase, renegotiate price and repair credits, or withdraw from the agreement. Before you get to this stage where you are paying a professional, though, closely check the condition of the house yourself.

For one thing, you'll need to get a general idea about the home's condition so that you can compare various properties to each other. Second, you can use any shortcomings you do discover to persuade sellers to offer a lower price, better terms, or an escrow credit for repairs. And third, you'll want to rule out some houses because they clearly don't fit your investment or operating strategy.

To go through a preprofessional inspection, here are six items to consider: (1) plumbing; (2) heating, ventilating, and air conditioning; (3) electrical; (4) ceilings, walls, and floor coverings; (5) cosmetics and floor plan; and (6) quality of materials.

1. *Plumbing.* To check the working condition of the plumbing in a house, first test the water pressure. Turn on a couple of baths or showers, then flush the toilets. What happens? Is the water pressure sufficient to maintain the water flows? Check all the water faucets for drips. Determine whether the water heater is large enough to allow all members of a family to take hot showers when everybody is trying to get ready at the same time. Inspect all the pipes and shutoff valves under sinks and cabinets. Is there any sign of leaking, rust, or corrosion? If the house has a basement or accessible crawl space, inspect the plumbing from that vantage point. What type of piping has been used—plastic, copper, galvanized steel, lead, or

something else? Each of these materials has its own advantages and disadvantages, installation procedures, and building code standards. Discuss these points with a professional inspector.

2. *Heating, ventilating, and air conditioning (HVAC)*. Depending on the season of the year, you may not be able to adequately test the HVAC system of a house. Nevertheless, at least note the placement and size of the duct vents. Do any rooms lack outlets? Are the vents positioned to evenly and efficiently distribute heat throughout the house? If the house (or specific rooms) lacks central heat or air (e.g., it has floor furnaces, wall furnaces, or window heat and air units), tenants may experience hot and cool spots throughout the house. Because most HVAC equipment has a limited life, ask the ages of various components. An age of more than 8 or 10 years may point to coming problems. Check with an expert.
3. *Electrical*. As with plumbing and HVAC systems, judge the condition of an electrical system by how well it will serve your tenants' needs and whether it meets modern standards of performance and safety. Reserve this latter question for experts. But you can evaluate the home's amperage (60, 100, or 200) and voltage (115 or 230); whether it has circuit breakers or an old-fashioned fuse box; and the number, location, and convenience of electrical outlets, switches, and built-in light fixtures.
4. *Ceilings, walls, and floors*. As you walk through a house or apartment building, examine the ceilings, walls, floors, and floor coverings. Note their condition, but also note any related problems. Water stains may indicate roof or plumbing leaks. Cracks may point to foundation problems. Check floors to see whether they are level. Would a marble placed in the center of the room roll swiftly to one side or the other? Don't feel as if you're out of line to pull back rugs, peek behind pictures, and look under furniture. More than a few sellers have been known to selectively place wall hangings, rugs, and furniture to hide stains, cracks, or other defects. I once pulled back a room-sized Oriental rug and discovered the underlying floor was particleboard.

5. *Appearance and floor plan*. A home may not *require* any redecorating, repairs, or remodeling. Yet it still may not look good. If that green shag carpeting or a closed-in kitchen doesn't meet contemporary tastes and preferences, you're going to have to spend some time and money to bring the house up to higher standards. But if you redecorate or remodel simply to suit your own preferences (as opposed to those of typical tenants), you may not be able to make money from your improvements. On the other hand, if you plan to own the house for the long term or rank tenant satisfaction above profit, then you still may want to change the home to match your extravagant tastes. Just keep in mind the difference between profitable and personal improvements. (Of course, in this instance you might profit from quicker renting, lower vacancies, and less tenant turnover.
6. *Quality of materials*. Note the quality of the materials used throughout the home's interior. The cost of carpeting, for example, may range from $10 per square yard up to $50 or more. Some interior flat-paneled, hollow-core doors can be bought for $10 to $15 each. Other doors, solid wood, stained, and decorative paneled, can cost upward of $500 each. You can buy a set of kitchen cabinets for $1,500 or $15,000. Low-grade vinyl floor coverings run $5 per square yard. Top-of-the-line can cost $25 per square yard or more.

   You can find similarly large differences in quality and costs for light fixtures, wood paneling, paints, wallpapers, sinks, bathtubs, faucets, and nearly all other interior building materials. Although cost seldom correlates one-to-one with value, you can reasonably expect to pay something extra for a property that includes better-grade materials. Such houses or apartments will rent faster and at higher rent levels. Just evaluate with caution. Make sure you will earn a good return on your investment.

Utility Bills (Energy Efficiency)

In some parts of the country, utility bills rank as the second- or third-largest expense in the budgets of many families. During months of peak usage, utility bills of $200 to $300 a month (or more) are not uncommon. As you compare properties, find out (1) which utilities are available to a house, (2) how much they will cost each month, and (3) what you can do to reduce utility expenses. Lower utility bills mean higher rents and less tenant turnover. Excessively high bills will create a tenant revolt.

What Utilities Are Available?

A friend of mine owns a rental house in Sarasota, Florida. He recently complained that he had to install a new sewage-disposal drain field at the property. He expected the cost to run around $1,200. As we talked about this repair, this friend admitted that when he bought the house he hadn't even realized that its sewage-disposal system wasn't connected to the city sewer. As an inexperienced investor, he hadn't even thought to ask. Don't make this same mistake. Before you offer to buy a house, ask what utilities are available (sewage disposal, water, electricity, natural gas, cable TV, digital high-speed cable, telephone, etc.). Many investors are surprised to learn that even properties located within a city may lack one or more of the utilities that they previously had taken for granted. For investors in properties located in suburban or rural areas, of course, the need to identify available utilities is even more pressing.

Identify Ways to Reduce the Utility Bills

Once you've checked a property's utility bills (obtained from either the sellers or the utility companies), look for ways to reduce these expenses. For example:

1. Would more insulation, caulking, or storm doors and windows significantly lower the costs of heating and cooling?
2. Has the water heater been wrapped with insulation?
3. Can you profitably switch from higher-cost energy (electric) to lower-cost (natural gas)?
4. Do utility companies offer special incentives to make the house more efficient? In some cities, natural gas companies will replace

electric water heaters with gas water heaters at no charge to the homeowner. Utility companies frequently give reduced rates to property owners or residents who agree to accept energy cutbacks during peak usage times. Many companies also will perform an energy audit on a property at little or no cost.

5. From time to time, the government, at the local, state, and federal levels, offers various tax credits, low-cost loans, and direct grants to property owners who upgrade to conserve energy. Are any of these benefits available for the properties that you're comparing?

Over a 10-year period, utility bill savings of just $100 a month would add up to nearly $18,000 (assuming interest compounded at 8%). Regardless of whether these dollars go directly into your pocket, they will eventually end up there—through either higher rents or less tenant turnover.

Summing Up

Many real estate investors err in one of two ways: (1) They judge a property only by the numbers (rent level, expenses, price), and thus they overlook the livability and practicality of the home for the tenants; or (2) they focus too much on their personal tastes and living standards and thus reject properties that would actually make good income investments. In contrast, the value investor pays close attention to the numbers but also closely judges the home or apartment units through the eyes and ears of the most desirable type of tenant that they would like to attract and retain. In other words, just as with stocks, value investors in real estate must collect and interpret a vast array of facts. It is only by paying attention to more details than the run-of-the-mill investor or home buyer that value investors become true experts in detecting, assessing, and creating property value.

Chapter 7

Is the Property a Good Buy?

Value investors rarely invest in a property (or stock) simply because it appears undervalued relative to the market prices of its peer group. To help figure out whether a property really offers good value, they routinely apply other benchmarks such as the following:

- Replacement cost
- Gross rent multipliers
- Per unit measures
- Cash flow (current return on investment [ROI])
- Discounted cash flow (DCF)
- Appreciation potential (see Chapters 8 and 9)
- Potential for creating value (see Chapter 10)

After reviewing these value benchmarks, you'll see that even a below-market price may not yield the rate of return and margin of safety that you would like. And contrary to popular belief, at times you can achieve a great return plus a margin of safety—even if you should pay above market value.

The trick, of course, is to know what you're doing and why you're doing it. Too many investors simplistically jump after below-market buys and reject in knee-jerk fashion all properties firmly priced above market. On closer inspection, either of these decision rules may err.

How Much Would It Cost to Rebuild the Property?

Naturally, when you invest in a property, you would like to profit as it appreciates in value. Over the long run, as construction costs go up and population increases, that's a safe forecast.[1] In the short run, though, current market values sometimes jump too far above building costs. Eyeing large profits, builders rush to construct new homes and apartments. The market becomes glutted. Property prices and rents stall or decline.[2]

The Construction Cycle

Here's how the construction cycle works: Typically, a city, town, or vacation area begins to boom. Jobs and wages go up. More people move in. Interest rates decline. Apartment rents and home prices start to take off. Vacancies disappear. Inventories of unsold homes decline. Pretty soon, existing homes or apartment units that could be built new for, say, $100,000 begin to sell at prices of, say, $120,000, $130,000, or more.

Builders Spy Opportunity

With market values of existing homes (or rentals) well above replacement costs, builders can quickly make a lot of money. Build at $100,000, sell at $130,000. That looks great—$30,000 of profit per unit. Unfortunately, in the past, too many builders often rushed in to earn such juicy returns. Then, because of these overly optimistic expectations, the supply of newly built properties multiplies. An earlier shortage becomes a surplus. Buyers who bought near the top of the cycle face disappointment (or worse) as home prices (or rent levels) stagnate or slide back to lower levels.

Recovery

Over time, builders pull back, and gradually excess inventories diminish.[3] Vacancies tighten, the inventory of unsold homes begins to fall, and potential buyers (renters) again outnumber the supply of available properties. Property prices and rents at first stabilize and then edge up. Eventually, as shortages again loom on the horizon, more buyers are drawn into the market. Prices take off on another short-term rapid run. The construction cycle turns another revolution.

Implications for Investors

The last major boom and bust construction cycle occurred in Texas in the mid- to late 1980s. Properties that could be built for $75,000 to $100,000 were selling for as high as $125,000 to $150,000. Condos and apartment projects, especially, multiplied with reckless abandon. Large real estate tax-shelter benefits added fuel to the fire. Just as what later occurred with the dot-coms and tech stocks, rapid price increases fed on themselves—until the bubble burst.

Pitfalls

Could investors have avoided getting caught in this downdraft? Absolutely. Had they kept an eye on construction costs, they could have anticipated impending problems. Whenever the selling prices of properties push more than 15% to 20% ahead of their replacement costs, the market is flashing yellow. Yet rather than cautiously slow down, most would-be buyers (and builders) speed up. Value investors, though, pay attention to this warning sign. They back off from new acquisitions or buy only when they can get their price—not the inflated (and soon-to-be-deflated) market price.

The lesson: Stay in touch with local builders or others who are in the know about contractor costs (e.g., building suppliers, lumberyards, appraisers, construction lenders). Or you might turn to one or more construction cost services. You can easily follow your local building costs through their manuals (at your library) or their Web sites.[4] When builder profit margins grow ever fatter, oversupply will surely result.

Profit When Values Drop Below Costs

Rents low? Vacancies climbing? Unsold homes piling up on the Realtors' Multiple Listing Service (MLS)? Builders going bankrupt? Lenders foreclosing? Great! That's the perfect time for value investors to buy—especially when market prices end up below replacement costs, because that means few builders will venture forth. Why pay more to build than you can get from a sale?

As long as emerging trends in the area point to a larger population, more jobs, and a growing economic base, prices (and rents) are guaranteed to rise. More demand pressing against a relatively fixed total supply will reward value investors with bountiful returns.

Cleanup Crews Earn Good Money

We frequently hear about the boom and bust cycles of real estate. But in fact, the notorious boom and busts of Texas, California, New England, New York City, and several other areas in the 1980s and early 1990s do not reflect the norm. Housing markets in most areas remain far more stable. The odds are that you will never experience that kind of shakeout. Though perhaps that's good in one sense, it's bad in another—because cleanup crews can make stupendous returns. Consider the Reichmans, who marched into New York City during its recession of 1974 to 1977. Within a relatively few years their $300 million of office building acquisitions (bought primarily with borrowed money) carried a value in excess of $1 billion.[5]

At the other end of the wealth spectrum, a former student of mine at Southern Methodist University in Dallas bought his first investment in 1992: a small foreclosed house for $8,000. After spending $1,500 for repairs and redecorating (most of which he performed himself), he leased the house for an off-the-chart return of $350 a month.

In buying during such hard times, were either of these investors taking a big risk? Quite the contrary. The purchase prices of their properties lay so far below replacement costs that they were taking virtually no risk at all. Both Dallas and New York City were (and remain) major capitals of industry and financial services. With their long-term growing base of jobs and population, a huge recovery in prices was only a matter of when, not if. In the meantime, the existing rents from the properties provided a more than ample cash flow to cover the costs of financing and still yield a strong cash-on-cash yield.

Have Money, Will Travel

Will similar local or regional shakeouts occur again? Probably. Although builders and construction lenders have supposedly entered a new era of disciplined building and lending, we've heard that story before. It seems that each generation forgets the mistakes of the past. They must relearn the lessons taught in earlier years.

Stay informed. Keep tabs on various cities and real estate markets around the country. Should property prices again plunge below their cost of replacement, don't miss that opportunity. Adopt the motto "have money (or credit), will travel." If the bargains don't come to you, then, as a value investor, prepare yourself to go to the bargains.

Local (Regional) Recessions

Even without serious overbuilding, property prices can sometimes fall below replacement costs due to job declines and recession. During the early 1990s, large layoffs in defense and aerospace firms created housing troubles in Southern California. We'll talk more about these economic base issues in Chapters 8 and 9. For now, just recognize that either overbuilding, job losses, or some combination of the two can offer up grand opportunities for value investors.

Market Value < Replacement Cost = Bargain Hunter's Delight

Tobin's q

Although the replacement cost method of valuing properties goes back to at least the 1920s, in more recent years the technique has also been applied to valuing the stock market. Developed by the Nobel-winning economist James Tobin, the technique in stocks has been dubbed Tobin's q.[6] In their excellent book *Valuing Wall Street*, Smithers and Wright used Tobin's q to forecast (quite accurately) a major stock market "correction." Smithers and Wright showed that the market value of stocks—and especially tech stocks—then sat at record high levels relative to the replacement costs of corporate assets.[7]

Market Prices Greatly Exceed Replacement Costs

Similar to what occurs in real estate markets, when Wall Street prices corporate assets at values far greater than the firms' costs to acquire (create) them, companies overexpand, just as builders tend to overbuild. Eventually, firms are stuck with excessive production capacity. Industry competition erodes profit margins. Unsold inventories accumulate and earnings turn into losses. Stock prices plummet (e.g., Nortel, Lucent, AT&T, Dell, and Compaq). Overinvestment leads to overcapacity.

The Tobin's q Case Against Stocks

Even after the 2000–2001 correction, stock prices for the S&P 500 still hang far above their historical levels relative to replacement costs. Are we in a new era where replacement costs no longer matter?[8] Or will most firms continue to face profit-killing competition until continuing operating losses and restructurings force many firms to abandon various lines of business?

Only time will tell. But if you bet on a new-era answer, you are *betting*, not investing.

Per Unit Measures

Real estate investors often rely on various per unit measures to help them decide whether a property looks like a good buy. Like all gross or rule-of-thumb measures, per unit figures signal whether a property tends to be priced over or under some benchmark norm. Though never compelling in isolation, these types of measures do provide meaningful benchmarks for investor comparisons.

Per Apartment Unit

Anytime you're looking at multiunit apartment buildings, you should divide the asking price by the number of apartment units in the property.

For example, for an eight-unit property priced at $450,000, you would calculate as follows:

$$\text{price per unit} = \frac{\$450{,}000}{8}$$

$$\text{price per unit} = \$56{,}250$$

If you know that other similar apartment buildings have typically sold for $60,000 to $70,000 per unit, you may have found a bargain. In addition, this and other per measures give you a quick way to compare prevailing prices when buildings differ in unit sizes. For instance, say you're comparing 6-unit, 9-unit, and 11-unit properties at the respective prices of $275,000, $435,000, and $467,500. By figuring per unit prices, you can more easily rank the properties from lowest to highest priced.

Size, Quality, and Location

Ideally, the units you compare should closely match each other. But if that's not possible, adjust your valuations to reflect size, quality, and location differences among properties. Especially consider all of the location, site, and building features highlighted in Chapter 6. I'm not trying to push you into the "analysis paralysis" so common in MBA programs. But by trying to spot those differences that make a difference, you can better rank properties according to their relative desirability and profit potential.

Opportunity Knocks (Arbitrage)

Primarily, price-per-unit measures can help you find bargain buildings. On occasion, though, this measure can help you spot opportunities in two other ways:

1. *Size*. Change the size of the units from smaller to larger, or vice versa. If large units of 1,200 to 1,400 square feet sell and rent at very substantial premiums over smaller 700- to 800-square-foot units,

buying a property with predominantly small units could pay off big when you reconfigure the building into one of larger-sized units.

2. *Conversion*. You might also profit by noticing that buildings with two-bedroom rentals typically sell in the range of $40,000 to $50,000 per unit. In contrast, in similar condo buildings, two-bedroom units sell in the $70,000 to $80,000 range. Or the price disparity could work in the opposite direction. Either way, you may be able to buy at the lower-priced use, convert, then sell (or rent) at the higher-priced use.

Although the preceding types of arbitrage do not occur often, they do arise every now and then. By always paying attention to relative prices, the value investor stays poised to buy when this type of arbitrage opportunity knocks.

Per Square Foot Measures

You've probably heard property buyers and sellers refer to a house or other type of property by noting that it sold for, say, $135 per square foot. Price per square foot (p.s.f.) represents one of the most widely used methods of benchmark pricing. Investors and home buyers alike rely on it to provide a ballpark measure of relative value. To calculate a p.s.f. figure, simply divide the total square footage of the unit (house, apartment, total building) into its price:

$$\text{p.s.f.} = \frac{\text{asking price}}{\text{square footage}}$$

$$\text{p.s.f.} = \frac{\$285{,}000}{1{,}900}$$

$$\text{p.s.f.} = \$150$$

If comparable properties typically have sold at $170 to $180 p.s.f., you may have found a bargain at a price of $150 p.s.f.

Caveats

If only it were so simple! Home buyers and investors both go wrong using p.s.f. figures because no uniform standards apply to square foot measures. In reality, all square feet are not created equal in terms of quality, design, and usability. So use p.s.f. figures with care. As pointed out in Chapter 6, converted garages, basements, and attics are worth far less per square foot than the main living area of a house. Also, be aware of size mismatches. Some houses are built with room counts or room sizes far out of proportion to each other, or to comparable sale homes.

I recently looked at a nearly new house (3,800 square feet) that included a huge great room, perhaps 800 or 900 square feet. Yet four of the home's five bedrooms were smallish and bland, about 10 by 12 feet. The remainder of the home's square footage was primarily taken up by a huge master bedroom and a glorious Roman bath. You've probably seen houses like this one—several giant rooms for show, others dysfunctionally small. The house fails as an integrated living unit. Accordingly, this house eventually sold at $70 per square foot. Other homes in the neighborhood typically achieved p.s.f. prices of $85 to $100. Use p.s.f. measures as a guide, but don't pay top-market prices for low-quality, dysfunctional space.

Land Value Caveat

Generally, when you look at p.s.f. pricing for existing properties, you'll find gross figures. This type of p.s.f. includes the value of the building, the site improvements (fences, decks, sidewalks, driveway), and the lot. As a rule-of-thumb benchmark, this technique works well—except when comparable houses sit on lots that differ greatly in value.

For example, say you're checking p.s.f. prices and find a couple of 1,400-square-foot houses that recently sold for around $125,000 each, or $89 per square foot. You find a very similar house two blocks away. It's priced at a p.s.f. of $75. Have you found a bargain? Apparently so—until, with a little more investigating, you learn that this house sits within the boundaries of a poorly regarded school system. As a result, its lot is worth $15,000 less than the lots of the comp houses. Of course, relative to its rent levels and appreciation potential, this $75 p.s.f. house still might make a good buy. But the p.s.f. price alone wouldn't tell you that. The lesson: Don't read too much too soon into per-square-foot price comparisons. Closely verify comparability.

Replacement Costs

When investigating replacement costs (see the preceding section), builders often quote construction costs in terms of price per square foot. Caveats apply here, too. First, unlike comparable sale p.s.f. figures, builder p.s.f. costs don't usually include the value of the lot. Second, if you've ever built (or bought) a new house, you know that cost figures can differ dramatically. Not only will they differ among builders, but they will differ according to types of materials, the quality of the finishing, and the brand of the built-in appliances.

Before you apply a price-per-square-foot construction cost figure to a property you're valuing, make sure you understand the precise nature of the estimate. In my area, the costs of construction for new homes range from $60 p.s.f. up to more than $100 p.s.f. As always, take care to match like for like.

Price per Front Foot

Although popular as a pricing metric for retail sites, price per front foot plays a relatively small role in valuing residential properties. Chiefly, home buyers or residential investors use it to benchmark waterfront sites. Because the most popular benefits of owning waterfront property are views and beach area, the larger a site's shoreline, the greater its desirability and the higher its value.

If waterfront is valued at $1,000 per front foot, a one-acre site with 125 feet of shoreline would sell at $125,000. If a site included only 80 feet of shoreline (other things being equal), its value would equal $80,000. Of course, it's that "other things *not* being equal" that can sometimes throw value estimates off track. But again, as a rule of thumb, price per front foot can convey a useful piece of information.

Gross Rent Multipliers

To value rental houses and apartment buildings, investors frequently compute monthly gross rent multipliers (GRMs) by dividing price by monthly rent. For example, an investor might check the sales of several comparable properties and discover the data shown in Table 7.1.

If you find a property for sale with a relatively low GRM, it could signal either a too-high price or too-low rents. Further checking would reveal the answer. Throughout the United States and Canada, I've seen GRMs as low as 50 or 60 (e.g., mobile home rentals or unpopular neighborhoods) and as high as 200 (coastal California cities). In my present university-dominated town, gross rent multipliers typically range from a low of 70 (unexceptional condominiums) to 130 (single-family houses in professional but not upscale neighborhoods).

As a rule (and depending on the costs and terms of financing), gross rent multipliers above 130 often produce negative cash flows—unless you increase your down payment to 30% or more. Because urban and vacation towns with high housing prices often produce GRMs of 150 or greater, value investors who live in those areas should buy their rental homes and apartments elsewhere. Alternatively, value investors can look for neighborhoods or market niches (condominiums, lower- or middle-income housing, suburbs, smaller outlying towns) that offer a better rent-to-price relationship.

***Table* 7.1 Calculating the Gross Rent Multiplier**

	Monthly Rent	*Sales Price*	*GRM*
2400 Flora	$1,100	$134,200	122
2790 Rose	$ 950	$121,600	128
3162 Pine	$1,250	$146,250	117

Capitalized Value

As another popular approach to value, most real estate investors use the following formula:

$$V = \frac{NOI}{R}$$

Where V represents the estimated value of the property, NOI (net operating income) represents the property's rents minus expenses; and R equals the capitalization rate. Essentially, this formula is the real estate investor's version of the price-to-earnings (P/E) ratio. To illustrate, Table 7.2 shows how this technique would look for a six-unit apartment building.

Calculating NOI looks relatively straightforward. If you're not careful, though, you can err in several ways. To alert you to these possible traps,

***Table* 7.2 Income Statement (Annual)**

1. Gross annual potential rents (4,725 × 6 × 12)		$52,200
2. Income from parking and storage areas		5,062
3. Vacancy and collection losses @ 7%		−4,009
4. Effective gross income		$53,253
Less operating and fixed expenses		
5. Trash pickup	$1,080	
6. Utilities	450	
7. License and permit fees	206	
8. Advertising and promotion	900	
9. Management fees @ 6%	3,195	
10. Maintenance and repairs	3,000	
11. Yard care	488	
12. Miscellaneous	2,250	
13. Property taxes	3,202	
14. Property and liability insurance	1,267	
15. Reserves for replacement	1,875	
Total operating and fixed expenses	$17,913	
16. NOI		$35,340

think about the following caveats and explanations (which match up numerically with the entries shown on the income statement):

1. *Gross annual potential rents*. For gross rents, use the property's existing rent levels. Or, if its current rents sit above market, use market rent levels. Verify all leases for rental amounts and lease terms. Do not use a rent figure that's based on your anticipated rent increases (if any).
2. *Extra income*. With many properties you can charge extra for parking, storage, laundry, party room, garages, and the like. Verify all such existing income. Don't project extra income that's not been proven by past operating experience or reasonable market data.
3. *Vacancy and collection losses*. Use market vacancy rates or the current owner's vacancies for the past year—whichever is higher. Also, when judging market vacancy rates, take your figures from the market niche in which this property currently operates. Vacancy rates may vary significantly by location, apartment size, quality, and rent level. In fact, as you compare vacancy rates by market niche, try to spot those segments that are experiencing the greatest shortages.
4. *Effective gross income*. It is from this cash that you will pay property expenses and mortgage payments. If you overestimate rent levels or underestimate vacancies, you may end up cash short.
5. *Trash pickup*. Verify rates and permissible quantities. Look for lower-cost alternatives.
6. *Utilities*. In addition to common-area lighting, some buildings include centralized heat and air systems. Verify with utility companies the amounts of these expenses. (Personal note: I would never again buy a building where apartment units lacked individual heating, ventilation, and cooling [HVAC] units—unless the price was extremely low or the HVAC system was extremely efficient. Centralized systems seldom distribute heat and air-conditioning uniformly. Tenants persistently voice complaints of being too cold or too hot.)

7. *License and permit fees*. On occasion, owners of rental properties are required to pay various municipal fees.
8. *Advertising and promotion*. Ideally, you will generate a good supply of rental applicants from free postings, referrals, and inquiries. Otherwise, you may need to advertise. Also, you'll probably need to pay for credit checks.
9. *Management fees*. Even if you self-manage your units, allocate some expense here for your time and effort. Don't confuse return on labor for return on investment.
10. *Maintenance and repairs*. As with management fees, enter an expense here to pay yourself or others. Taking care of something yourself shouldn't mean that you will work for free.
11. *Grounds maintenance*. Yard care entails mowing the lawn, trimming hedges, removing snow, cleaning up leaves, and so on.
12. *Miscellaneous*. You will incur such odds-and-ends expenses as lease preparation, auto mileage, and long-distance telephone charges.
13. *Property taxes*. Verify the amount, tax rate, and assessed value. Check for accuracy. Note whether the property is subject to any special assessments (e.g., sewer, sidewalks, water reclamation).
14. *Property and liability insurance*. Verify your exact coverage for property and types of loses. Increase deductibles and limits on liability.
15. *Reserves for replacement*. Eventually you'll need to replace the roof, HVAC, appliances, carpeting, and other short-life items. Allocate a pro rata annual amount here.
16. *NOI*. Subtract all expenses from effective gross income. You now have the numerator for V = NOI/R.

As a general principle, value investors first use a conservative approach to figuring NOI. They don't make grand assumptions about potential rent increases. They don't omit necessary expenses. They try to verify and double-check all expense figures. They charge for their own labor (if any), and they allocate reasonable amounts for replacement reserves. In addition, as a value investor, you'll ask to see the sellers' Schedule E, where they have reported property revenues and expenses to the Internal Revenue Service. (You get resistance to this request. But carefully weigh the sellers' response.)

Estimate Value

To calculate value via the capitalized income approach, you next need to come up with an appropriate capitalization rate (R). Essentially, this rate represents your unleveraged annual return, just as the dividend yield represents your unleveraged annual cash return on stocks. Fortunately for real estate investors, R typically dwarfs the now diminutive dividend yield.

Calculate R

You calculate your capitalization rate by comparing the NOIs of other similar properties to their respective selling prices. To come up with this type of information, you can talk with competent realty agents who regularly sell (and preferably own) rental properties, other investors (from a local realty investment club, for example), or recent sellers. People in real estate generally tend to help each other and share information freely. In terms of format, you would display these market data as follows:

Property	*Sales Price*	*NOI*	R
Hampton Apts. (8 units)	$452,900	$43,211	9.54%
Woodruff Apts. (6 units)	$360,000	$35,900	9.97
Adams Manor (6 units)	$295,000	$28,440	9.6
Newport Apts. (9 units)	$549,000	$53,700	9.78
Ridge Terrace (8 units)	$471,210	$42,409	9.0

From the various comparable property cap rates (R), you would select those buildings and locations most comparable to the property you're evaluating, say, 9.0 to 9.5 percent. You would then calculate a market value range as follows:

$$1.\ V = \frac{\$35{,}340\ (\text{NOI})}{.09\ (\text{R})}$$

$$V = \$392{,}666$$

$$2.\ V = \frac{\$35{,}340\ (\text{NOI})}{.098\ (\text{R})}$$

$$V = \$360{,}612$$

Throughout the country, cap rates for small rental properties may run from as low as 6% or 7% up to 12%, 14%, or higher. Generally, a low cap rate occurs when you're valuing highly desirable properties in good to top neighborhoods. On the other hand, relatively high cap rates tend to follow less-desirable properties in so-so neighborhoods. Apartment buildings with condo conversion potential also tend to sell with low cap rates.

If you find that cap rates in your area are too low across the board, search other areas. High cap rates (lower earnings multiples) typically offer lower risk and higher cash yields.

P/E Ratio Analogy

Stock market investors may see the parallel between cap rates and the P/E ratio. If a property sells with a cap rate of .085, that figure would represent a P/E multiple of close to 12. Or, conversely, a stock with a P/E multiple of, say, 14 would show an earnings yield (cap rate) of 7.1%. Either way, these very similar techniques both try to show the relative valuation of a stream of income—with stocks, a stream of corporate earnings; with real estate, a stream of rental earnings.[9]

Likewise, over time these yields will move up or down according to growth potential, interest rate outlook, income quality, and various risk factors. No single rate can ever represent the "correct" rate. You must always investigate specific conditions of the relevant property market and submarket.

Anticipate the Future; Pay for the Present

In the preceding example, we used conservative income and expense figures drawn primarily from the property's current operating history. More than likely, though, you will make some changes to the property through improvements, better management, and perhaps even neighborhood revitalization. These changes may dramatically boost net income and lower the appropriate cap rate. Taken together, these changes can dramatically boost a property's value.

So here's where you need to exercise caution. When negotiating to buy, focus on the present, not your vision of the future. Investors who anticipate great profits often pay too much. They let the sellers capture the value potential that they plan to create. (Remember the once accepted yet fallacious value metric for tech stocks—growth at *any* price.)

Reason and Judgment

When you buy conservatively, you enhance your margin of safety. However, on occasion, you may run across a super property at a relatively high price. Should you automatically reject it? Not necessarily. But before you buy, check, verify, and recheck your optimistic expectations. Sometimes a fully valued property with extraordinary potential will outperform a bargain-priced property that merely shows moderate potential.

In doing so, be sure to note the risks you're taking. Unnoticed perils have brought down many a sure thing. Guide such buys with cool reason and keen judgment.

Mum's the Word

Novice investors, especially, tend to give away too much of their plans for a property. To buy at a conservative price, don't turn your cards so that the sellers can see them. If you explicitly question the sellers in ways that reveal your value-creating ideas, the sellers will likely use that potential to strengthen their own negotiating position. In most cases sellers already hold inflated ideas about all the great things you can do to enhance their property—which, regrettably, they say, they never had the time (or money) to accomplish. With such ploys common, you need not load the sellers with even more ammunition to fire back at you.

Cash-on-Cash Return

As covered in an earlier chapter, many investors judge their properties by the cash-on-cash rate of return they can achieve. As a result, investors scrutinize the cost and terms of their financing as much as they do a property. To illustrate, let's bring forward that six-unit apartment building discussed earlier in this chapter. Assume that you can buy that property for $350,000, or just under $60,000 per unit. You talk to a lender and tentatively arrange a mortgage for $280,000 (an 80% loan-to-value ratio). The lender wants an 8.0% interest rate with a 25-year term. You would need to come up with $70,000. Here are the relevant figures:

Loan amount	$280,000
Annualized mortgage payments @ 8.0%; 25 years	25,932
Net operating income (NOI)	35,340
Less mortgage payments	25,932
BTCF	$9,408

$$\text{Cash-on-cash return} = \frac{\text{BTCF}}{\text{Down payment}}$$

$$= \frac{\$\,9{,}408}{\$70{,}000}$$

$$= 13.44\%$$

Not bad. But say this investor's hurdle rate equals 15%. What might she do to boost her cash-on-cash return? For starters, she could try to get the lender to extend the loan term to 30 years. If successful, her annualized payments (assuming no change in interest rate) would drop to $24,652. Thus BTCF would increase to $10,688 (35,340 – 24,652):

$$\text{Cash-on-cash return} = \frac{\$10{,}688}{\$70{,}000}$$

$$= 15.3\%$$

If she doesn't want to extend the loan term to 30 years, she could try to push the lender down to a 7.625% interest rate. In that case, her annualized mortgage payments (25-years) would total $25,102. This investor's BTCF would equal $10,238 (35,340 – 25,102):

$$\text{Cash-on-cash return} = \frac{\$10{,}238}{\$70{,}000}$$

$$= 14.28\%$$

That lower 7.625% rate won't quite do it. But as an enterprising investor, she might pursue any number of other options:

1. Try for an even lower interest rate (7.5% would work).
2. Ask the seller to take back a balloon note for five years at 7.0% for, say, $20,000.
3. Negotiate a lower price for the property.
4. Switch from a 25-year fixed-rate mortgage to a 7.0% 5/20 adjustable-rate mortgage. This tactic would work especially well if she planned to sell (or exchange) the property within five years.
5. Look for reasonable and certain ways to boost the property's net income. Increase rent collections, raise occupancy, cut expenses.
6. Agree to pay the seller a higher price in exchange for owner financing on terms more favorable (lower interest rate, lower down payment) than a bank would offer.

Any or all of these techniques could work. An investor would just have to experiment with the numbers and negotiate for some mutually agreeable solution. The point is that for an investor in real estate, the market never provides a definitive return. You provide your own return based on the price, terms of financing, property improvements, and management strategy that you negotiate and implement.

Discounted Cash Flow

In the recent *Smart Money* article, "Value Rules: The Best Strategy Ever," Warren Buffet is quoted with regard to value investing.[10] Using the same definition as John Burr Williams in *The Theory of Investment Value*, Buffet says that the "intrinsic value" of an investment equals "the discounted value of the cash that can be taken out . . . during its remaining life." Clearly, value investors in both stocks and real estate use a wide variety of value metrics to help them select their winners. In the end, though, the decision comes down to discounted cash flow (DCF): Will the present value of the cash flows exceed the amount of your original cash investment when discounted at your required rate of return?

Calculating Present Value

Although the complex mathematics of DCF go beyond what I want to explain here, the principles are quite simple, and you can make the appropriate calculations with a $29.95 financial calculator. Essentially, to calculate present value, you need to lay out three factors: (1) the cash flows you expect on a year-by-year basis; (2) the reversion value, which is the cash you expect to receive at the time you sell; and (3) the discount rate (i.e., your required rate of return).[11] Once you have discounted your cash flows and reversion at the required rate of return, you sum your results. Next, compare these results to the original amount of your investment. If the results exceed your investment, your income flows are said to provide a positive net present value (NPV). Your investment meets your rate-of-return criteria.

Income Taxes

Because nearly all stock return figures are quoted gross of taxes and expenses, I have followed this same convention. Nevertheless, several strong advantages for real estate deserve mention. When held outside of a tax-deferred retirement plan, real estate offers four distinct tax advantages over stocks.

1. *Depreciation*. You can shelter part of your cash flows with depreciation deductions. For example, on a $100,000 rental house, these annual deductions could amount to around $3,000 and could save you more than $1,000 in payments to the IRS (depending on your tax rate).
2. *Capital improvement deductions*. Generally, income tax law requires property owners to amortize long-life items such as new roofs, kitchen remodeling, or a garage conversion. However, to simplify bookkeeping, the IRS permits small real estate investors to write off these types of capital expenses each year up to the amount of $10,000. In other words, this IRS rule gives property owners a large deduction that immediately reduces (or eliminates) their liability to pay income taxes.
3. *Capital gains*. If you sell rental real estate, your proceeds will be taxed as capital gains in essentially the same manner as stocks. However, smart real estate investors don't sell; they trade up, tax free. In clear advantage over stocks, by executing a continual series of Section 1031 exchanges, you can pyramid your real estate holdings completely free of federal taxes.
4. *Tax-free withdrawals*. If you ever need money for business or personal reasons, you can tap your real estate equity with a cash-out refinance or a second mortgage. You can pocket these funds free of all income taxes.

Read the footnoted tax references and check with your tax advisor.[12] You'll find that real estate not only offers value investors higher pretax returns than stocks, it also offers far superior after-tax returns.[13]

Real Estate Investment Trusts

If after completing this book you still choose not to directly own real estate, consider buying into one or more real estate investment trusts (REITs). REITs permit you to become a part owner of virtually any class of property. You can buy REIT shares in world-class hotels, warehouses, office buildings, apartment complexes, and shopping centers.[14] Some REITs specialize in one of these property categories. Others may mix and match. With more than 100 REITs traded on the major U.S. stock exchanges, you can find nearly any type of REIT that you might want.[15] In addition, you can buy mutual funds that specialize in holding REIT stocks or stocks in other real estate–related companies such as home builders and mortgage companies.[16]

Valuing REIT Shares (Asset Play)

Theoretically, a REIT's shares should sell for a price that reflects the values of the properties it owns. As a practical matter, though, REIT share prices jump up and down far more than the values and income streams of their properties. As a result, in some cases, value investors can make great asset plays in REIT stocks. For example, at the beginning of 2000, REIT shares were trading at a 20% to 25% discount from net asset value. In other words, you can sometimes buy an interest in the properties that a REIT owns for as little as 75 to 80 cents on the dollar.

Discount the Income Stream

In contrast to the stocks of most companies traded on the major stock exchanges, REITs typically pay very high dividends. In recent years, many REITs have registered yields of 5.5% to 9.0%, sometimes higher. During 2000, Shurgard (an owner of "mini warehouse" storage centers) paid a cash dividend of $2.04 per share and its stock price traded within the range of $22 to $27 per share. Using the standard dividend discount model, a dividend growth rate of 2.0% (Shurgard's recent five-year average), and a required rate of return of 11%, we can compute this REIT's intrinsic value as follows:

$$V = \frac{\text{dividend}}{r - g}$$

$$V = \frac{\$2.04}{.11 - .02}$$

$$V = \$22.66$$

If we drop our required rate of return to 10%, Shurgard's intrinsic value would total as follows:

$$V = \frac{\$2.04}{.10 - .02}$$

$$V = \$25.50$$

Using this accepted valuation technique, Shurgard looked reasonably valued relative to its intrinsic value. However, relative to the stock market as a whole, Shurgard looked substantially undervalued. Recall from Chapter 3 that when the dividend discount model was applied to stocks, our portfolio appeared overvalued by a factor of three.

So had you performed this kind of calculation in late 2000, you would have found Shurgard (and most other REITs) to have provided strong relative value. And you would have been right. By late 2001, the S&P 500 was down around 20% from earlier in the year, whereas Shurgard was trading at over $30 per share (up 25%), and REITs in general were up by around 5% to 10% —in a bear market!

Advantages of REITs

REITs pay high dividends relative to other types of stocks for two reasons: (1) To maintain favored tax status, REITs are exempt from paying federal and state income taxes—they must pay out (return to stockholders) at least

90% of their annual earnings; and (2) REITs typically earn strong, reliable cash flows from the rents they collect on their properties.

Diversification

REITs permit investors to diversify their stock holdings into defensive positions. (Now, presumably, a stock that pays strong dividends in a dependable manner is *defensive!*) Because of their high payout ratios, REIT shares tend to hold up better (or even advance) in down markets as compared with those stocks who run with the growth and glamour crowd. In addition, REITs permit individual real estate investors to diversify their real estate holdings among geographic areas and classes of properties.

Liquidity and Management

Because REITs are shares of stock, they can be sold easily and quickly just as most other actively traded shares. (Of course, just as with other stocks, REIT liquidity guarantees a sale, not a price. If your REIT shares are trading at 75 cents on the dollar, then that's the price you're going to get. Take solace, though; at least you'll be selling to a fellow value investor.) As to management, REIT investing appeals to many real estate investors because it frees them from the effort of buying, managing, and selling properties.

Should You Invest in REITs?

For value investors, REITs provide a good choice—as long as the yield and price look favorable. Throughout much of the 1990s, REITs provided good and reliable returns. However, REITs lack flash. Most sound REITs plug along. They tend to trade within plus or minus 20% of their underlying asset value. You're not likely to score a 10-bagger with an REIT. On the positive side, absent highly unusual events, neither will you see a well-managed REIT plunge in price by 40% or 50%.[17]

What about REITs versus direct ownership? Direct ownership wins hands down. Only direct owners of properties can earn those outsized returns that go to enterprise and intelligence. As a REIT investor, you invest passively. You won't be able to capture superior returns through sharp negotiating, finding bargains, employing leverage, or creating value. Neither can you reap the tax advantages that individual investors can avail themselves of. Nevertheless, as a direct owner who wishes property diversification, putting part of your portfolio into REITs can provide capital gains, income, and growth—all without a steep downside.

Chapter 8

Look Beyond Market Value

Several years ago, Amazon.com was trading at $200 per share.[1] If an owner of Amazon stock had then offered you 1,000 shares at the below-market price of $150 per share, would you have bought? Sure—if you could have turned around and immediately resold these holdings at $200 per share. But what if you had to agree to a lock-up period of 12 months? Would you then have bought? Not if you were following the principles of value investing.

The Market Value Mistake

Almost universally, books on real estate investing tell you to search for properties that you can buy at a bargain price. Sounds good, except that nearly all of these books define bargain price only in terms of buying at less than market value. But unless you can immediately flip this property and take a quick profit, it may or may not prove to be a bargain. As with Amazon .com and most other stocks, property prices can go up, or they can go down. You must look beyond the less-than-market-price approach to finding a bargain.

The Million-Dollar Loss

Consider this experience: In mid-1999, the Haskells of Palo Alto, California, thought they had scored a real coup when they found a great four-bedroom, three-bath home not far from Sand Hill Road for just $1.8 million. Comparable homes had sold recently at $2.1 to $2.4 million. By mid-2001, though, John Haskell had lost his dot-com job, his stock options, and his ability to make the mortgage payments on their newly acquired home. They faced no other choice—the house had to go. After four months of nail biting and sleepless nights, the Haskells finally closed a sale of their home at $1.3 million—just enough to clear their mortgage and brokerage commissions. "That house was the worst investment we ever made," John Haskell lamented.

"The way home prices were skyrocketing in the Valley, we didn't think we could lose.[2] In fact, six months ago, we thought we could have easily sold our house for $2.5, maybe $3.0 million. We were thinking of building our dream home. Our house appreciation would have more than covered the down payment. Now, those dreams have been erased by nightmares."

Media Hype

In ferreting out home-buying "nightmares" similar to the Haskells', reporters once again are setting out to warn Americans against the dangers of investing (sic) in real estate. The cover of a recent issue of *Forbes* featured a photo of a mournful couple with the caption, "Their house lost $1 million in value. It could happen to you." The story inside the magazine went on to detail the tough times facing many homeowners (now hope-to-be-sellers) who bought expensive homes at or near the peak of the market.[3]

As to that couple featured in the Forbes cover story, don't feel too badly for them. Although the market value of their house fell from its $2 million peak, they still sold the house for $1.04 million—almost $200,000 more than the $856,000 they had paid two years earlier.

Leave the Party Early

Do not confuse going to a wildly escalating housing party with value investing. And if you do go, plan to leave early. Don't wait for the police to come and arrest those unsustainable rates of appreciation. Buying in a speculative boom—even at a below-market price—does not guarantee profits.[4]

As a value investor, you must realize that some housing markets go through repeated boom and bust cycles. No one should watch property prices jump 10%, 20%, or 30% a year and then foolishly conclude that such extravagant price increases can play a role in one's long-term (or even shorter-term) financial planning. Such booms always give lie to the popular cliché "Buy in the areas where prices are appreciating the fastest."

Unless sound fundamental reasons support forecasts of future appreciation, you've no right to expect continuing outsized price increases.[5] As with the market price of Amazon.com stock at $200, real estate market values tell you nothing about the future. Nor does a less-than-market value price tell you whether you're getting a good buy.

How to Define Bargain

Warren Buffet has said he would rather buy a great company at a fair price than get a lousy company at a bargain price. Of course, ideally, the goal of every value investor is to get both: (1) a great company (property), and (2) a below-market price (as Buffet did with the *Washington Post*).

Essentially, Buffet made his statement in response to the simplistic and frequent reporting that value investors are bargain hunters. Buffet wanted to emphasize that to value investors, the term bargain does mean absolutely low-priced, but only low-priced relative to an investment's expected future cash flows (income and appreciation). No one should interpret bargain-priced to narrowly mean low-priced relative to the present or the past.[6]

How does it profit you to buy Amazon.com at $50 off its market price of $200 a share if, in fact, its intrinsic value could easily sit at less than $10 per share? The same principle is true in real estate. Yes, do look for a property that you can buy for less than its market value. But before you commit, make sure that market fundamentals point to increases in market values, not declines (as Silicon Valley home buyers are now experiencing).

Appraisals Shortchange Fundamentals

As a starting point, of course, closely calculate the market value of every property you're interested in. Normally, that value should set the top limit for your purchase price. If you pay more than market value for a property, even with market appreciation you could wait years before the market catches up to the price you overpaid.[7] On the other hand, if you buy an appreciating property for less than its market value, you create an instant boost to your equity in excess of the amount of your down payment.

Notwithstanding the preceding, even though an appraisal may help you decide how much to offer for a property, in and of itself, a market value appraisal can never tell you whether you *should* buy a property—regardless of how much of a below-market price you expect to get. Why? Because market value appraisals do the following:

1. *Focus on the past*. By drawing data only from past (albeit the recent past), appraisals say nothing about the future.
2. *Ignore other areas*. By drawing sales prices from comparable homes in the same location, appraisals say nothing about the relative price advantages or disadvantages of homes located elsewhere, near or far.
3. *Shortchange area economics*. Most market value appraisals shortchange the economics of an area. Because market value appraisals look chiefly to the sales prices of comparable properties, they do not thoroughly discuss issues such as jobs, incomes, population trends, new developments, land-use controls, and other fundamental factors that push up (or pull down) property values.

Focus on the Recent Past

Value investors in real estate must realize that market value appraisals represent a snapshot of the recent past. Essentially, they say, "Since these similar properties have sold for these prices, then this subject property should sell for this price." As a practical matter, though, the sales of those comparable homes may actually have occurred three to six months ago—sometimes longer. In fast-changing markets, such out-of-date comparable sales not only fail to speak to the future, they do not even speak to the present.

If a market has recently slowed, an appraiser's (or your) estimate of market value may overshoot the correct mark. You can easily err in this way when property prices have been marching up by 1% or 2% a month for a year or more. You look at recent comparable sales, extrapolate from recent trends, and set a market value figure. You bid 15% less. After negotiations, you buy at a perceived 10% discount.

In this case, you think you paid less than market. In fact, though, due to the economic slowdown that you have not yet picked up on, you really paid above market. Naturally, given these difficulties, you should always keep in mind that comparable sale data often will leave you with much less market knowledge (present and future) than you actually need.

Appraisals Ignore Other Areas

In any given urban area, some neighborhoods, subdivisions, or communities may offer far better value for the price than others. Yet appraisals concentrate their attention on properties all drawn from the same location. As a result, many investors never think to compare the strengths and weaknesses of various locations and rank them according to their relative prices and benefits.

By remaining fixated on buying at a below market price, these investors miss another type of bargain hunting: buying in an undervalued neighborhood, subdivision, or community.

Appraisals Shortchange Economic Fundamentals

Imagine the year is 1975. Assume you must buy one of two investment choices:

1. *Berkeley Hills, California*. This three-bedroom, two-bath home is firmly (non-negotiably) priced at $65,000. Its market value sits at $55,000.
2. *Terre Haute, Indiana*. You can buy this three-bedroom, two-bath home for $40,000. An accurate appraisal shows a market value for this home at $50,000.

Which of these properties would you choose? If you define a bargain or good buy as a price less than market value, you would choose the house in

Terre Haute. If you were astute enough to understand the importance of economic fundamentals, you would have chosen the Berkeley house—even though you must pay an above-market price. Since the mid-1970s, houses in the Berkeley Hills have multiplied in value at least sixfold, whereas similarly constructed houses in Terre Haute have little more than doubled.

Economic fundamentals account for this huge difference. Yet had you compared market value appraisals on these properties, you would not have been able to detect serious mention of any of these fundamentals.

Summing Up: The Market Value Mistake

Many real estate investors mistakenly believe that market value represents the ultimate touchstone for finding a bargain. When they buy for less than market value, they brag to the world about the "good buy" they snagged. When they can't negotiate a sharp deal, they walk.

Value investors take a more complex approach. Yes, they would like to acquire each of the properties they do buy at a price less than market value. But they also realize that the real test of a bargain price comes on the date of sale—not the date of purchase. To achieve success toward that end they supplement their market value appraisals with more extensive market information.

Current Market Data

In addition to recent comparable sales data, your investigation of the current market should include several other market facts. These facts can help you develop a better picture of the here and now, as well as help you forecast short-term changes. Available primarily from local Realtors and mortgage lenders, these data include the following:

1. Time on market
2. Asking price/selling price
3. Inventory of unsold homes

4. Properties under contract
5. Mortgage applications, delinquencies, and foreclosures
6. Vacancy rates/for-rent ads

Time on Market

In most areas of the country, Realtors keep tabs on how long it takes for listed properties to sell. When the real estate cycle starts to cool, homes sit unsold for greater periods of time. If last year homes sat with for-sale signs in their front yards for an average of 77 days and now the time on the market stands at 98 days, be careful.

The previously cited *Forbes* article, for example, reports that in Manhattan between 2000 and 2001, time on market increased from 118 days to 132 days.[8] As the time on the market lengthens, the slowdown is signaling that sellers are asking too much for their properties. What is true of the market in general is also true of particular properties. Before you put in an offer for a property, find out how long it has been up for sale—not just with the brokerage firm that has the current listing, but also any other firm with which the property was previously listed unsuccessfully. As a rule, the slower the market, the longer a specific property has languished unsold, the more carefully you should weigh your buying decision.

Asking Price/Selling Price

In very strong markets, homes sell quickly at (or sometimes in excess of) their asking prices. Bidding wars and multiple offers create buyer panic. On the down cycle, the reverse occurs. Not only do homes take longer to sell, but on average, the eventual selling price might fall to, say, only 80% to 85% of its listing price. Either of these types of markets should cause you to step back and evaluate where the market is likely to head in the near future.

The need to exercise caution in a slowing market is obvious. But why be cautious in a super-hot market? Because buyer panic, bidding wars, and multiple offers often push prices up too quickly (e.g., Silicon Valley, 1997–2000). Once the buying fever passes, prices get a dose of market reality. In 1984, when I put a property up for sale in Dallas, I got three offers at the full asking price. Buyers were in a frenzy. Eight years later, the people I had sold to put the house back on the market at the same price they had paid. In contrast, I had picked up a 30% gain in two-and-a-half years of ownership. (Note: Had I continued to own that rental property for those eight years of zero appreciation, I would still have earned a very high rate of return on my initial investment. That's because during that eight-year period rents increased by more than 50% and interest rates fell from 13.5% to 7.0%. My annual cash flow would have jumped by 150%.)

Inventory of Unsold Properties

In slowing markets the inventory of homes for sale steadily piles up. Buyers tend to disappear. Everybody wants to sell. During San Diego's early 1990s down market, the local Realtors' Multiple Listing Service (MLS) accumulated more than 18,000 listings. By the time the area's recovery was in full swing, the number of listings had shrunk to fewer than 14,000 homes. Between mid-2000 and mid-2001, the nationwide Realtor MLS inventory of unsold homes increased from 1.4 million to 1.72 million—and accurately signaled the subsequent market slowdown.

Now contrast this recent slowing with a previous scarcity. Illustrating this point, in 1998 a Vermont sales agent reported, "We're not in a sellers' market, but inventory is depleted and prices are tending to go up." In contrast, this agent reports, "In 1991, I had a ski resort condo complex with fifty-two units on the market. Now only seven are for sale. I'm begging owners to list."

Keep an eye on the number of homes for sale. When realty agents first begin to beg for listings, the market typically is signaling "buy now," and price increases are nearly certain. A piling-up inventory of unsold properties indicates that prices may sit above the price levels buyers are able and willing to pay. That's the time that value investors hang back and wait for sellers to become desperate and thus far easier to work with.

Properties Under Contract

You can also detect market tempo by keeping count of properties going under contract. Realtors typically track homes by the number listed, the number going to contract, and the number of closed sales. Essentially, the going-to-contract number represents a pipeline for property sales just as the new orders figure represents pipeline activity for manufacturers.

When the number of properties going to contract heads up relative to the number of new listings, the market can be expected to tighten and prices will increase. When contracts begin to decline relative to the number of new listings and closed sales, you can expect the market to cool and prices to soften.

Mortgage Purchase Applications, Delinquencies, and Foreclosures

Because mortgage financing plays such a key role in real estate markets, as a value investor you should keep a record of mortgage trends, especially as they relate to new buyer mortgage applications, payment delinquencies, and foreclosures.[9]

Mortgage Applications

Relatively few home buyers or investors pay cash for their properties. So tracking new mortgage applications (as opposed to refinancing) over the past 6 to 12 months can further signal whether the market is picking up (or losing) steam. In addition, learn whether lenders are easing up on credit standards or pulling back.

Starting in the mid-1990s, mortgage lenders created an enormous array of easy-qualifying, little- or nothing-down mortgage loan programs for first-time home buyers, minorities, inner-city neighborhoods, the credit impaired, and innumerable other segments of borrowers. Some lenders were even making investor loans with 90% loan-to-value ratios. “Have money, will lend” became the bankers’ motto.

This aggressive lending helped to fuel the late 1990s real estate boom. Low interest rates and the National Homeownership Strategy also played a big role. Now, though, with subprime lenders, the Federal Housing Administration, and the Department of Veterans Affairs taking some hits, you might find that mortgage lenders will return to a more prudent approach to qualifying borrowers and setting loan terms.[10]

Is a slowdown coming? As always, when lenders tighten their lending after a run of easy money, they choke off property financing and sales. In turn, fewer sales build up larger inventories of unsold homes and place downward pressure on property prices.

Delinquencies and Foreclosures

Under such adverse circumstances, out-of-work or otherwise financially strapped homeowners (mostly overextended recent buyers) can't sell at a price high enough to cover their outstanding mortgage balance and selling expenses. Mortgage delinquencies and foreclosures tend to increase, causing more downward pressure on property prices and more opportunities for value investors.

Regulatory law requires most mortgage lenders to report their 30-day, 60-day, and 90-day delinquencies. By following these trends, real estate investors can forecast a likely fall (or stabilizing) in market values. In addition, mortgage delinquency gives advance notice on foreclosure rates. Because foreclosures compete with owners who are trying to sell their properties, a larger inventory of foreclosures adds to their difficulties.

From the mid-1990s to mid-2001, most areas of the country experienced very small inventories of foreclosed properties—especially as compared with the tumultuous late 1980s and early 1990s. During these more recent years, value investors found slim pickings in the foreclosure files. However, as lender excesses come back to haunt them, you can expect to see a big increase in the number of foreclosures in those areas of the country where job losses spike up.

In any event, staying abreast of delinquencies and foreclosures provides an early warning system to real estate investors. Falling rates signal market recovery and rising prices. Upward trends in late payments, foreclosure filings, and foreclosure sales signal a market slowdown or housing recession.

Vacancy Rates

Because you will want to get your properties rented quickly, you also should survey vacancy rates and rental amounts for apartments and single-family houses.[11] Vacancy rates (and rent levels) don't necessarily move in the same direction as property sales prices. For example, falling interest rates improve home buyer affordability and can draw people out of rentals and into home ownership. On the other hand, fear of falling home prices scares off many would-be home buyers. They cling to their rentals, and vacancy rates tighten. Rents may even go up.

Summing Up: The Current Market

Even when comparable sales data seem to show that you're buying at a bargain price, you still need to look for other confirming (or conflicting) evidence. Comparable sales data lags the market. Other indicators such as time on market, selling price, asking price/selling price ratios, inventories of unsold homes, mortgage applications, mortgage delinquencies, and mortgage foreclosures tend to lead the market.

So in addition to market value, look to these leading indicators to help you spot markets that are about to turn up or down. Value investors avoid bubbles about to burst; and they arrive early for the next housing party. When you stay tuned to leading indicators, you materially decrease your chance of loss and disappointment; more profitably, you position yourself to gain from quick jumps in the rate of appreciation.

Boom and Bust Cycles

Most efficient (or quasi-efficient) stock market theorists believe that market timing never works. Random walks prevail. You might as well throw away your charts of past stock price and volume movements. Whether or not you accept this efficient market theory for stocks, you certainly want to reject it for real estate. Time lags in new construction; selling periods; shopping time; employment trends; and other slower-paced factors of building, buying, and selling mean that you can accurately forecast (more or less) short- to midterm market movements.

Unlike stocks, housing prices do not wander around like a drunk in a parking lot looking for his car. Nor does housing experience massive sell-offs that immediately send property prices plunging by 50% or more. Nor can massive buying at the click of a mouse immediately push housing prices skyward.

Boom and Bust Myth

Although some residential property markets throughout the United States and Canada do swing in so-called boom and bust cycles, most do not. During the late 1980s and early 1990s, the national media published a continuing stream of negative articles that would have led any foreign observer to conclude that housing nationwide was suffering a cataclysmic and never-ending downturn. In part, this negativity was fueled by a famous article by two Harvard researchers entitled "The Baby Boom, the Baby Bust, and the Coming Collapse of Housing Prices."[12]

However, if the journalists (and professors) who were writing these stories had traveled outside of the Boston-to-Washington, D.C. corridor and California, they would have cured their myopia. They would have found some housing markets going strong, others in modest slowdown, and a relatively few markets in severe distress (Texas, for example).

Media Distortion versus Local Market Experience

Like all of us, national journalists tend to extrapolate from the experiences they are close to. With severe housing recessions (following extravagant booms) in Manhattan; Boston; Washington, D.C.; and Los Angeles, the national press imagined that real estate markets everywhere else must be facing similar difficulties. But they weren't. And they won't.

Before you accept the real estate boom and bust myth, check the experience of your local market. You will likely find relatively modest ups and downs. More importantly, market segments matter. The media tend to focus on homes in the higher price ranges ($400,000 and up). Naturally, because rent levels typically won't come close to supporting such high prices, this segment of the housing market will show far more price volatility than lower-priced housing. Whenever your cash flows support the price you pay (as they should), you need not fear a bust. Even if property prices fall in the short run, your annual returns will persist. Even better, maintain a strong position of cash and credit. Use downturns to pick up true bargains.

The Market versus Market Segments

In the early 1990s when $1 million homes in La Jolla, California, were falling in value by $200,000 to $300,000, home prices in nearby Clairemont were holding firm. When $5 million homes in Beverly Hills were falling in market value by $1.5 million, homes in Watts (South Central Los Angeles) were continuing to climb.

Whenever you hear about the real estate market doing one thing or another, probe further. Ask, "Which market?" Condos, co-ops, single-family houses, apartment buildings, retail, or offices? Which communities or neighborhoods? What price ranges? What rental rates? What sizes (square footage, room counts)? What types of buyers? What types of tenants? Even within the same local area and within the same period of time, various real estate submarkets may buck against the prevailing market conditions and trends.

Don't jump to conclusions about the market until you know what precise market segment you're referring to. Just as with stocks, gross perceptions about the market frequently mislead. You may believe that the market is overpriced, suffering too-high vacancies, or is bereft of good tenants. But none of these or any other generalizations are likely to apply wholesale. Market segments matter.

When discouraged by overall market trends, don't give up. Look for undiscovered submarkets. I have never seen a time when a local market did not offer at least a few opportunistic paths to follow. Similarly, don't naively fall for talk of a market boom, either. Just as busts don't affect all properties equally, neither do booms. For value investors, a strong market never displaces the need for thorough analysis.

In fact, because booms tend to dull reasoned thought, too many investors adopt a "can't-wait, must-buy-now, prices-can-only-go-up" mentality. Avoid this amateurish mistake. Before you quickly buy into an apparent boom, play devil's advocate with yourself. Honestly evaluate whether you've really discovered the best market segment in which to invest. A quick trip through the condominium experience can illustrate this point.

Condominiums: Boom, Bust, and Recovery

Some years back, Paul Maglio bought a two-bedroom condominium located near Boston Harbor. He paid a peak-market price of $120,500 for the unit. At the time Maglio bought, 200 other potential buyers had put their names on the complex's waiting list. Everyone wanted this surefire investment opportunity. With then recent appreciation rates running at 20% a year, condominiums were geese laying golden eggs.[13]

Then the geese died. Throughout Massachusetts, as well as other areas in New England, New York, much of the Southwest, and Southern California, many condominium (and co-op) prices fell 30% to 70% off their peaks. Bruce Hopper, another Bostonian who lost a bundle on his condominium, sadly regrets his decision to buy. "It's too bad," Hopper says, "because condos were the ideal situation for a lot of people—first-time home buyers who wanted the American dream. But it didn't pan out and now we're stuck." Upon hearing about experiences like these, many investors hesitate to buy a condominium. They fear getting stuck with a condo that can't be sold for anywhere near its purchase price.

Don't Prejudge: Weigh Risks against Potential Rewards

Such concerns about condos are justified. But as with all investments, weigh potential risks against potential rewards. Dismissing condos as poor investments without closely looking at a sample of condo projects and complexes that exist in your area could be a mistake. When compared to the prices of single-family homes in many cities, condos once again appear to offer good value and good opportunity for moderate appreciation. Search the market and the odds are at least 50–50 that you can find a condo bargain.

How to Spot a Condo Bargain

In nearly every case, the majority of condo buyers and investors who have lost money have been those who bought within a year or two of the top of the market. Longer-term owners nearly always have come out ahead. Second, condo investors who could see the market softening and sold out near the top often made tens of thousands of dollars. Third, buyers today who can learn to spot opportunity (and smell potential danger) do stand to make good profits.

By learning the lessons of history, you can reasonably judge whether condo prices in your area stand a good chance of going up. Here are the signals to look for:

1. Nearly everyone is pessimistic about future appreciation rates. (Yes, condo contrarians frequently do make money.)
2. The monthly after-tax payments for principal, interest, property taxes, insurance, and homeowner fees total less than monthly rentals on comparable apartments. In other words, you can generate positive cash flows—right now.
3. The market values of existing units are substantially below the cost of constructing similar new units.
4. Vacancy rates for rental apartments are less than 5%.
5. Local economic indicators (number of people working, personal incomes, retail sales, new car sales, bank deposits, new business starts, etc.) are showing strong positive gains.
6. The condo units that you are considering enjoy some unique and highly desirable advantages (design, views, location).
7. Very few new apartment or condominium complexes are being built or planned. No major conversions of apartments to condominiums are under way or planned. Government restrictions limit apartment conversions.
8. Compared to single-family houses, condo prices (especially when calculated on a price-per-square-foot basis) sit relatively low.
9. The condo complex you are looking at is stable: strong financial reserves for repairs and replacements, no pending litigation, few units

occupied by renters (fewer than 20% is good; fewer than 10% is excellent), relatively little turnover of owners and residents, well-maintained common areas, and cooperative relations among owners.

On the downside, history shows that, in most cases, a fall in condo prices usually is foreshadowed by one or more of these danger signals:

1. A sharp downturn in local employment.
2. Large numbers of apartments being converted to condos, especially when accompanied by easy-qualifier financing.
3. Large amounts of new condo or apartment construction.
4. The current monthly costs of owning greatly exceed the monthly costs of renting.
5. More than 30% to 40% of a complex's units are investor owned and are occupied by renters (or, even worse, are vacant).[14]
6. Everybody believes that values are going up at least 10% to 15% a year. The market runs rampant with speculation.

Past experience has taught lenders, investors, and overly optimistic home buyers that a condominium isn't a printing press for money disguised as a place to live. Nevertheless, with speculation squeezed out, condos in many cities once again offer good long-term investment potential. Even ignoring appreciation, if you can earn a good positive cash flow, your condominium may yield an attractive financial return. As you pay down the mortgage balance, you will build up your equity. For investors who want an inflation-protected income stream, owning one or more investment condominiums can prove quite profitable. In addition, because the home owner's association will take care of all (or most) external upkeep and maintenance, condos make for low-effort investments. So explore this market segment. Contrary to popular belief, condo investments can outperform stocks. Run the numbers for a sampling of condominium complexes. You may discover some very profitable opportunities.

Chapter 9

Predict the Future

Would you have given your eyeteeth to have seen the future of Intel or Cisco Systems circa 1985? I suppose most people would. But alas, that's the trouble with stocks. Timely prediction of winners from all of the contenders requires the unique power of Nostradamus. Few can do it successfully. But here's the good news. As a value investor in real estate, you don't need a prophet or fortune-teller. Before long-term prices and rents begin to move up (or down) in a neighborhood or other defined geographic area, they give plenty of cues. Just stay alert and you will be able to see the future.

Discover the Next Harlem

During the late 1980s and early 1990s, you could have picked up a decent townhouse in Harlem for $150,000, maybe $200,000 at most. By the year 2000, after only modest refurbishing, you could have sold that property for $500,000 to $700,000, possibly more. Why the big jump in prices? Because relative to other Manhattan neighborhoods, Harlem had been greatly undervalued. Compared to the $2 million it would take to buy a similar townhouse in, say, the East Village on East 7th Street or on the Upper East Side at East 82nd Street, Harlem looked like a real steal.

Gentrification and Other Value Plays

In large- and medium-sized cities across the United States and Canada, gentrification has pushed home prices through the roof in neighborhoods like Kerrisdale (Vancouver), Buckhead (Atlanta), South of Market (San Francisco), Chicago's North Side and Westside, College Park (Orlando), M Street (Dallas), and Coconut Grove (Miami). Most of these neighborhoods have become name brands. In earlier years, though, they were modest- (even low-) priced neighborhoods. Several of these areas, such as Chicago Near North and San Francisco South of Market, even included substantial industrial and commercial properties.

In each instance, however, the in-close accessibility of these neighborhoods overwhelmed their negatives. Prior to their entering prime time, these neighborhoods provided residents an easy walk, drive, or commute to major job districts. And as in Harlem, their prices looked dirt cheap when compared with conveniently situated premier neighborhoods.

Unfortunately for value investors, many gentrified name brand neighborhoods no longer represent good value. That's not to say that these areas won't show strong future appreciation. But as a rule, their current rents probably won't cover a reasonable-sized mortgage payment plus property expenses. (However, you may be able to find individual properties or market niches where this general rule does not apply. At least it may be worth your time to look.)

How to Spot the Next Harlem

Although it may be difficult to find a profitable income investment in Harlem or Buckhead, this fact also shows a bright side. When a neighborhood's prices jump too high for value investors, they also jump too high for many would-be home buyers. That means these buyers must look elsewhere. The question is: Where? What neighborhoods or communities are now attracting the younger, upwardly mobile professionals?

Ask Realtors

To most easily identify these soon-to-be up-and-coming neighborhoods (or communities), talk with Realtors who cater to this clientele. Ask where their disappointed buyers are now choosing to relocate. Often, tenants who rent in gentrified areas first look to buy in the same neighborhood. When they find they can't afford it, they settle for their second- or third-choice area.

As other buyers choose this same area, property prices edge up. A new up-and-coming neighborhood begins to bid for recognition. Chic shops and restaurants open. A Starbucks or Peets arrives. Older, established property owners step up their selling. Young buyers ambitiously renovate and remodel their properties. New buyers or home builders may begin to replace tear-downs with more lavish homes.

Continuing Cycle

In the stock market, value investors may emphasize relative stock prices and P/E ratios. They may look for the stocks of companies that sell at a discount relative to the stocks of other companies that display similar characteristics. Value investors in real estate adopt this same way of thinking.[1] Instead of companies with relatively favorable P/Es, however, they search out neighborhoods with relatively low cap rates (or other measures of valuation).

As a rule, unjustifiably wide disparities in prices won't last forever. The more this gentrifying neighborhood (or community) gets discovered, the higher its prices. Then, as its prices go higher, affordability again becomes a problem. Disappointed buyers are pushed to find another hidden-value area. The cycle continues. New opportunities continue to arise.

Discover Undervalued Areas

To secure a bargain, you can buy a property for less than its market value. Or you can try to locate a neighborhood or community that offers great benefits for the money. When people begin to say, "Sure, I would *like* to live in Highland Park. But for $200,000 less, I much *prefer* to live in Crestview. You get a lot more for your money in Crestview," you've probably found an up-and-coming area.

Pay Attention

Besides talking with Realtors, here are some other ways you can learn about undervalued areas:

1. Talk with home buyers and other investors.
2. Read local and community newspapers.
3. Talk with your government planning office.
4. Study a map.

Talk with Home Buyers, Investors, and Everyone Else

When you bought your home, you probably surveyed friends, relatives, colleagues at work, and anyone else you could think of. Follow this same strategy now. Ask where people are buying (or renting) and find out why. What do people like and dislike? How do prices (rents) compare with those in other neighborhoods or communities? Has the rate of appreciation been slow or fast? (Slow is usually better unless the fast is sure to have legs.) The people you know and the people they know comprise a vast web of information and market knowledge. Use it. You won't find a cheaper or easier way to discover potential opportunities.

Read Local Newspapers

Most regional, city, and community newspapers include some type of "Homes and Living" section that regularly spotlights good-value neighborhoods. Go down to your local library and pull out issues from the past 6 to 36 months. Read through the articles on neighborhoods. What kinds of comments do residents and recent home buyers make? Here are two examples of what I mean:

> After moving from the Midwest to a high-priced part of the country, I thought I'd never be able to buy anything here. At first, I wanted the college area or Atlantic Park. But after looking for several months, I learned cheap [in those areas] meant $150,000. Just as I was about to give up, a Realtor friend suggested I take a look at Rogers Point.
>
> Rogers Point? All I knew about Rogers Point was crime, vandalism, and school busing. But the neighbors take a lot of pride in their homes, and around here you really feel like you're in the

> country, with the hills, grassy knolls, and even horses galloping by my living room window. I was able to buy a great two-bedroom with a large yard for my three Irish setters to run around in. I've no problem handling the monthly payments.
>
> From my experience, here's the advice I would give first-time buyers: Don't let certain parts of the city scare you away. Don't be biased because of what you've heard. You can buy. You may not get everything you want, but you've got to start somewhere.[2]

In speaking of his recently purchased home in a neighborhood called Avondale, Richard Winston says,

> Some people believe that this is a 3-G (gangs, gunfire, and graffiti) neighborhood. It's not. Some hoodlum types do hang out over on Lincoln Boulevard, but in our area, it looks like Beaver Cleaver Street. To tell the truth, my wife wasn't so excited about buying here. She was a little afraid, and we had a lot of work to do on the inside of the house before we could move in. But now we can say it's ours. We earned this. So she's coming around. When we're all finished and it's nice and we sell it for a lot more, she'll be happy. I'm sure.[3]

During the past 5 to 15 years, many previously marginal neighborhoods have revitalized and gentrified—but are now priced beyond the means of many first-time home buyers: the Wrigley section of Long Beach, California; South of Market in San Francisco; South of Houston in Manhattan; Lincoln Park–DePaul in Chicago; and Capitol Hill in Washington, D.C. are just a few examples. "Boy, I wish I had gotten into Rockridge [Oakland, California] ten years ago," someone recently said to me. And on my last trip to Chicago, I talked with a now not-so-young couple who complained, "In the early eighties, we could have bought a house on a decent block in Hyde Park for $62,000. But we eventually decided against it. Now we can't find anything like it for less than $200,000."

Ten to fifteen years ago, every one of the previously mentioned neighborhoods was experiencing its share of the urban problems typical of larger cities everywhere. And none of these neighborhoods is free of problems today. But each of these neighborhoods has enjoyed renewed popularity and price increases of 100% or more.

What's advantageous for your investing future, though, is that hundreds of somewhat similar neighborhoods are positioned for turnaround or gentrification during the coming 10 years. As good people are priced out of "highly desirable" neighborhoods, they move into "less desirable" neighborhoods. But that's not where the story ends. As home buyer counselor Mary Ortez advises people, "Home buyers have to realize that they can make any area nice."

Neighborhoods aren't inherently good or bad; it's the people in them and the standards and values they enforce that determine a neighborhood's future. No one would encourage you to invest in a neighborhood where kids dodge gunfire as they walk to school, or a neighborhood where residents post signs in their car windows that read, "Please don't break in. Radio already stolen." But standing in between so-called worst and best neighborhoods are many areas that are increasing in value and livability because the people living in them are working to make better lives for themselves and their families. Just as important, houses, duplexes, and apartments in these areas can still yield great cash-on-cash returns.

You can spot these emerging areas when you put on a first-time-home buyer hat. As an investor, you're looking for the best value at an affordable price. First-time home buyers also seek value at an affordable price. Learn where these buyers are beginning to buy, and you will achieve income and growth—the foundation of good value.

Good Value. "We bought in Brentwood because we had to buy at the low end of the market," says recent home buyer Peter Shapiro. "It's one of the few neighborhoods in the Washington, D.C., area where single-family homes could still be bought for less than $100,000."

Talking about Dumfries, a small town outside of D.C., Alfredo Calerdon says, "For me and my wife, this was the only affordable place we could find to live. Most of the people who live here are working-class people who moved here to buy an affordable home, the same as we did."

Portland, Oregon, resident Larry Hollibaugh had wanted to buy in a southeastern neighborhood of Portland. But he couldn't find the home he wanted at a price he was able to pay. So he switched his search to the North Portland neighborhood of St. Johns. There he found an 1,800-square-foot home priced at just $46,000. He bought it.

In Richmond, California, a historically distressed city on San Francisco Bay, the Marina Bay redevelopment project succeeded because it offered waterfront homes at prices 30% to 60% below other communities around the Bay. With home prices ranging between $150,000 and $300,000, no one would call Marina Bay prices low in any absolute sense. Yet compared to most other San Francisco Bay communities, as well as some outlying suburbs, Marina Bay offered excellent value for the money. Although the new residents of this formerly abandoned shipyard must work to change the negative image associated with a Richmond address, they gained "one of the last opportunities to live on the water at an affordable price this close to San Francisco," says Kenneth Ambrose, an executive of the firm that redeveloped the area.

By the time you read these words, each of the just-mentioned neighborhoods and communities will have experienced substantial jumps in the prices of their properties. Nevertheless, they all illustrate the same profit-making point. Whenever possible, value investors go for bargain prices in two ways: (1) They try to find (or negotiate) a purchase price that falls below a property's market value; and (2) more importantly, they look for neighborhoods and communities that offer low prices relative to other neighborhoods that display similar features and in the past attracted similar types of first-time, or move-up buyers.

Strong Sales. In addition to good relative value, look to see whether homes in a neighborhood are selling relatively quickly at close to their asking prices. Realtor Larry Strong has said of the Brentwood neighborhood, "The market was extremely strong because it was affordable. A lot of people were so happy to get a house here."

In Candler Park, a now popular neighborhood in Atlanta, Bud King, president of the Candler Park Neighborhood Association, says, "People pass the word when they're ready to sell, and the houses are gone." Candler Park resident and Realtor Mary Durham paid $18,000 for her home in the late 1970s. "The average price of a house here now exceeds $125,000.

Things were really moving in that price range. It's the one people are looking for," reports Durham.

Of course, you shouldn't push the "strong sales" criterion too far. Before you invest, remember to get completely current market information. Make sure prices still sit well below their reasonable (intrinsic) value relative to rent levels and other comparable neighborhoods and communities.

Consult Government Agencies

Every city, town, and county throughout the United States and Canada operates one or more government departments dedicated to development, redevelopment, and community revitalization. Their personnel assume responsibilities such as land-use planning, building permits, urban renewal, housing and housing finance, transportation, public safety, urban renewal, parks and recreation, and business (industrial) development.

As a rule, before anything major (or minor) moves forward that may enhance (or diminish) property values in an area, one or more of these government departments will know about it. As a minimum, lead times of 6 to 12 months are common. In many instances, though, these agencies will know years in advance.

Centre City Development Corporation. In speaking of a San Diego neighborhood that's poised for turnaround and redevelopment, city planner Lori Weisberg has said, "To the outsider, there's very little here that seems inviting. . . . Yet whereas most people see a shabby area . . . visionaries see an exciting new downtown neighborhood adorned with a grand tree-lined boulevard, a central plaza, artisans' studios, and loft housing, crowned with a sports and entertainment center. . . . [Already] there are pockets of gentrification—a budding arts district, scattered loft conversions, and . . . structures well suited for preservation. . . . But [the total revitalization and redevelopment] does have to be imagined."[4]

"There's no doubt," says Pam Hamilton, an executive with San Diego's Centre City Development Corporation, "this project will happen—it's just a question of when." Sounds like a great opportunity for value investors. Buy at today's depressed prices, get the future for free (or at least at a bargain price).[5]

Homes for Dallas. To meet their obligations under the Community Reinvestment Act, many mortgage lenders are now working hard to revitalize urban areas. One could say that lenders are "greenlining." They're targeting some cities and neighborhoods for easier-qualifying home mortgages and home improvement loans. Instead of pulling out of these areas, many mortgage lenders are pouring money into them.[6]

In Dallas, city council member Charlotte Mayes recently has exclaimed, "I'm so excited, I'm so enthusiastic. . . . It's really exciting news for renters of low-income status to be able to have an opportunity for once . . . I could just kiss Fannie Mae." The object of Mayes's excitement was the newly announced "Homes for Dallas" home-ownership initiative struck by the city of Dallas, a group of participating mortgage lenders, and Fannie Mae (Federal National Mortgage Association).[7]

Under the original Homes for Dallas initiative, 15,000 renters who bought a home within the city limits of Dallas—and in some instances, within certain targeted neighborhoods—would become eligible for a variety of special financing programs that include grants and loans for down payments and closing costs, lease-purchase programs, flexible underwriting standards, home improvement loans, and home-buyer counseling (to be offered in both English and Spanish).

Naturally, as home financing in targeted areas becomes easier, these neighborhoods become positioned for appreciation. With mortgage money more widely available, residents who are renting today will become home owners tomorrow. As these home owners renovate and remodel their properties, the character of their neighborhoods will improve. To identify this type of investment potential, discover those neighborhoods where community redevelopment or community reinvestment monies are targeted to flow. As home owners and community groups revitalize their neighborhoods, property values will head up.

Use Creative Cartography

In most cases, you look at a map to figure out how to get to where you want to go physically. But with creative cartography, you can use or design maps to help you get to where you want to go financially. Here are just a few ways that map reading or mapmaking might help you spot communities or neighborhoods with above-average appreciation possibilities. Gather up some maps and look for some of these clues:

1. *Accessibility*. Do you see any relatively undervalued areas with convenient access to job centers? Do you see any areas where accessibility will increase due to new or widened roads and bridges, additional public transportation, or other improvements?
2. *Overflow from congestion*. Do you see roads or interchanges clogged with congestion? What alternative locations might provide relief from these traffic hassles?
3. *Demographics*. Try to identify areas that are moving (or about to move) upscale. In which areas are younger, more affluent buyers displacing older, working-class households?
4. *New employment/Shopping centers*. Are any new (or expanded) large- or midscale employers about to locate in an area? What neighborhoods or communities will attract their employees? The same goes for retail and professional offices.
5. *Property prices*. Plot property prices by neighborhood, subdivision, or community. Do you see anomalies? Do some areas stand out as underpriced relative to other nearby areas? Can you reasonably expect these imbalances to experience a "correction"?

Everyone now relies on maps. Using modern software and vast data sources, government workers, college professors, and researchers in private market-analysis firms are generating maps to show in graphic detail almost any type of conceivable facts and figures. Talk with these professionals. Talk also with demographers, geographers, planners, housing analysts, and development specialists. Try your local utility companies, too. Because utility companies need to plan long-term building and capacity-expansion projects, they typically keep track of and forecast population growth throughout their service areas.

Expand Your Search

In searching for areas that show great promise for appreciation, you might profitably expand your search beyond the neighborhoods and communities located within (or nearby) your current city. Often you can spot undervalued communities by comparing prices among locations quite distant from each other. In one of my earlier books, for example, I compared Siesta Key and Captiva Island as follows:

> Captiva Island and Siesta Key are two popular Florida locations. Captiva is located over the north-end bridge of Sanibel Island about forty-five to sixty minutes from Ft. Meyers. Siesta Key is located about fifteen minutes from downtown Sarasota. To my way of thinking, Siesta Key offers superior value. It has prettier beaches, less traffic congestion, a greater choice of nearby restaurants, and a more convenient location than Captiva. It's closer to major shopping and commercial districts, health-care facilities, a major airport, and other attractive resort and vacation destinations such as Busch Gardens, Disney World, and an excellent selection of golf and tennis clubs. Siesta and Captiva both prohibit major commercial development. Lush vegetation beautifies the environment of each area. And residents in both communities enjoy a sense of isolation, privacy, and security.[8]

I then pointed out that even though (in my analysis) Siesta proved equally desirable to Captiva, Siesta's housing prices languished far below those of Captiva. What has happened since I wrote that comparison four years ago? Property prices on Siesta have jumped 50%.

Likewise, in the same book, I included several other comparative analyses:

- "The Irish property market has seen a sharp rise in prices over the past year, which means that it does not offer quite such exceptional value as it did. . . . [Now] areas nearest the border with Northern Ireland represent the best value for the money. The countryside is lovely and there are some excellent properties." (*Sunday Times* [London], October 18, 1998)
- "The value of prime cottages in rural locations straddling the M4 corridor west from London has rocketed . . . although there are a few bargains if you are prepared to travel further west. . . . Unfortunately, this forces up prices for second-home buyers who don't live in London. Cottages in Wales, the traditional cheap weekend retreat, are now averaging (pounds) 145,000. . . . those whose resources are more limited will find East Anglia their best bet." (*The Independent* [London], June 7, 1998)
- "There's better value in some lovely unspoiled areas just south of Norwich. One pretty three-bedroom house just sold for £110,000. The area is still affordable because it hasn't been colonized yet by the second-home brigade." (*The Independent*, June 7, 1998)
- "As the Costa del Sol becomes overrun with sun-seeking holiday makers, people searching for a peaceful second home start to look elsewhere. . . . One less frequented area is the Costa Blanca. . . . Orihuela Costa is a well-kept secret. Thousands of Britons have purchased in Spain, yet few have found this part of the coast." (*Sunday Times* [London], September 20, 1998)
- "Italy's housing market is emerging from recession as overseas investors pour millions of dollars. . . . Brick for brick, like for like in location and quality, Italy is relatively cheap compared with France and Spain. . . . Some British buyers also were snapping up homes in Marche, close to [higher-priced] Tuscany, where prices were lower. . . . In Sicily, a new studio flat . . . can cost as little as £20,000." (*The Times* [London], August 17, 1998)[9]

What can we get for our money? Whether people are buying first homes, second homes, or investment properties, they all ask this basic question. In 1990, housing prices in Portland, Oregon, were only 20% to

30% of those in Berkeley, California. Yet both Portland and Berkeley appealed to similar types of people. With such wide disparities, Portland prices had to jump considerably.

In 1990, housing in Silicon Valley was priced two to three times higher than in Austin, Texas. Yet Austin was emerging as one of the country's premier new economy centers of technology growth. It did not require elite expertise to see that Austin housing offered great bargains vis à vis the San Francisco–San Jose corridor.

Unwarranted Pricing Gaps Don't Persist

Unlike stocks, real estate markets don't shift at the speed of light—or even the click of a mouse. Pricing gaps can linger for years. In the short run, price increases in higher-cost areas can feed on themselves. Higher prices beget even higher prices. People are priced out of entire urban areas, not just neighborhoods. For a time, people do squeeze to pay $250,000 for that dilapidated, three-bedroom, one-bath starter home. Eventually, though, a few people notice that another area (often in another county or state) offers far more house for the money. Then the migration begins.

What's the Lesson for Value Investors?

As a value investor, you should expand your investing horizons. Pay attention not only to your local neighborhoods and communities, but also to other areas located throughout your state, the country, or even the world. Wherever you travel, compare prices among areas. Take advantage of open houses. Read through newspapers. Pick up copies of those free "Homes for Sale" publications. Talk to friends and family who live elsewhere. Go on the Web and explore property prices in various locations. Educate yourself. Then stay alert for great bargains, because you will find them.

Undervalued Lakefront?

Just recently, I had some business in a small, pleasant town located in south central Florida. As always, I began glancing through a local "Homes for

Sale" magazine. I couldn't believe what I saw: Lakefront lots at $15,000. Three- and four-bedroom (2,000–2,400 square feet) lakefront homes at $115,000 to $175,000. Do these properties represent undervalued bargains?

I haven't yet had time to study the area enough to know the answer to this question. But given the fact that comparable lakefront lots in larger cities 45 to 90 minutes away typically sell for upwards of $200,000, I plan to investigate further. As larger Florida cities become ever more expensive and ever more congested, I am forecasting a large migration to the outlying (though not necessarily remote) Florida areas. Likewise for the migration of Northern retirees: When I think about prices in this outlying Florida community relative to those in Indianapolis or Milwaukee, they look like a steal.

What do you see in your travels? Keep your mind open to possibilities. You too will be able to discover potential bargain-priced areas.

Jobs, Incomes, Population

Up to this point, we've tried to identify areas poised for appreciation because they offer good relative value. When you compare property prices among neighborhoods, communities, or even cities and states, you will always find some areas that appear undervalued. But now we need to turn our attention to an area's economic base. Before you choose an area in which to invest, check its expected growth in jobs, income, and population. Then compare this growth potential to the supply and costs of buildable land.

Since 1990, property prices have increased much faster in Seattle, Washington, than in Wheeling, West Virginia; much faster in Austin, Texas, than in Lincoln, Nebraska; much faster in Winter Park, Florida, than in Tallahassee, Florida. What accounts for the major differences among these paired cities? Rapid growth in jobs, household incomes, and population pressing against the ever-more-costly, shrinking supply of land that's available for building and development.

Though over time, nearly all viable cities and metropolitan areas experience some increase in property prices, the most rapid price increases occur when too much money and too many people chase after too few properties. If you can spot areas where growth will soon take off, you can ride the next cycle of rent and price increases.

Basic Employment: The Foundation of Buying Power

How do most towns and cities grow in wealth? They find some way to bring money into their areas from beyond their borders. Hollywood brings in movie ticket revenues from all over the world. Seattle, through Microsoft and other software companies, brings in billions of software dollars from all over the world. Bloomington, Indiana (Indiana University), brings in several billions of dollars from the taxpayers of Indiana and the spending of 30,000 out-of-town and out-of-state students.

Why have West Virginia and other lagging state and local economies failed to become wealthy? Because they lack the entrepreneurial talents and resources to bring in money. Why did the Texas economy falter in the late 1980s? Because revenues from oil exports and oil production fell. Why did Southern California falter in the early 1990s? Because its defense contractors lost huge amounts of revenues when the U.S. government cut military spending. Why will Silicon Valley housing prices slide in the early 2000s? Because the fiscal boost it previously gained from many of its dot-com and technology companies has dwindled.

Real Estate Follows the Local and Regional Economy

We commonly speak of investing in real estate. Instead, we should probably say that we're investing in our local and regional economy. Consequently, as a value investor, you should judge an area according to its potential for growth and its history of stability. First, check with local and regional government economic development agencies. What's the outlook for growth in basic (income-generating) employers? Second, learn whether the area is highly cyclical or if its employment and the local "GDP" tend to increase steadily with only mild downturns.

Investors can buy trouble if they ignore a local area's economic foundation. On the upside, though, when you choose areas with reasonable prices, reasonable growth, and a stable and diverse economic base, you will enjoy good long-term returns plus a margin of safety.

More Jobs + Higher Incomes + More People = Higher Property Values

"They Ain't Making It Any More"

"Buy land—they ain't making it any more." This oft-quoted quip attributed to Will Rogers sums up the long-term advantage of investing in real estate. In many areas of the country, the supply of buildable land falls far short of demand—especially land that is situated conveniently near employment centers. Even better, at least from the standpoint of real estate investors, government regulations of all sorts severely limit development, even when the acreage may be physically available.

Ahmanson Land Company

For the past 15 years, the Ahmanson Land Company has been trying to build houses in Ventura County, just north of Los Angeles. Given the high cost of California housing, you would think Ahmanson would have met with cheers and encouragement. But no, because this is the United States, Ahmanson has been stuck in litigation. It seems that the Ahmanson site of 13,000 acres gives habitat to the San Fernando Valley spineflower and the California red-legged frog.[10]

To save these ecological rarities, Ahmanson has already agreed to set aside 11,050 acres of its land. The Save Open Space environmentalist group, though, won't accept that compromise. This band of activists is pushing for a total ban on development. Will Save Open Space win its fight? Check back in two years. That's how long Ahmanson now must wait for further environmental study. All the while, Ahmanson's interest costs and legal fees continue to climb into the millions of dollars.

The Regulation and Litigation Maze

Even when not faced by endangered frogs and wildflowers, developers and home builders face a maze of different types of (often contradictory) regulations and restrictions, such as the following:[11]

- Environmental (endangered species, water and air quality, open spaces)
- Growth management (limits created by the diminished capacity of schools, roads, utilities, and waste disposal)
- Agricultural preservation (saving farmland)
- Historical preservation (saving ancestry)
- Rent controls (no more greedy landlords)
- Condominium conversions (saving rental apartments)
- Coastal preservation (saving beaches)

In addition to these regulations, of course, are typical restrictions such as zoning and building regulations and health and safety codes. Yet even if builders and developers satisfy all the regulators, they still must face (litigate) any number of preservationists, environmentalists, and NIMBYs ("not-in-my-backyard" groups of nearby property owners).[12]

What's the Land Development Situation?

You can count on growth in jobs, incomes, and population to push property values up. But when these pressures push against land shortages—whether actual or artificially created by government regulations and activist protestors—you can score from first base. As part of your value analysis, check out the land development situation in the areas where you plan to invest. Or, alternatively, look for those communities where "they ain't making it any more." Will Rogers knew what he was talking about.

What Is a Bargain Price?

All value investors try to buy their properties at a bargain price. But you can't truly answer this question at the time you buy. You can answer it only at some point in the future. The real test for bargain price comes on the date you sell (or exchange) the property. Do look for and try to negotiate a below-market purchase price. But don't stop there.

Envision the future. Do you see strong reasons why the rents and value of this property will increase during the coming years? Does the price of the property you're planning to buy compare well with the prices of similar properties in more-distant neighborhoods and communities? Does the area show growth potential for jobs, incomes, and population? How many different ways (i.e., benchmark metrics) does the property seem undervalued? Relative to rental income? Relative to the present market? Relative to other local neighborhoods? Relative to other communities? Relative to its possibilities for growth? When a property passes all (or even most) of these tests, you know that you've found a sure future winner.

Chapter 10

Create Value Now

Several years back, just as California was heading into its worst recession since the 1930s, Ann Williams and her husband split up.[1] Out of work with two children to support, Ann needed to make some money quickly. So she decided to become a value investor in real estate. Given the deteriorating economy in the Golden State, you might think that Ann was misguided. But she knew what she was doing.

During the next five years, as many California home prices fell by 20% to 30%, Ann bought and resold six homes. After each sale she banked between $20,000 and $40,000. Her total profits exceeded $150,000. What was her secret? A keen eye for a bargain, hard work, and perseverance. "The deals are not marked with a big red flag," Ann says. "I had to weed through a lot of properties and get up to speed on the market."

When Ann says she had to "weed through" a lot of properties, she means that literally as well as figuratively. Relying on seller financing, Ann's value strategy was to ferret out and buy rundown, bargain-priced houses known as fixer-uppers or fixers. Applying the knowledge she had gained about the market, Ann would next renovate and revitalize these properties to enhance their value. She would then sell at a higher price. With her quickly learned savvy, Ann didn't wait for the California real estate market to turn around. She created her own housing appreciation.

Value Investors Don't Wait for Market Appreciation

With stocks, value investors must wait for the market to turn before they can profit from their bargain buys. Not so in real estate. Through savvy purchases and property improvements, real estate investors can create their own appreciation. Once again you can see that in real estate the idea of market returns fails the simplest test of common sense. In real estate, value investors can create large returns (as did Ann Williams) through applied intelligence, market knowledge, and shrewd observation.

All Properties Are Fixers

Most real estate books speak of fixers with terms such as "handyman special," "distressed property," or "needs work." In other words, they limit the term fixer to the types of rundown properties that Ann Williams fixed and flipped. But in fact, from the perspective of value investing, virtually all properties qualify as fixers. In this sense, I mean that through creative improvement, you can change any property for the better.

The property can be new or old, urban or rural, in good condition or poor condition. When you train yourself to look for ways to enhance a property, you will always find them.[2]

Woodpecker Haven

When Raymond Brown and his wife, Annie B., bought their California vacation retreat home, Woodpecker Haven, Raymond says, "I thought it was a done property. It was only five years old."

Annie B., though, viewed the home from a different perspective. As an interior designer with a forward-looking imagination, Annie B. simply said the home "had great potential." As Raymond points out, "Here are some of the improvements my enterprising wife accomplished to transform a livable property into an exquisite home."

- Landscaped the front and rear yards.
- Installed a drip irrigation system.

- Built a stone fence around the pool.
- Added decks around the rear of the house.
- Installed French doors in both bedrooms that led out to the decks.
- Remodeled the guest bedroom and bath to create a master bedroom for visitors.
- Built in a fireplace, bookshelves, cabinets, and track lighting in the living room.
- Trimmed overgrown trees and shrubs to enhance a picture-perfect view from the front porch.

Although Raymond and Annie B. invested $75,000 in these and other improvements, they added around $175,000 in value—throughout a falling market. "We bought our Sonoma retreat," says Raymond, "in August 1988 as home prices were peaking, and sold in April 1993, two months before prices bottomed out. . . . Yet we made a $100,000 profit. Our secret? Woodpecker Haven was a fixer-upper we renovated inside and out."

As the Browns' experience demonstrates, a fixer is any property that could look better, live better, and feel better than it does. (Remember, at the time they bought, Woodpecker Haven was only five years old.) The name of the property-improvement game is profitable creativity. Fixing up a property may require you to scrape encrusted bubble gum off floors and counters, patch holes in the roof, fight a gnarled mass of weeds and debris in the backyard, or pull out and replace rusted and obsolete kitchen and bathroom plumbing fixtures. But fixing up a property also can mean visualizing ways to redecorate, redesign, remodel, expand, or romance the property.

In fact, to profit from fix-up work, you don't even have to get your hands dirty. Yes, sweat equity can pay big dividends. But so can creativity, imagination, and market research. To create value you can (1) look for properties that obviously need work; (2) focus on properties whose creative possibilities most buyers would overlook; or (3) find a property that, to a certain extent, fits both descriptions. Overall, the better you can envision opportunities that other buyers mistakenly pass up without thought, the greater your potential for profits.

Research, Not Rules

When you create value, no set rules apply to all cities or all types of properties. Features that one person loves, another may hate. What's popular in California may look out of place in Kansas. Today's most faddish options may become outdated tomorrow. What suits you may not appeal to the tastes and lifestyles of most buyers or tenants. Money spent for a remodeled bath in Atlanta may pay back $3 for each $1 invested. In Milwaukee, returns for the same improvements may fall to 50 cents per dollar spent.

With so many variables entering the value equation, before you plan your improvements, profits dictate that you learn what features your future buyers or tenants will pay for. When you plan to create value, you can't let your personal tastes or preconceived notions stand unchallenged. Instead, like smart home builders who want their homes to sell, you've got to research your market. You need to develop a market-based improvement strategy.[3]

Ask local Realtors and property managers to tell you about buyers' and tenants' turn-ons and turnoffs. Identify unique niches for uncommon yet highly desired features. Tour new home and apartment complexes. Notice colors, decorating themes, floor coverings, and floor plans. Discover the models, features, and amenities that are renting or selling best. Which ones are rarely chosen? Which features are functional rather than merely glitzy?

To excite your creative impulses, visit open houses. Look for ways others have remodeled, redecorated, or redesigned their properties to make them more livable or more appealing. Talk to friends, relatives, or acquaintances who have previously improved their properties. At the supermarket or bookstore, buy a box full of guides with titles like *101 Ideas to Improve Your Home*. Go to your library. Flip through the pages of back issues of *Apartment Life* and *Journal of Property Management*. The more creative ideas you can come up with, the better you can design a profit-generating improvement strategy.

Attitude and Insight

Your success in creating value will depend on your ability to develop a positive approach that's bolstered by sharp insight. Instead of looking for what's wrong, ask yourself, "How can I make this right? How can I turn this feature into an advantage?" Puzzle over possible solutions. Look for ideas in those home-improvement publications. Solicit ideas from specialists. (Or even friends or family. Remember, Donald Trump enlisted his then-wife, Ivana, to design the interior of his Grand Hyatt hotel.)

In contrast to an insightful solutions-directed approach, most people will inspect and evaluate a property to discover its flaws and shortcomings. Some first-time buyers or investors adopt a supercritical attitude as a subconscious defense to alleviate their fear of making a mistake. As long as they supposedly can't find what they're looking for, they tell themselves they should just keep looking. Yet they never find the property they want because they demand perfection primarily to avoid commitment.

Other buyers and investors simply lack the will or ability to exert their imaginations. Either way, you gain. Less competition and less insight by others means a greater chance for your profitable improvement.

Creative Improvement

Recall the basic value formula discussed previously:

$$V = \frac{\text{net operating income (NOI)}}{R}$$

You will create value for a property any time you increase its NOI, or whenever you can enhance its investment potential and as a result reduce the capitalization rate that your buyers will apply to the property's income stream. For example, say you buy a property that is currently producing a net operating income of $15,000. Its market cap rate is 9.75%. Thus,

$$V = \frac{\$15,000}{.0975}$$

$$V = \$153,846$$

Now, let's say that through your efforts to create value, you boost this property's net income to $17,250. In addition, because your property and other properties nearby now display greater curb appeal and less risk, your cap rate falls to 9.0%. Accordingly, you have created $37,821 of value:

$$V = \frac{\$17{,}250}{.09}$$

$$V = \$191{,}666$$

Are such large changes in value possible within a short time? Absolutely. To achieve this size gain, you face the same challenges and opportunities that corporate CEOs must address when they want to quickly boost their company's share price: (1) search for ways to increase earnings, and (2) search for ways to raise investor expectations for the company's future performance.

When successful at both of these tasks, corporate management can enjoy outstanding gains. The same is true for owners of income properties. To achieve this goal, you can pursue some combination of the following six strategies:

1. Develop an investment plan.
2. Develop a market strategy.
3. Develop a legal strategy.
4. Improve the physical property.
5. Reduce expenses.
6. Change the location of the property.

Develop an Investment Plan

With such unlimited opportunities available, value investors in real estate should first analyze themselves. You can't do everything. You can't become proficient at every managerial and operational activity. You will find it impossible to learn about all types of properties, neighborhoods, and communities. You will face limits of time, money, talent, and effort. You need an investment plan.

In contrast, unsuccessful investors flounder. Without an investment plan that matches their capabilities and motivation, they ricochet from idea to idea, property to property, neighborhood to neighborhood. They stretch themselves too thin. They take on projects for which they are unsuited. They fail to achieve economies of scale. They never climb the learning curve because they think they already know all they need to know. When things go wrong, they blame others. ("Those sellers deceived me." "You can't find good tenants." "Those zoning clerks are nothing more than bumbling bureaucrats.")

Your Personal Profile

As a value investor in real estate, you can choose from any combination of time, money, talent, effort, and knowledge. You can choose to delegate almost everything, or you can actively execute. You can accumulate detailed market knowledge, or you can tell real estate agents exactly what you want and let them do your searching. You can "fix and flip," or you can buy and hold. You can invest hundreds of thousands of dollars, or you can easily get started with $10,000 or less. So before you begin to seriously look for properties, take inventory of yourself.

Time

How many hours a week, month, or year are you willing to devote to becoming financially secure and independently wealthy? Unless you earn in excess of $100 an hour, your time in real estate will almost surely pay you more than your employment. Nevertheless, maybe you value your time for activities other than work. That's okay. The key point here is for you to accurately assess the amount of time that you're willing to invest. Then choose an investment plan to match.

Cash

What amount of cash will you set aside for your real estate investments? This amount should include money for down payments, improvements, and cash reserves. You can begin in real estate with a fortune already made or little more than a hope and a prayer. Just realize that your available cash must fit your investment plans. Don't take foolish risks if you're cash short. Don't buy with little or nothing down without a firm idea of where you can raise the cash or credit for rent shortfalls, expense overruns, or unexpected emergencies.[4]

Credit

Realistically review your credit record and borrowing capacity. Those who are "credit challenged" can buy properties. But perhaps a dose of financial discipline should take first priority if your credit difficulties arose from unwise spending and borrowing.[5]

Experience

Because we all live in houses and apartments, we all possess basic experience in real estate. That's why those who apply themselves can succeed. Nearly anyone can learn how to tell a good buy from a bad buy. Nearly anyone can develop the talent and skills necessary to improve a house or apartment building. Yet even though you don't need investment experience per se, you do need a willingness to learn and enhance the knowledge you do possess. The best real estate investors read widely, talk to everybody, and stay alert to change. In real estate, experience sets the stage for future growth in understanding.

Specialized Skills

Do you have a flair for design? Do you enjoy remodeling and renovation? Are you good at the physical work? Can you work effectively with people (especially tenants)? Do your powers of observation and analysis enable you to spot and create market opportunities? Are you willing to learn? If none of these activities appeals to you, then you should adopt a simple long-term buy-and-hold strategy. Delegate almost everything. If, on the other hand, you are willing to learn several of these specialized skills, you will be able to multiply your returns and build wealth much faster. In real estate, enterprising investors can definitely outperform passive ones.

Financial Goals

How much, and how fast? Real estate investing provides you the surest and safest path to building wealth, financial security, and a retirement income. Yet the amount and timing of your gains depend on the plan of investment you choose to pursue. Even though your personal profile of wants versus don't-wants, likes versus dislikes, and skills versus talent void should influence your investment plan, perhaps you should begin your plan with your financial goals. Then adapt your personal profile to match. Many people never realize that it is their personal profile that blocks their ability to build wealth.

Rich Dad, Poor Dad

In their book *Rich Dad, Poor Dad*, Kiyosaki and Lechter draw this distinction between those who achieve their goals and those who accumulate excuses and assign blame.[6] The successful, Kiyosaki and Lechter emphasize, stay focused on their needs (goals). Then they do what's necessary to achieve them. In the words of Stephen Covey, the successful begin with the end in mind, then map a way to get there.[7]

In contrast, the whiners and complainers speak like children: "I don't want to go to bed, I don't want to do my homework, I don't want to eat my spinach, I don't want to go to college—I'm tired of school." Unfortunately, say Kiyosaki and Lechter, too many adults still carry around their childish "don't-want" mindset. In consequence, they ignore their true long-term needs and wants in favor of short-term pain avoidance.

Implications for Real Estate

From my years of experience in teaching, investing, and conducting investment seminars, I'm convinced that most people fail to invest in real estate for two reasons: (1) they falsely believe that they can safely and surely build wealth in stocks, and (2) the "don't-want" mindset. Like children, they automatically erect the don't-want obstacle: "I don't want to deal with tenants, I don't want to worry about something going wrong, I don't want to fix toilets in the middle of the night, I don't want the hassles." Although without doubt, the adverse nature of these don't-wants is greatly exaggerated, that's not the real issue. The real questions are: What do you need, and how do you *plan* (not hope) to get there?

What Do You Need?

As I emphasized earlier in this book, we face a demographic age wave. More people now than ever before need to build wealth for retirement. Yet our economy can't possibly fulfill everyone's retirement dreams unless those who continue to work accept a reduced standard of living and a reduced quality of life. For seniors to live the life they want, workers must sacrifice their current (and future) lifestyles.

As a result, neither stocks, nor employer pensions (which depend on stocks), nor Social Security can provide a firm foundation for your retirement or other wealth-building goals. At today's prices and rent levels, only real estate can meet this need. So, before you let your don't-want obstacles block you from this superior investment alternative, focus on what you're giving up in later life. Focus on your financial goals. If not real estate, then what other source of wealth and income can you dependably count on?

Multiple-Choice Possibilities

The value-creating strategies set forth in this section will give you multiple possibilities for enhancing the returns of your properties. In addition, they will provide you with criteria for selecting the properties you do buy.

Once you develop an investment plan, you will learn to spot those properties that best serve your personal profile and financial goals.

As a beginning investor, buy only those properties that fit your investment plan. Don't jump for the random "good deal." Don't respond to realty agents who persistently try to entice you with "sure things," "super buys," and other "won't last" opportunities. To create value, first map your journey, then steer along the route you've chosen.

Develop a Market Strategy

Amazingly, few small real estate investors develop any type of sophisticated market strategy. They may think they have a strategy ("we rent to the college market"). Or they may follow some routine practices that experience has taught them to follow. But in reality, a market strategy involves much more. And it pays off in large dividends.

Journal of Property Management

Thumb through the *Journal of Property Management*. Although this magazine primarily directs its articles to owners, property managers, and consultants who operate large apartment complexes, everyone who owns rental properties can gain useful insights from it. Notice the repeated mention of terms like competitive market analysis, target markets, market segmentation, and resident services.

In reading through these articles, you'll learn that a true market strategy will work to give you a competitive advantage over other property owners. With this approach, you'll be able to achieve some combination of the following:

- Higher rents
- Higher occupancy
- Lower tenant turnover
- Fewer collection losses
- Lower costs of advertising and promotion

In essence, your market strategy will permit you to offer your tenants a preferred value proposition (PVP). Nearly all tenants actively compare at least three or four properties before they sign a lease. By researching a market, you can create a PVP that will make your properties the preferred choice for the types of tenants that you want to attract and retain.

Creating a Preferred Value Proposition

Few owners of rental properties conduct any market studies. When you begin looking, you'll find properties mismatched with their rent levels. You'll find properties just begging for profitable improvement. You'll find properties where most tenants exit as soon as their leases expire. And you'll find properties that stand vacant for a month or longer—even in strong rental markets. Why? Because their owners (managers) lack either the ability or the willingness to creatively and systematically explore the rental market.

As a value investor, you won't make these mistakes. By conducting some basic market research you'll seek answers to these questions:

1. What types and sizes of properties lease the fastest?
2. What features create the "wow" factor among tenants?
3. What types of tenants tend to stay the longest in their rentals?
4. What complaints do tenants voice most often about property owners and property managers?
5. What kinds and sizes of properties tend to experience the most frequent and longest vacancies?
6. What neighborhoods tend to experience the most frequent and longest vacancies?
7. What tenants experience the largest gap between the properties that are available and the qualities of the properties that they're actually willing and able to pay for?"
8. How might you especially tailor your properties to uniquely meet the needs and wants of a particular niche of tenants?

You see the idea. Learn as much as you can about tenants and properties. Go out and inspect rental properties as they come onto the market.

Note how long it takes for them to rent. Pay attention to size, features, and location. Stop by and talk with the tenants after they move in. Learn why they chose this property over others. Question everyone and everything.

Looking for Opportunity

Your market research will reveal the information you need to shape your PVP. Most owners of rental properties think they're in the rental property business. Value investors realize that they are in the business of wooing high-quality, financially responsible tenants. Most owners of rental properties think the market sets their rental rates. Value investors know that (within reason) tenants will pay more than market when they find properties that stand out and stand above their other choices.

Develop a Legal Strategy

Recall from an earlier chapter how Vancouver developer Andre Molnar created his highly profitable loft-enhanced condominiums. He studied the pertinent zoning and building regulations, then ferreted out a loophole that added $10,000 per unit to his condo selling prices.

You might be able to achieve something similar. Quite often existing properties have not been built to the full extent of the permissible zoning and building rules and regulations. By spotting underbuilt (and underperforming) properties, you might be able to create value through an addition, a conversion, or even a change in use. Apart from pursuing some type of regulatory loophole to change a property, though, you should always acquaint yourself with zoning and building regulations before you buy a property.

In some towns and cities, even small changes to a property can raise a regulatory inquiry. In any event, be aware that your right to use, occupy, repair, redecorate, remodel, renovate, or even rent out a property may be restricted by a tangle of federal, state, and local laws. Piled on top of these are private deed restrictions and homeowner association bylaws, rules, and regulations. Don't assume that you can build a second story, create an accessory apartment, add a fireplace, put in a circular asphalt driveway, or rebuild the boat dock. Check all potential restrictions before you buy with the idea of property improvement.

Allan Funt's Surprise

Consider what happened to Allan Funt, popularly known for his *Candid Camera* movies and television shows. Allan bought 1,200 acres of land near Monterey, California. He intended to construct four buildings on the site: a house, guest house, barn, and stable. The California Coastal Commission (the zoning authority over the 1,200 acres) refused permission. Instead, the commission allowed Funt to build just two structures and ordered him to grant the public a 300-acre scenic easement through the site. To top that, the commission further specified that Funt position and landscape his home such that after dark, no passersby along the Pacific Coast Highway would be able to see the home's lights.[8]

Many Types of Regulations

Let's hope government won't regulate you to the same degree that the California Coastal Commission has regulated millions of Californians. Yet here are some of the types of restrictions you might face concerning your properties:

- *Height restrictions*. Most properties must fit within a specified height. You may not be able to add a second or third story. In addition, even though you don't exceed the maximum regulatory height, your plans could be curtailed. Neighbors to the property might complain that your proposed second story will block their view, or maybe even their sunlight.
- *Side yard, front yard, and backyard setbacks*. Land-use laws typically require a home to be set back a certain distance from each of the site's boundaries. You may not be able to extend the house, garage, or outbuildings.
- *Floor area ratios (FARs)*. FAR regulations limit the maximum square footage of a property. For example, say the FAR maximum is 1:3. If

your lot size equals 7,500 square feet, then the house and garage cannot exceed 2,500 square feet.

- *Energy conservation*. Energy conservation laws may apply to anything from window size and placement to retrofitting toilets with water-saving devices. Such restrictions might even exclude certain types of grass or landscaping that require sprinklers.
- *Architectural review boards*. These boards may regulate everything and anything that involves how a property will look to passersby; for example, roof color and composition; curtain and drapery liners; home color and building materials; driveway size, placement, and composition; and, of course, overall home design.
- *Environmental controls*. Will your plans to add on a room require you to cut down a tree? Better check the environmental restrictions. Want to add a wood-burning fireplace? It may be prohibited under a clean air restriction. Want to build a boat dock or fill in some "wetlands?" Be prepared to hire an experienced environmental lawyer. (I place "wetlands" in quotation marks because state and federal Environmental Protection Agency officials define wetlands far more broadly than most property owners find reasonable. That's certainly been true for megamillionaire commodities trader Paul Tudor Jones. He served six months in jail for "wetland" offenses he allegedly committed on his own Virginia farm.)

Permissible, Prohibited, or "Let's Argue About It"

When it comes to government restrictions controlling things you may want to do, the general categories are (1) permissible ("Yes, you can paint your bedroom green, as long as you're not covered by historical 'purity' regulations"); (2) prohibited ("No, you can't dump your used motor oil down the storm sewer"); and (3) maybe yes, maybe no ("let's argue about it").[9]

Unfortunately, far too many property rules and regulations fall into the "let's argue about it" category. As a result, the rule of law is violated time and time again. You may never know for sure how you might proceed until an assortment of disgruntled neighbors; planning agencies; development boards; review commissions; county councils; and, all too frequently, judges have had their say.

Property Improvements: America's Favorite Pastime

Lest you think the situation impossible, it's encouraging to note that every year millions of property owners, building contractors, and housing developers do successfully complete building projects. The Home Depot has created a multibillion-dollar business catering to do-it-yourselfers and small contractors. Property improvement has become America's favorite pastime. Through redecorating, remodeling, renovating, and restoration, owners are making their properties more useful, enjoyable, and valuable. In fact, you may have already joined this group in connection with your principal home.

Today, however, land-use laws and property restrictions can regulate everything from fireplaces to clotheslines, septic systems to roofing, landscaping and yard care to window shutters and flower boxes. Nearly everyone agrees that these rules and restrictions often boost property values. They can assure clean air and water, preservation of natural habitats, aesthetic attractiveness, and safer buildings. But here's the rub: too often, the rules trivialize their true purpose. They entangle unwilling victims in a labyrinth of meetings, bureaucracies, and public hearings. In contrast to the rule of law, outcomes sometimes depend as much on who you are, the amount of your political power (compared to your opposition), and the cleverness of your lawyer.

Other Regulatory Concerns

Even if you don't plan to renovate or remodel a property, as a precaution verify whether the property you're buying meets all current building codes, ordinances, and restrictions. Otherwise, you unknowingly run the risk of noncompliance, and then later, if for some reason the authorities discover a violation, you could be forced to remedy it.

I once owned a rental house that had an old-fashioned 60-amp electrical system. Current building codes specified a minimum of 100-amp service.

One night the home suffered a small fire and some of the wiring was damaged, but the building inspector wouldn't simply allow a small repair. Instead he required me to completely rewire the house to comply with lawful standards. A $200 fire cost $2,000 to repair. (I sold the house for a $22,000 gain, so this expense fortunately did not materially affect my returns.)

Throughout the United States, as many as 50% of houses and small apartment buildings may violate some neighborhood zoning ordinance, building regulation, or environmental restriction. Especially if you're buying an older property, you may not be able to avoid some type of violation. Just don't buy blind. And if you do discover violations, think through the risks they might present. As the risks grow larger, your offering price should drop. If you're expected to bear the risk of legal noncompliance, then the sellers should discount their price to make up for it.

Never merely accept the glib response, "Oh, those regulations are never enforced." Even if that claim is true, who's to say what the future holds? A shift in the political winds can easily bring about stricter enforcement practices. Or a small necessary repair might trigger a more costly compliance remedy. You want to make improvements that will create value, not merely satisfy bureaucratic appetites.

Ideas to Improve the Physical Property

Most owners of rental properties fail to design their overall property-improvement program to accomplish any particular effect. Sure, they want their properties to look better, lease faster, and rent for higher amounts. But because they don't perform any market research, they fail to target their improvements to a specific profitable segment of tenants.

Run-of-the-mill investors often think of improvements in narrow terms such as paint, carpeting, and yard work. In contrast, value investors think in terms of tenant benefits. Though of course there's some overlap, value investors approach their improvement work with more innovation, more flair. They don't just focus on the obvious; they focus on tenant needs and wants, then try to shape the property accordingly.

Here are eight areas you can address:

1. Clean thoroughly.
2. Add pizzazz.
3. Create usable space.
4. Create a view.
5. Capitalize on builder mistakes.
6. Eliminate a negative view.
7. Bring in more natural light.
8. Reduce noise levels.

Thoroughly Clean Your Properties

Many owners of small rental properties do not realize the basic necessity of spotlessly clean apartments or houses. Many owners seem to take the view, "Why clean the place thoroughly? The tenants will leave it like a pigsty anyway." But actually it's this bad attitude that often brings about the undesired result. When rental units aren't meticulously maintained, top-quality renters are turned off. They go elsewhere. On the other hand, those tenants who accept units with dirt-encrusted windows and light fixtures, stained carpets, grease-layered stoves, and dust-laden window blinds are the same tenants who are likely to treat your property as a pigsty.

If you display a pride-of-ownership cleanliness, not only will you attract a better class of tenants, you'll also demonstrate to your tenants the degree of cleanliness you expect. When I first became a landlord, I confess that I operated with the "why clean thoroughly" attitude. After seeing tenants wreck a property, it's easy to reduce standards. But I soon learned that that's a self-defeating downward cycle. On the other hand, once I began to offer units that stood head and shoulders above the competition, I was always able to choose excellent tenants from a long list of applicants.

Add Pizzazz with Color Schemes, Decorating Patterns, and Fixtures

Before you paint or redecorate your rental units, go out and tour several new home developments and new upscale apartment projects. Also look through a variety of home decorator magazines. Can you enhance the appeal of your units with more modern color schemes, wallpaper patterns, or special touches like chair railings, mirrors, fancy plumbing, light fixtures, or patterned tile floors? Don't go wild with the outlandish, but just the right amount of pizzazz can make your units stand out from the crowd.

Create More Usable Space

Have you seen ads for California Closet Company or any of its imitators? This company took the simple idea that closet space could be used more efficiently and turned it into a $50 million a year business. Now the company is following the same principle with garages, workshops, and home offices. You can do the same thing. Figure out how to create more usable space and you will increase the value of your property.

But don't just mull over using existing space more efficiently. Maybe you should convert an attic, garage, or basement to additional living area. Or you might consider enclosing a porch or patio, adding a second story, or building an accessory apartment. Keep asking yourself, "How can I use or create space to generate more income from these units?"

You might also think about "rightsizing" the living area within the units. Rightsizing means reducing the size of large rooms by adding walls or separate areas, or perhaps combining small rooms to make larger areas. In other words, every storage and living area within a house or apartment should be proportionate to market tastes and preferences. When areas are perceived as too large or too small, you can't get top rents. By rightsizing, you better fit the space to tenant needs.

In another sense, rightsizing can refer to making units themselves larger or smaller. For example, several years ago a Manhattan investor noticed that two-bedroom apartments were a glut on the market and rent levels were severely depressed. On the other hand, those few buildings that offered four-bedroom apartments had long waiting lists. So he bought a building of two-bedroom apartments at a steep discount, combined the apartments into four-bedroom units, and rented them all immediately at premium rent levels.

Create a View

Some years back when I was looking for a lakefront home in Winter Park, Florida, I discovered a basic flaw in home building. Many builders had used standard building plans even when they built on lots with views. As a result, a great majority of the older lakefront houses I looked at failed to fully capture the view potential of the properties. Similarly, not long ago I was touring a new home development in northwest Albuquerque when I came across a home situated such that it could have offered spectacular views of the Sandia Mountain Range.

As I entered the house full of anticipation, disappointment soon set in. None of the rooms downstairs even had windows facing the mountains. Surely, though, the upstairs would be different, I thought. I imagined a master bedroom suite with large windows and perhaps a deck facing out to the mountains. But again, no. The master bedroom was situated to look straight at the house next door. And on the mountain side of the house was a small child's bedroom with no view window.

Capitalize on Builder Mistakes

If you can find older (or even newer) homes or apartments that fail to fully capture a potential view of a lake, ocean, mountain range, park, woods, or other pleasant surroundings, you may have discovered a great way to add value to a property.

What's surprising is that often the owners of such properties have become so accustomed to the property as it exists that they don't even realize its possibilities. As noted previously, after remodeling my lakefront home in Winter Park to achieve views from eight of its nine rooms, Mrs. Seller stopped by and exclaimed, "Wow! If we could have imagined these changes, we might never have sold the house."

This example emphasizes my overall theme that profitable improvement begins with market research and creative imagination. Don't rush into your property fix-up without first considering all types of possibilities. As mentioned, too many property owners define property improvement as slapping on a fresh coat of white paint and laying new beige wall-to-wall carpeting. Though such improvements may help, don't limit yourself to such routine ideas.

Eliminate a Negative View

Some buildings suffer diminished value because their windows look out directly onto an alley, another building, or perhaps a tangle of power lines. For such properties, your goal is to eliminate a negative view and convert it into a positive whenever possible. For example, can you change the location of a window? Can you plant shrubbery, bamboo, or leafy trees? Can you add decorative fencing?

At the Black Oak Bookstore in Berkeley, California, the owners transformed an area that had looked out directly at a plain concrete-block wall. To remedy this negative, the owners planted ivy to climb up and cover the concrete wall and added hanging plants, a rock garden, and wooden latticework. The results are quite stunning and a 200% improvement over the old, plain concrete wall.

Enhance the Unit's Natural Light

Today, most home buyers and tenants prefer homes with loads of natural light. You can achieve this effect by adding or enlarging windows, changing solid doors to those with glass, or installing skylights. In addition to the positive influence of the sunshine itself, brighter rooms seem more spacious. To enhance this effect, determine if you can add volume to interior rooms by tearing out a false ceiling; or at times it can even pay you to eliminate attic area. When you add skylights and volume simultaneously, you can dramatically improve the way a home lives and feels.

Consider the experience of property owner Joan Phelps: "The previous owners had brick all across the inside wall, so it was very dark and dreary," says Joan. To solve this problem she and her husband spent $2,620 to tear out much of the brick and add windows on each side of the fireplace. The result was dramatic. When they put their home up for sale, "We had two offers and a backup buyer the first weekend. First impressions really sell," Joan advises.

Not only did the Phelpses get the price they wanted, but another nearby home with the same old brick-wall design sat on the market unsold for months. People (tenants and buyers) will pay a premium for a bright, cheery home. Can you add windows, skylights, or different window treatments (get rid of those heavy dark blinds or drapes)? Can you rip out those low ceilings? With more height, you can bring in more light as well as eliminate that closed-in feeling created by low ceilings.

Reduce Noise

Home buyers and tenants also will pay for quiet and discount heavily for noise. More home insulation, trees and shrubs, soundproof windows, caulking, and earth berms are all possible solutions.

I recently attended a home improvements fair where one exhibitor had a boom box blasting hard-rock music. But this offensive noise machine sat behind the exhibitor's product: sound-insulating windows. As shoppers approached, the man at the exhibit closed the window, and the noise disappeared. Quite an effective demonstration of how soundproof windows can muffle or eliminate outside noise.

If you're thinking of buying a multiunit building, make sure you test the soundproofing between units. If you can hear a television, people walking or talking, or toilets flushing, beware. Unless you can figure out a solution to the noise problem, you will face repeated problems in retaining tenants and keeping them satisfied.

Estimating Costs to Repair, Redecorate, or Remodel

In planning improvements, here are three tips to keep in mind: (1) little things can mean a lot; (2) beware of hidden costs; and (3) know the difference between do-it-yourself, self-contracting, and full-service retail cost estimates. Cost overruns can spoil a great improvement project.

Little Things Can Mean a Lot

Each time you note something to change in or around a property that you're inspecting to buy, write it down. "When we were buying our first investment," recalls Shannon Grimes, "we never made a list of everything we wanted to do. We just made mental notes like, 'We can repaint those rooms, retile the bath and kitchen, add a window, install new blinds, recarpet the living room. . . . ' Since we didn't write out a complete list and then figure all the costs, we underestimated expenses by around $2,500. Were we surprised! I guess it's true what they say, little things can mean a lot." To avoid this type of oversight, list each change you would like to make to a property. Go into your purchase negotiations with a good idea of your proposed repair, redecorating, and remodeling costs. Otherwise, you risk paying more than you should.[10]

Beware of Hidden Costs

I was recently looking at a house that needed a new roof. "That's not a problem," the seller said. "You'll spend about $2,800 to replace it with a new one, and we're willing to give you an escrow credit to cover it." Now the question is, "Could a buyer replace that roof for $2,800?" Maybe, maybe not. The potential problem is that even if the roof costs $2,800 to replace, total repairs could run much more. If the sellers had played the "notice a leak, patch it; notice another leak, patch it" game for very long, that house could require repairs for wood rot and plaster damage. But you may not be able to tell for sure until after the old roof has been removed.[11]

To address this potential problem, anticipate whether your repairs or remodeling plans may discover hidden damages. If the answer is yes, then ask the sellers to either satisfactorily repair all damage or set up an escrow credit that will pay for basic repairs as well as contingent damages. Alternatively, ask the sellers to drop their price. If before you buy you can't pin down how much you must pay for repairs or improvements, it's not unreasonable to ask the sellers to price their house to offset these uncertainties.

Who Will Perform the Work?

Some years ago, I gutted the kitchen in one of my homes and spent $8,000 to completely renovate it. I did the design, shopped for the materials, and scheduled the work for all of the manual and skilled labor (electrical, cabinetry, appliance installation, and roof cuts for skylights). If instead I had performed the labor myself, I could have spent as little as $5,000. On the other hand, had I employed a kitchen design firm to do the full job from start to finish, the same remodeled kitchen would have cost more than $12,000.

This example illustrates the difference between do-it-yourself, self-contracting, and full-service retail cost figures. When you're talking cost estimates, keep in mind which type of figure you're referring to. Will you perform all of the labor yourself? Will you serve as the general contractor? Or will you delegate responsibility for the entire job to someone else? There are large differences in costs among these choices. Remember, too, should you choose to do some or all of the work yourself, budget a dollar amount for your time. Keep your investment returns separate from returns due to your physical labor.

Cut Operating Expenses

As a rule of thumb, every dollar you slice from your property's operating expenses can add $10 or more to your building's value. With figures like that, you should meticulously keep track of all expenses. Then make continuous efforts to reduce, shift, or eliminate them. Here are some ideas.

Energy Audits

Nearly all utility companies will help you discover ways to reduce your gas and electric bills. Some will even perform a physical audit and inspection of your property. Others will provide booklets or brochures and perhaps a customer service department to answer specialized questions. You can also find dozens of articles and books at your local library that discuss energy conservation.

Because each type of building construction and area of the country presents different problems and opportunities, seek out information that fits your particular situation. In addition, be aware that site placement and window placement can dramatically increase or diminish your energy costs.

In fact, energy audit a building before you buy it. Then you can judge beforehand the extent to which you can feasibly reduce these costs. Or, alternatively, avoid buying an energy glutton for which no economically practical solution exists.

Maintenance and Repair Costs

Value investors also need to reduce or eliminate money-wasting property maintenance and repair expenses. In my experience, I would encourage you to focus on these five measures:

1. *Low-maintenance houses and apartment buildings*. When shopping to buy, favor those properties that are constructed with materials, HVAC, and fixtures that require less maintenance. Nothing beats a property that's built to last with minimal care. The same goes for yards, shrubs, and landscaping.
2. *Tenant selection*. Just as there are both low-maintenance and high-maintenance houses and apartment buildings, so too are there low-maintenance and high-maintenance tenants. Avoid the latter and select the former. Personally, I watch out for chronic complainers and people who show no "house sense." Overall, I believe that more than half of rental property maintenance, repair, cleaning, and wear and tear costs can be cut by selecting only tenants who have consistently demonstrated personal responsibility. Contrary to the claims of some tenants, things seldom break by themselves, nor do toilets stop up and overflow as an act of God.
3. *Repair clauses*. To further promote tenant responsibility, a growing number of property owners shift the first $50 or $100 of every repair cost onto their tenants' shoulders. Also, I favor high security deposits.
4. *Handyman on call*. Nothing eases the drain on your time and pocketbook as much as having a trustworthy and competent all-around handyman (or other service providers) to take care of property maintenance and repairs. With service calls now costing upward of $100 in many cities, establishing a relationship with those you

can regularly depend on will save you time and money—and many bottles of Excedrin.

5. *Preventive maintenance*. If you're not pennywise and pound foolish, you subject your car to periodic maintenance and inspection. Likewise with your income properties. The operative advice is to anticipate and alleviate when the cost is relatively small. Also, always ask your maintenance experts how you might replace high-maintenance items with low maintenance ones.

Property Taxes

"If you think that your property taxes are too high," writes tax consultant Harry Koenig, "you're probably right! Research shows that nearly half of all properties may be assessed illegally or excessively."[12] Though Koenig probably overstates the situation somewhat, there's certainly no doubt that millions of property owners pay more in property taxes than they need to. With just a little attention and planning, you can avoid falling into this trap by taking several precautions:

1. *Check the accuracy of your assessed valuation*. Usually, tax assessors base their tax calculations on a property's market value. Look closely at the assessor's value estimate on your tax bill. Can you find comp sales of similar properties that would support a lower value for your property? If so, you may have grounds to request a tax reduction. (See Chapter 6 for more details on market value appraisal.)
2. *Compare your purchase price to the assessor's estimate of market value*. Apart from providing comp sales, if you can show the assessor's office that you recently paid $190,000 for a property that it has appraised at $240,000, you've got a prima facie case for lower taxes.
3. *Look for unequal treatment*. Under the law, assessors must tax properties in a neighborhood in an equal (fair) and uniform manner. This means that you might be able to successfully argue for lower taxes even though the assessor has accurately estimated the market value of your property. How? By showing that the assessor has assigned lower values to similar nearby properties. (All property tax

data are publicly available.) If faced with this issue, the assessor will have to cut your taxes because once everyone's tax notices have been sent out, it's not politically feasible (even if lawful) for the assessor's office to start telling people it's made a mistake and they actually owe more than what is stated on their tax bills.

4. *Recognize the difference between assessed value and market value*. Typically, property taxes are based on assessed value, which is calculated as a percentage of market value. If your tax notice shows an assessed value of $80,000 and you know your property's worth $120,000, don't necessarily conclude that you've been underassessed. If tax law states that assessed values should equal 50% of market value, then your assessed value should come in at $60,000 (0.5 x $120,000), not $80,000.
5. *Determine if your property suffers any negative features that the assessor has not considered*. Even though comp properties may appear similar, are there really significant differences? Does your property abut railroad tracks or a busy, noisy highway? Does it lack a basement, built-in appliances, a desirable floor plan, or off-street parking? Does it have a flat roof? (In some areas, flat roofs reduce value because they tend to leak and are costly to replace.)
6. *Find out whether you or your property qualify for any exemptions*. Most property tax laws grant preferential treatment to various persons or properties. For example, veterans, seniors, blind persons, and hardship cases may be entitled to reduced assessments based on their special status. Similarly, historic properties, properties in areas designated for revitalization, energy-efficient properties, or properties rented to low-income households may be eligible for reduced assessments. Check with your assessor's office to see what exemptions might apply in your city or county.
7. *Verify that your assessment meets all technical requirements specified in the law*. Tax assessors and the legislative bodies that levy property taxes must operate within a set of rules, regulations, laws, and even constitutional requirements. For instance, some technical or procedural requirements may pertain to assessed value ratios, property classification, land-improvements ratio, conducting public hearings,

notice of public hearings, permissible valuation techniques, and allocation of assessed value between real and personal property.

8. *Learn tax assessment laws before you improve or rehabilitate a property.* The property tax laws of every state list the types of property improvements that are taxed and the applicable rates. Once you discover the detailed nature of these laws, you then can develop an improvement strategy that adds value without adding taxes.[13]

A related issue is building permits. Some investors contract for remodeling and renovations without securing the appropriate permits. The thought is that the government can't tax what it doesn't know about. The danger with this approach, though, is that at some later date a building inspector may discover your unpermitted work. In some cities, that means the inspector can require you to tear out the work and do it over. This is especially a risk where unpermitted work doesn't meet code requirements. In the past, governments often overlooked unpermitted work and failed to keep their property tax records up to date. But now, with computer data banks, buyer prepurchase inspections, and seller disclosure statements, such work is more likely to be discovered. Furthermore, in their unrelenting quest for greater tax revenues, local governments recognize that unreported remodeling and renovations are costing them millions of dollars each year in lost tax revenues.

As a result, the trend throughout the country is toward more thorough property investigations and harsher penalties. Though many city and county governments still lack the personnel, resources, or political will to change their careless practices, do you want to bet that these assessment inefficiencies will continue forever?

Mortgage Interest

Without a doubt, your mortgage interest expense will dwarf all of your other expenses. When buying, don't just think price; think financing. Always try to arrange at least some low-cost owner-will-carry (OWC) financing. In more than half of my purchases, sellers have carried back some or all of the financing.

Mortgage Assumptions

Although mortgage assumptions are not as common now as in years past, you will run across them every now and then. Stay alert for sellers who offer this advantage. Mortgage assumptions often can save you thousands of dollars in costs and fees. Plus, in times of high interest rates, a low-rate mortgage assumption can save you thousands of dollars a year in interest expenses.

Adjustable-Rate Mortgages

Adjustable-rate mortgages (ARMs) rise and fall in popularity. In periods with high long-term interest rates and much lower short-term rates (i.e., a steep yield curve), an ARM can save you thousands of dollars in the early years of your loan—especially if you can secure a very attractive teaser rate that lasts a year or more.

Because the costs, terms, and conditions of ARMs do change, it's impossible to say whether ARMs beat fixed-rate mortgages or vice versa. It all depends on the specific credit environment in which you're looking for financing. On occasion, too, a majority of mortgage lenders may shut investors out of fixed-rate mortgages and force them to accept an ARM.

Nevertheless, even when you can borrow with a fixed-rate loan, don't rule out an ARM. Shop and compare carefully. You may be able to find a deal that gives you short-term savings that are large enough to offset the risks of higher rates in the longer-term future. Of course, if you plan to hold a property for, say, just two to five years, you will almost certainly find an ARM that will permit more cash to flow into your pockets.

Refinance

With interest rates always bouncing up and down, always stay tuned for the chance to reduce your interest expenses through a refinance. Set up a rate-monitoring system, or tell your mortgage broker to put your name into his file to be notified when refinancing rates are favorable. In addition, if you ever get the chance to finance or refinance with a low-rate mortgage that your property buyers can later assume, take it! When interest rates go up, investors and home buyers will often pay a premium price to sellers who can pass along their low-rate mortgage.

Change the Location of the Property

"Florida's new urban entrepreneurs have the vision to see a bustling district of sushi bars, loft apartments and boutiques on a glass-strewn lot or rat-infested warehouse," writes Cynthia Barnett in the August 2001 issue of *Florida Trend.*[14]

Phil Rampy is proud to have been one of those early entrepreneurs. Twelve years ago, Rampy bought a house in the then-shunned Thorton Park neighborhood near trash-strewn Lake Eola (or, as they used to call it, Lake Erie-ola). Today, times have changed. Thorton Park has climbed up the status ladder to rank among the trendiest addresses in Orlando. That $60,000 bungalow is now valued at more than $200,000.[15]

You Can Change a Location

Virtually every supposed expert in the field of home buying and real estate investing thoughtlessly repeats the same cliché: "What are the three most important features of real estate?" They answer, "Location, location, location. You can change anything about a property except its location."

Quite plainly, such clichéd advice and commentary stands quite opposite to the facts. As the Thorton Park experience proves, you can change a property's location. The term location does not refer primarily to a fixed and unmovable site on the face of the earth. Rather, as you saw in Chapter 6, location encompasses an expansive constellation of attributes such as the following:

- Aesthetics (sounds, sights, smells)
- School district
- Crime rates
- Zoning

- Convenience and accessibility
- Demographics
- Government services
- Shopping and restaurants
- Parks and recreation
- Private services

Now, substitute the term neighborhood for location and ask, "Can the residents and property owners in a neighborhood work to successfully improve it?" Of course, the answer is, "Definitely." Consider these possibilities.

Improve Appearances and Aesthetics

Put together a civic pride organization. Organize a cleanup and fix-up campaign. Plant trees, shrubs, and flowers in yards and in public areas. Lobby the city to tear down or eliminate eyesore buildings, graffiti, or trashy areas. Try to reduce on-street parking. Get immobile or abandoned vehicles towed. Enforce environmental regulations against property owners and businesses that pollute (noise, smoke, odors). Walk the neighborhood. Closely observe and note any value-diminishing negatives. Then do what's necessary to change, remove, or alleviate them.

School District

The *Wall Street Journal* reports that all across the country, "Parents and property owners have become increasingly aggressive about trying to improve the public schools."[16] When you think that in many areas, parents spend \$3,000 to \$10,000 a year to send their kids to private schools, why not rechannel those monies and support into the neighborhood schools?

In some cases, too, the neighborhood schools may not truly deserve their dismal reputations. Or perhaps a strong-performing school (at least in some areas of specialization) isn't receiving the favorable notice it deserves. Improvement in such instances might focus more on publicity and press releases. Let potential home buyers, tenants, and Realtors know the positive facts. Because better schools and better school reputations boost property values, neighborhood improvement can easily begin with enhancing the schools.

Reduce Crime

"While it may seem that everywhere crime is on the rise," write Stephanie Mann and M. C. Blakeman (*Safe Homes, Safe Neighborhoods*), "in many neighborhoods the opposite is true."[17] In cities and towns across the country, local crime prevention groups have reduced burglaries and car break-ins; helped catch muggers, rapists, and kidnappers; established Block Parents and other child-safety projects; driven out drug dealers; eliminated graffiti; and, in general, made their homes and streets safer. All it takes is a few people to get things started. By identifying and focusing on a neighborhood's main concerns—and working with police and each other—neighbors can make a difference."

Change the Address

Some good friends of mine used to live in Miami, Florida, but now they live in the upscale Village of Pinecrest, Florida. Did they move? No. They and their neighbors lobbied the post office to give them a new address so they could distinguish themselves from that diverse agglomeration known as Miami.

Will Cauldron used to own an apartment building located at 466 Lexington Avenue in Manhattan. But now he owns a rental property located at 230 Park Avenue and has boosted his rent collections by 20%. Did Cauldron buy a new building? No. Through an ingenious agreement, Cauldron linked his building to the property that actually occupies the site at 230 Park Avenue. Being able to use the highly desirable Park Avenue address permitted Cauldron to substantially raise his rents—although nothing changed but the address.

People pay for addresses. To boost your rents and property value, change the name of your property's street, neighborhood, community, or even the building itself. (Who would want to live at Terrace Arms Apartments?) Property owners use this technique all the time. They know the answer to the question "What's in a name?" is money.

Accessibility

Would a stoplight, wider road, or new highway interchange improve accessibility to the neighborhood? How about better (or lower-priced) bus or commuter train service? Greater convenience means higher value. On the other hand, perhaps the neighborhood is too convenient and accessible. You get too much traffic. In that case, put in speed bumps. Or, as in some Berkeley, California, neighborhoods, pressure the city to put up intersection barriers that block flow-through traffic.

Zoning and Building Regulations (Legal Environment)

Are too many property owners in the neighborhood cutting up single-family houses and converting them into apartments? Do too many residents run businesses out of their homes and garages? Are high- or midrise buildings planned that will diminish livability? Are too many commercial properties encroaching on the area? Then lobby for tighter zoning and building regulations. On the other hand, do areas within the neighborhood and nearby make more intense use of neighborhood properties desirable? Then lobby the city to rezone the area to apartments or commercial.

Because zoning and building regulations affect property use, they can dramatically affect property values. When value-creating changes are warranted, pressure the politicians and planners to accommodate you.

Increase Rents, Lower the Cap Rate

When you and other property owners improve a neighborhood, you achieve two goals: (1) You attract more desirable tenants who will pay higher rents, and (2) because of lower risk and greater attractiveness, that neighborhood will command lower capitalization rates (the R in V = NOI/R) and higher gross rent multipliers. Contrary to the advice of so-called experts, you can and should work to change and improve the location of your properties. With these efforts, you can multiply your equity by a factor of two, three, four, or more within a period of just a few years. When you work to create the next up-and-coming area, you will earn ample rewards for your investment of time and money.

Boosting Value: Some Final Words

For the past 10 to 15 years, we've heard about corporate managers who repeatedly downsize, rightsize, restructure, and slash expenses, all the while searching for new customers, new products, and new ways of doing business. Surely, some of these corporate efforts were nothing more than cheap attempts to excite cheers from Wall Street. But far more importantly, these management efforts illustrate how creative, strategic thinking and the never-ending search to improve can push dollars to the bottom line and boost stock prices.

This same principle applies to value investing in real estate. When you approach your rental business with the attitude that you can design and develop more-profitable (less-costly, higher-yielding) ways of operating these properties, you will far outperform the results of other owners. The investor-owners of large shopping malls, office buildings, and apartment complexes have long proved the merits of market research, strategy, property improvement, and cost reduction.

It's now time for individual owners of investment properties to adopt a similar pattern of thinking—and doing. For those enterprising investors who follow this approach, the rewards of increased property values and super returns remain readily available.

Conclusion

You *(Not Everybody)* Ought to Be Rich

In 1929, the *Ladies Home Journal* published its now infamous article, "Everybody Ought to be Rich."[1] In this advice piece, John J. Raskob, then a well-known financier, told Americans that they owed themselves a duty to get rich by investing in stocks.[2] How did Raskob define rich? "Let us say," Raskob continued, "that a man is rich when he has an income from invested capital which is sufficient to support him and his family in a decent and comfortable manner—to give them as much support as he has ever been given by his earnings. That amount of prosperity ought to be attainable by anyone."[3]

How Much Wealth? How Much Income?

Raskob went on to say that an average worker who invested just 10% of his monthly wages and reinvested all dividends would after 20 years hold wealth valued at $80,000.[4] Assuming future dividend yields at 6%, Raskob predicted that this worker would then be able to receive a yearly income of $4,800, or $400 per month.[5] Based on the consumer prices of those times, that worker could enjoy financial security: an income for life without spending capital.

Oops!

As we now know, things didn't quite work out the way Raskob projected. At the exact time his *Ladies Home Journal* article was published, stocks began a downward slide that didn't end until 1932, when the market had lost 90% of its 1929 high.[6] Had a 1929 worker actually invested according to Raskob's advice, by 1949 this worker's accumulations of 20 years would have totaled just under $9,000—not quite the $80,000 that Raskob had forecast. And even though dividend yields were strong in 1949, this worker could hardly have lived on the meager $50 or so a month those dividends would have provided. Given this sorry turn of events, writers have been ridiculing Mr. Raskob and his projections ever since.

Reputation Revived?

Writers up until Jeremy Siegel, that is. In his book *Stocks for the Long Run*, Siegel tries to revive Raskob's reputation. Admittedly, Siegel agrees that Raskob's projections for 1949 fell drastically short of the mark. But Siegel argues that had this worker continued this investment plan for just another 10 years (another 10 years!), his retirement wealth would have grown to around $60,000.[7] Although still far short of Raskob's promise, Siegel nevertheless celebrates the fact that over the full 30-year period (1929 to 1959), this worker-investor would have earned a "fantastic 13 percent on invested capital," far exceeding the returns earned by those conservative investors whose fear of the stock market pushed them into Treasury bonds or bills.[8]

Siegel Misses the Point

Once again Siegel appears to miss the point. Raskob did not offer his advice to help investors outperform Treasury bonds and bills. His goal was far more important, and far more relevant to Americans today. Raskob wanted to show Americans how they could become rich in stocks, rich according to Raskob's definition, rich enough to live a comfortable life on dividends without consuming their seed corn.[9]

In trying to revive the reputation of Raskob, Siegel ignores Raskob's central point, just as Siegel ignores this central and critical point throughout his entire book. Although we all want to earn a competitive rate of return, the rate of return is the means, not the end. Would anyone care a whit about having beaten bonds if they ended up in their later years eating at soup kitchens and living in an SRO (single-room occupancy) hotel for the down-and-out?

Income, Not Just Rate of Return

When viewed in terms of income, this investor-retiree would not have fared well at all. Assuming a generous 4.0% dividend yield, in 1959 his stock portfolio would have paid him and his wife only $200 per month.[10] Although slightly above the poverty level, $200 a month, even in 1959, would hardly have provided a decent and comfortable life. But this retiree's situation gets worse—much worse.

Let's assume our stock investor/retiree lives another 20 years. Between 1959 and 1969, stock prices rose about 40%.[11] Let's say by 1969, our retiree now has $85,000. On the downside, though, throughout the 1960s dividend yields averaged around 3.5%. So after factoring in a 25% increase in consumer prices, our retiree's dividend checks (now $250 a month) barely kept pace with inflation.

The 1970s, unfortunately, were not so kind. Between 1969 and 1979, the *nominal* value of this retiree's stock portfolio would have shrunk from $85,000 to $78,000. Still, with a boost in the dividend yield to around 5.5%, our retiree's monthly dividend advanced to $361. Now for the bad news. In terms of 1959 buying power, the inflation of the 1970s whittled the real value of that $361 monthly dividend down to around $150—25% less than he was receiving 20 years earlier. (Note, too, I have ignored income tax payments that may have been owed by this investor.)

Can You Get Rich in Stocks?

What does all of the preceding prove? It proves that both Raskob and Siegel err. Most Americans cannot reliably count on stocks to provide themselves a comfortable, inflation-protected retirement income. Neither recent experience, history, or reason supports such a confident claim of prediction.

You must face the fact that no one knows—no one can know—what the future holds for the stock market. Record-setting advances in stock prices from 1980 to 2000 may foreshadow much lower rates of appreciation in the future. Record-low dividend yields (1.25% or so) certainly imply paltry levels of income even from relatively large accumulations of (illusionary?) stock market wealth. Even if the economy stays on a steady path of growth (as most people expect), stocks could advance in exuberance, slip sideways, or slide toward the basement. Yet, without strong dividends or exuberant appreciation, how could you believe that stocks will fulfill your retirement wants and needs?

Work the Numbers

Before you commit yourself to a retirement income based on stocks, work the numbers yourself. Go to one of those retirement-calculator Web sites.[12] Plug in the numbers. How much will you invest each year? How much will you accumulate? At what rate of return? At what rate of withdrawal? How will taxes and inflation slice the true buying power of your withdrawal? Evaluate your results. In light of long-term experience, do your assumptions seem reasonable? In light of long-term experience and present market conditions, how much confidence can you place in your numbers? If you answer with any level of confidence exceeding 50%, you are fooling yourself.

Just remember what happened to that retiree of Raskob and Siegel who earned a "fantastic return" of 13%. Of course, on the optimistic side, you may invest a higher percentage of your income than he did. And your wage income may advance considerably over time. On the pessimistic side, though, your returns and dividend yields will likely fall well below his. So what's the conclusion? Will you get Raskob rich in stocks? Maybe, but probably not.

Can Everybody Get Rich in Stocks?

Siegel maintains that "everybody" can get rich in stocks. Indeed, an Amazon.com reviewer of *Stocks for the Long Run* gives the book a five-star rating (the highest possible). "Professor Siegel," opines this reviewer, "does a great job advancing the thesis that everyone can get rich in the stock market."[13] Other reviewers similarly lavish Siegel's thesis and exposition with remarkable praise. Yet Siegel and his reviewers err egregiously. For reasons laid out in the introduction to this book, neither everyone, nor any substantially large number of Americans, can ever accumulate enough real wealth in stocks to live on the earnings from capital. Even Raskob noted in 1929 that production must precede consumption.[14] We cannot consume what we fail to produce. Speculative increases in stock prices, increases that far surpass the level supported by dividend income and economic growth, do not create spendable wealth and real consumable goods and services.

Anyone, Not Everybody

In fact, Raskob actually said that becoming rich ought to be attainable by *anyone*, not *everybody!* Undoubtedly, the headline writer, not Raskob, placed the word "everybody" into the title of the article. Yet today, stock enthusiasts like Siegel seem to avoid this subtle but all-important difference.

Granted, Raskob did believe that channeling capital into productive plant and equipment would eventually lead to increased standards of living for nearly everybody. But that's a long way from saying that we can all become rich by trading stocks with each other at ever-higher prices.

Everybody Can't Get Rich

Karl Marx once described how socialism would create so much wealth for society that average workers would merely have to spend a little time at their jobs in the mornings. In the afternoon they could fish or take walks, and in the evening paint or perhaps attend a concert or symphony.[15]

It seems that our stock enthusiasts have given Karl Marx a new twist. Under their forecasts, 50 million retired Americans will be able to skip their morning work altogether and jump directly to fishing, painting, and enjoying the arts. Sadly, these predictions by the stock market enthusiasts will prove just as dangerously false as Marx's predictions for a life of ease created by socialism. At any reasonably anticipated future level of production, everybody can't get rich.[16]

You Can Get Rich, Safely and Surely

Everybody can't get rich in stocks. Everybody can't get rich in real estate. But at today's (but perhaps not tomorrow's) levels of property prices and rents, *you* can secure your financial future by value investing in real estate. Look again at Tables 3.1, 3.2, and 3.3 on pages 72–73. Relish the amounts of income and equity that you can build with just one rental home under relatively conservative assumptions. By applying any or all of the techniques of enterprise discussed throughout this book, you can surely beat these commonplace results—if you're willing to put forth the intelligence and effort. Moreover, these examples assume that mortgage payments will pull off substantial amounts of your cash flow. Yet after 30 years of ownership (or sooner if you choose), you can eliminate this expense.

So, all you need to do is determine how much income you would like to enjoy during your later years. Then begin buying the appropriate number of investment housing units. No need to fool with speculative projections for stock market returns.[17] No need to worry about outliving your capital because you've consumed your seed corn (as most stock market retirees must do). Implement this simple real estate investment program and not only will you outperform stocks and bonds, you will achieve your financial goals. You will live a secure and adventurous retirement.

Real Estate: The Superior Way to Get (Raskob) Rich

Given the uncertainties of stocks, I cannot figure out why more investors have not discovered the power of real estate to produce a safe and sure income. Undoubtedly, the "I don't want the bother" attitude accounts for some reluctance. Two decades of spectacular increases in stock prices also deflected attention away from real estate. But perhaps as much as anything, it's investor complacency.

The persistent journalistic drumbeat of "stocks for the long run" and "stocks outperform all other assets" has dulled investor thinking.[18] But look at history. What asset has best maintained its value through all types of post–World War II economic cycles? What asset shows the most persistent record of year-to-year and decade-to-decade increases in value? What asset has, dollar for dollar, always yielded the highest income and returns? What asset enjoys the most advantageous treatment by the Internal Revenue Code? What asset nearly guarantees an inflation-protected income for life—no matter how long you live? What asset best preserves the value of your estate for your children?[19] Each of these questions has the same answer: *income properties*.

Value Investors Win

History proves that value investing outperforms speculation, gambling, and taking a flier. Value investing outperforms fads, momentum, and growth. But what is value investing?

The first rule of value investing is price. Does the price of the investment sit below its intrinsic value (the discounted value of its reasonably expected cash flows)? The second rule is margin of safety. Do history and reasonable expectations guard you against a serious and permanent loss of capital (both nominal and real)? And the third rule of value investing is enterprise and intelligence. Does the investment promise reduced risk and superior returns to those investors who apply enterprise and market savvy?[20]

What type of investment outperforms all others on these three cardinal principles of value investing? Residential income properties. If you wish to achieve the wealth-building power of value investing, you will choose residential income properties.[21]

Notes

Introduction Rethink Your Financial Future

1. I omit bonds from this list of retirement funding alternatives because today (and historically) bonds have yielded very low (sometimes negative), real (inflation-adjusted), after-tax rates of return. If you wish to build real wealth, own real estate. If you wish to protect the wealth you've already accumulated against economic crisis and asset deflation, then buy U.S. government bonds. For a good introduction to the bond market, see Michael B. O'Higgins, *Beating the Dow with Bonds* (New York: Harper Business, 1999).

2. I do not mean to imply that Social Security will go broke or that stock prices will collapse as they did between 1929 and 1932. I mean only that these sources of funding incorporate too much uncertainty to provide a firm foundation of benefits of a knowable amount. Therefore, you cannot safely or surely plan your retirement with these sources as the base.

3. Peter G. Peterson, *Gray Dawn: How the Coming Age Wave Will Transform America—and the World* (New York: Random House, 1999).

4. Formally, this economic principle is called the fallacy of composition. Imagine that you know of an undiscovered route that leads from the Inland Empire to downtown Los Angeles that remains free of traffic congestion. How long will this route continue to offer a quick trip to Los Angeles? For only as long as the route remains undiscovered. If large numbers of drivers choose this option, the route will soon fail to provide its promised benefit. Likewise, stocks, pensions, and Social Security can provide good incomes for the relative few but not for a substantial majority.

5. Thornton Parker, *What If Boomers Can't Retire?* (San Francisco: Berret-Koehler, 2000), 15.

6. I emphasize *hope*. Already, with the 2000–2001 stock market downturn, the personal finance magazines are replete with stories of investors whose hopes for an early retirement have been dashed. For example, see the letter from Arthur Moriarity in *Worth*, October 2001, 26.

7. Tom Redburn, "No Easy Fix for Social Security," *New York Times*, September 2, 2001, sec. 3, p. 2. "The economy cannot support millions upon millions of healthy people not working year after year." Precisely my point.

8. Of course, paying for such medical treatment will also bear heavily on then existing workers.

9. In the short run, individual firms can boost stock prices through company stock repurchases. Over time, though, aggregate stock prices will tend to track the growth rates experienced in the real economy. That's certainly the position of most economists. Moreover, whether buybacks at high P/Es make economic sense is clearly open to serious question. See Jonathan Clements, "Companies' Cash Piles May Not Help You," *Wall Street Journal*, October 30, 2001, C1.

10. Thornton Parker, "No Accounting for Gains," *Barron's*, October 29, 2001, 49.

11. Here, I am assuming that by some stroke of magic, this buying power of stock market retirees is not merely siphoned off from workers.

12. Indeed, to justify current stock market valuations, many stock enthusiasts point to low interest rates on bonds. Yet they fail to point out how a strong upward move in nominal bond yields could decimate stock prices. Some say tax efficiency justifies low dividend yields. The slightness of that defense is addressed later.

13. Indeed, with future stock price appreciation rates in doubt, many investors have already begun their flight to those few stocks with higher yields. See Henry Sender, "Current Rich Dividends Demand Caution," *Wall Street Journal*, October 25, 2001, C1. Also, Sandra Ward, "Seeking Yield: Dividend Stocks Are Back in Style," *Barron's*, October 1, 2001, 20.

14. *The World Almanac and Book of Facts* (Mahwah, N.J.: World Almanac Books), 133.

15. "Stock Market Drop Pinches Young and Old," *Wall Street Journal*, September 24, 2001, A2. Also, Lisa A. Kiester, *Wealth in America: Trends in Wealth Inequality* (New York: Cambridge University Press, 2000).

16. As another danger, beware of holding more than 10% or 15% of your retirement wealth in the stock of your employer. See "Buying into the Company," *Kiplinger's Retirement Planning Guide*, October 2, 2000, 53–55.

17. For an extended discussion of the Social Security private account debate, see the transcripts of various public hearings held by the President's Commission to Strengthen Social Security. You can access these through www.google.com.

18. Robert Reich, "Surplus Silliness," *Wall Street Journal*, August 29, 2001, A14.

19. *FY 2000 Budget*, Analytic Perspectives, 337.

20. Steve Forbes, "Stop Shafting American Workers," *Forbes*, November 12, 2001, 31–32.

21. I was one of the first to write on this topic. See my scholarly article, Gary W. Eldred, "The Development of Factors to be Examined in the Termination of the Social Security Coverage Agreement," *Journal of Risk and Insurance* (September 1975): 443–446.

22. Robert Shiller, *Irrational Exuberance* (Princeton, N.J.: Princeton University Press, 2000), 96–132.

23. Ibid., 106.

24. Ibid., 116.

25. Lester C. Thurow, *The Zero Sum Society* (New York: Basic, 1980).

26. Jonathan Clements, "Investors Optimistic," *Wall Street Journal*, June 2, 2001, C1.

27. For example, "The market since 1926 has returned an average of 11% per year and can serve as a pretty good forecast as what you should expect . . . over time." James K. Glassman, "Forget the Fed," *Kiplinger's Personal Finance*, December 2001, 50.

28. James K. Glassman and Kevin A. Hassett, *Dow 36,000* (New York: Times Books, 1999).

29. Ibid., 3, 22.

30. For example, "For retirement six to ten years away . . . you'll still want to put all of your money in stocks. . . . In fact, we advise you to put all of your long-term money into stocks" (30–31). Steven T. Goldberg, "Be Your Own Investment Guru," *Kiplinger's Stocks 2002*, Winter 2001, 28–31.

31. For a good summary, see A. Wayne Thrope, "Lakonishok Value Approach," *AAII Journal* (April 2001), 26–31; Lauren Young, "Value Rules: The Best Strategy Ever," *Smart Money*, August 2001, 83–92; and Warren Buffet, "The Superstars of Graham-and-Doddsville," in Benjamin Graham, *The Intelligent Investor* (New York: Harper Business, 1973), 291–313.

32. Peter Lynch, *One Up on Wall Street* (New York: Simon and Schuster, 1989), 15.

Chapter 1 Value Investing: The One Best Way

1. Benjamin Graham and David Dodd, *Security Analysis* (New York: McGraw-Hill, 1934). Although four later editions were written, this first edition remains in print and is the edition favored by many (if not most) value investors.

2. Ibid., 3.

3. Lawrence Chamberlain and William Hay, *Investment and Speculations* (New York: Henry Holt, 1931), 57.

4. Ibid., 5.

5. Ibid.

6. For the best modern restatement of Graham and Dodd, see Bruce Greenwald et al., *Value Investing from Graham to Buffet* (New York: Wiley, 2001).

7. Of course, the notion that stocks represent speculations did not simply arise after 1929. "The desire for sudden wealth is strong in all parts of our American community. Men want money, and women too for a score of reasons—some good, some bad—and the stock market is the magical place where miracles occur and dollars multiply themselves overnight. The agent for all the cupidity in the world is the stock-broker. . . ." Thomas W. Lawson, *Frenzied Finance* (New York: Ridgeway-Thayer, 1906), 80. Interestingly, *Frenzied Finance* appeared just before the stock market crash of 1907. And the market could not sustain the level it reached in 1906 until 1925.

8. See *Stock Exchange Practices, Hearings Before the Committee on Banking and Currency*, U.S. Senate, 73d Congress, 1st Session, 1933 (10 volumes).

9. Also, in an effort to reach out to the middle and professional classes, Merrill Lynch began running its famous 6,000-word full-page advertisement that was headlined, "What Everybody Ought to Know . . . about This Stock and Bond Business." Although low key and not expressly intended to draw inquiries, this ad's first placement in the *New York Times* drew requests for 20,000 copies. Julian Lewis Watkins, *The 100 Greatest Advertisements* (New York: Dover), 164–165.

10. At the time, highly rated investment grade bonds yielded 4.0% to 4.5% in interest, whereas dividend yields had fallen to 3.0% to 3.5%. In 1958, respectively, the yields were 3.34% and 4.01%. "Bond and Stock Yields: 1857–1970," *Historical Statistics of the United States* (Washington, D.C.: U.S. Bureau of Census, 1975), 1003.

11. Right around 750. See B. Mark Smith, *Toward Rational Exuberance* (New York: Farrar, Straus, and Giroux, 2001), 196.

12. The most famous gunslinger of the day was Gerald Tsai with his Manhattan Fund. Half of the companies held in this fund lost more than 90% of their market value. Ibid., 197–217.

13. Graham, *Intelligent Investor*, ix.

14. To calculate the P/E ratio, divide a company's current stock price by its annual earnings. On the difficulties of calculating a reliable P/E ratio, see Jonathan Weil, "What's the P/E Ratio?" *Wall Street Journal*, August 21, 2001, A1, A8.

15. Graham, *Intelligent Investor*, 37, 39.

16. Smith, *Toward Rational Exuberance*, 218, 250.

17. Ibid., 196, 250.

18. "The Death of Equities," *Business Week*, August 13, 1979, 79.

19. Ibid., 81.

20. Ibid., 79.

21. Ibid., 77.

22. Ibid., 84.

23. Graham and Dodd, *Security Analysis*, 11.

24. Ibid., 28–29.

25. Ibid.

26. Indeed, after September 11, 2001, the financial press inundated their readers with the message "To bail is to fail." See, for example, the cover story, "It's Time to Buy Stocks," *Barron's*, September 24, 2001, 1, 19.

27. Cited in Chamberlain and Hay, *Investment and Speculation*, 7.

28. "Fund Managers Illustrate Importance of Company Fundamentals, *Wall Street Journal*, July 9, 2000, R3.

29. *New York Times*, July 9, 2000, A1.

30. Ibid.

31. Ibid., A12.

32. Ibid.

33. Graham, *Intelligent Investor*, 1.

34. Ibid., 277.

35. Ibid., 283.

36. Ibid., 4.

37. Ibid., 4.

38. For fun-to-read accounts of losing traders, see Anonymous Investor, *Wiped Out* (New York: Simon & Schuster, 1966); and John Rothchild, *A Fool and His Money* (New York: Viking, 1988). Rothchild was also the writer who penned both of Peter Lynch's best-sellers, *One Up on Wall Street* and *Beating the Street*.

39. See "He Never Saw the Sun," *Kiplinger's Personal Finance*, August 2001, 40–45. "It's said that 90% of brokerage profits come from the 10% of its [trader] clients" (45).

40. For a brief look at this debate, see Peter Chambers, "The Folly of Value Investing," *Financial Times* (London), February 21, 2001, 21; and the critical response that reads, in part, "Mr. Chambers, in addition to many in the media, seems to lack an understanding of what true value investing is. Value investing is not merely buying stocks with the cheapest valuation metrics. Rather, it is buying companies with the best cost-to-worth profile.

Value investors like growth and premier companies as much as the next man. They are not just willing to pay over the odds for them." Paul Hechmer, *Financial Times* (London), February 28, 2001, 14.

41. Graham, *Intelligent Investor*, 4.

42. Graham and Dodd, *Security Analysis*, 55.

43. Graham, *Intelligent Investor*, 5.

44. Although still advocating stocks for the long run, even Jeremy Siegel now says, "I'm just not at all confident that in 5 to 10 years, we're going to match or exceed the long-term historical norm." See Jeffrey Kosnett, "History Takes a Detour," *Kiplinger's Stocks 2002*, Winter 2001, 40.

45. William Reichenstein, "What Do Past Stock Market Returns Tell Us About the Future?," August 6, 2001. Unpublished research report for TIAA-CREFF, one of the world's largest pension funds. Obtained through personal correspondence.

46. Graham, *Intelligent Investor*, 24.

47. Ibid., 25. The other fields Graham discussed (quite unfavorably) include gold, artwork, and collectibles.

Chapter 2 The Case Against Stocks for Retirement

1. "Workers Come Up Short on Retirement," *U.S. News & World Report*, December 11, 2000, 74.

2. Parker, *What If Boomers*, 15.

3. Jeremy Siegel, *Stocks for the Long Run*, 2d ed. (New York: McGraw-Hill, 1998), 5.

4. Ibid., 290.

5. See, for example, Fidelity's two-full-page confidence-building ad that ran in *Barron's*, the *Wall Street Journal* and other print media cf. *Barron's*, October 15, 2001, 2–3.

6. Mike McNamee and Marcia Vickers, "Where Should I Put My Money?" *Business Week*, July 2, 2001, 80.

7. Professor Siegel's influence is also heightened by the fact that he is a star on the lecture circuit and the most popular speaker at the Wharton School's annual seminar for business writers.

8. Graham, *Intelligent Investor*, ix.

9. Jeremy Siegel, "More than Ever, Go Long," *Mutual Funds*, November 2001, 46–47. Also see Kosnett interview of Siegel, "History Takes a Detour," 38–42. "I think stocks are still the best choice for long-term investors," says Siegel (40).

10. As noted, in recent interviews Siegel continues to tout stocks, but he cautions investors not to expect a quick repeat of the double-digit returns they witnessed during the 1980s and 1990s. Kosnett, "History Takes a Detour," 40–42.

11. Edgar Lawrence Smith, *Common Stocks as Long-Term Investments* (New York: Macmillan, 1924).

12. Ibid., 4.

13. Ibid., 80.

14. Ibid., 91.

15. See Chamberlain and Hay, *Investment and Speculations*, 9.

16. Siegel, *Stocks for the Long Run*, 52.

17. E. L. Smith, *Common Stocks*, vi.

18. Indeed, in private correspondence, a former colleague (and professor of finance) has informed me of some current research in progress that shows that balanced portfolios (stocks and bonds) may actually have outperformed stocks during the period between 1994 and 2001. Obviously, though, all such studies depend upon a multitude of arbitrary assumptions. Nevertheless, contrary to the stock enthusiasts, under some circumstances balanced portfolios outperform portfolios of 100% stocks, yet still show less volatility.

19. Siegel, *Stocks for the Long Run*, 282–290.

20. Ibid., 290.

21. E. L. Smith, *Common Stocks*, 17.

22. Ibid., 79.

23. For daily bond yields see the latter pages of the Money and Investing section of the *Wall Street Journal*. As I write, a flight to yield and quality has driven down bond interest rates to 30-year lows.

24. As you might guess, only the stocks of real estate investment trusts (REITs), which we will discuss in Chapter 7, meet Smith's income test.

25. E. L. Smith, *Common Stocks*, 91.

26. J. Siegel, *Stocks for the Long Run*, xvii.

27. Sources for the five quotes in this list are as follows: Douglas Sease, *Winning with the Market* (New York: Simon & Schuster, 2001), 53–54; Lewis Schiff and Douglas Gerlach, *The Armchair Millionaire* (New York: Pocket Books, 2001), 20–21; Jean Sherman Chatzky, "Can Real Estate Make You Rich," *Money*, June 2001, 102–103; Jane Bryan Quinn, "To Bail Is to Fail: Stick with Stocks," *Newsweek*, June 4, 2001, 61; McNamee and Vickers, "Where Should I," 80.

28. Glassman, "Forget the Fed," 50.

29. Of course, to a certain degree, many investors have already reignited their interest in real estate. My book *Investing in Real Estate*, 3d ed. (New York: John Wiley & Sons, 2001) is selling more copies now than at any previous time during its 15-year history.

30. Graham and Dodd, *Security Analysis*, 47.

31. Chelcie C. Bosland, *The Common Stock Theory of Investment* (New York: Ronald Press, 1937), 4.

32. Buffet, "Superstars of Graham-and-Doddsville," in Benjamin Graham, *The Intelligent Investor* (New York: Harper Business, 1973), 291–313.

33. Ellen Hoffman, "Opening Your Nest Egg Without Breaking It," *Business Week*, July 30, 2001, 92–93.

34. Beardstown Ladies Investment Club, *Beardstown Ladies' Common-Sense Investment Guide* (New York: Hyperion, 1994).

35. The ladies now claim that their book wasn't intended to show people how to make money. Rather, they say they wanted to motivate people to educate themselves about the stock market. For their recent apologia, see Amy Rauch Neilson, "The Beardstown Ladies' Phenomenon: Promises Kept," *Better Investing*, October 2001, 34–41, 82–83.

36. Actually, stock researchers (both modern and from days past) have constructed a wide variety of indexes and data bases. Yet no matter which data researchers have used, none includes a constant set of companies because no such data set exists.

37. Of course, improvements in the quality of most goods and services account for some of these price increases.

38. Some observers have perceptively remarked that calculating synthetic returns with indexes merely reports history being written by the winners.

39. Neither J. Siegel nor any other buy-and-hold stock advocate endorses such stock-trading tactics. Yet, in encouraging all investors to buy and hold for the long term, they divert investor attention away from the fallacy of composition. A long-term system ostensibly worked in the past only because so few investors actually followed it.

40. For then contemporary accounts of Wall Street practices and actual investor (speculator) experience, see Matthew Hale Smith, *Twenty Years Among the Bulls and Bears of Wall Street* (Hartford: J. Burr, 1870); Henry Clewes, *Fifty Years on Wall Street* (New York: Irving, 1910); Fred Schwed Jr., *Where Are the Customers' Yachts* (New York: Wiley, 1940).

41. Gary Belsky and Thomas Gilovich, *Why Smart People Make Big Money Mistakes* (New York: Simon & Schuster, 1999). Interestingly, these authors, too, fall for the myth of the 11% return. In remarking on a "sophisticated investor," they say, "Good for her, considering that stocks have offered the best average annual return of all investment categories over the past 70 years—about 11% . . . " (44).

42. Schwed, *Customers' Yachts*.

43. Steve Liesman, "Spate of Write-Offs Calls into Question Lofty 1990s Profits," *Wall Street Journal*, July 13, 2001, A1, A4; Jonathan Weil, "What's the P/E Ratio? Depends on What Is Meant by Earnings," *Wall Street Journal*, August 21, 2001, A1, A8; Steve Liesman, "NASDAQ Companies Erase 5 Years of Profit," *Wall Street Journal*, August 16, 2001, C1, C4.

44. Nevertheless, the stock enthusiasts are still developing rationales for unprecedented P/E levels. See Burton G. Malkiel, "Don't Sell Out," *Wall Street Journal*, September 26, 2001, A20; and for an opposing view, Mark Farber, "Seeing the Future," *Bloomburg Personal Finance*, November 2001, 69–73.

45. Andrew Smithers and Stephen Wright, *Valuing Wall Street* (New York: McGraw-Hill, 2000); and for an update, Smithers and Wright, "Bear Bottom," *Barron's*, November 12, 2001, 29.

46. Johnson Pantolope, "There's No Place Like Rental Property," *USA Today*, August 31, 2001, B1; and Sheila Muto, "Apartment Buildings Are a Choice Investment," *Wall Street Journal*, November 14, 2001, B10.

47. "Resetting the Gold Watch," *Kiplinger's Retirement Planning Guide*, October 2, 2000, 51.

48. McNamee and Vickers, "Where Should I," 80.

49. Burton G. Malkiel, *A Random Walk Down Wall Street*, 4th ed. (New York: W. W. Norton, 1985), 305.

50. Siegel, *Stocks for the Long Run*, 118.

Chapter 3 The Case for Real Estate

1. J. Siegel, *Stocks for the Long Run*, 37.

2. Cynthia Crossen, *Tainted Truth: The Manipulation of Fact in America* (New York: Simon & Schuster, 1994). See also Joel Best, *Damned Lies and Statistics* (Berkeley: University of California Press, 2001); and David Murray, Joel Schwartz, and Robert Lichter, *It Ain't Necessarily So* (Boston: Rowman and Littlefield, 2001).

3. Roger Ibbotson and Rex Sinquefield, *Stocks, Bonds, Bills, and Inflation: 2000 Yearbook* (Chicago: Ibbotson, 2000).

4. Roger Ibbotson and Laurence Siegel, "Real Estate Returns: A Comparison with Other Investments, *AREUEA Journal* 12, no. 3 (1984): 219–240. In this article Ibbotson and Siegel admit the serious inadequacy of their data and methodology. Moreover, during the period they studied, individuals gained extensive tax shelter benefits from real estate, which these authors completely ignore.

5. Charles D. Ellis, *Winning the Loser's Game*, 2d ed. (Burr Ridge, Ill.: BusinessOne Irwin, 1998), 105.

6. See also Neil Weinberg, "Rescuing Your Retirement," *Forbes*, November 12, 2001, 104–112. "No, your house is unlikely to be a racy investment . . . house prices have appreciated just 6.8% since 1968. After inflation, the figure falls to 1.5%. That's less than long-term Treasuries pay . . . " (112). Because such analytically feeble thinking runs rampant among so-called financial experts, it's no wonder that most Americans erroneously believe that "stocks outperform all other assets."

7. I did briefly address the topic in one of my previous books. See Gary Eldred and Andrew McLean, *Investing in Real Estate*, 3d ed. (New York: Wiley, 2001), 1–14.

8. Of course, the nationwide intensive promotional campaign for stocks as advanced by self-interested mutual funds, financial planners, personal finance magazines, and television shows facilitates this indoctrination.

9. In other words, if in your area home prices run upward of $150,000 to, say, $300,000, then as a value investor, you should also look for rents that are proportionately larger than those shown here. If you can't find value according to the metrics and opportunities explained throughout this book, then look in outlying areas, smaller cities or communities, or multifamily properties instead of single-family houses. Note, too, in these examples, I have used a currently above-market interest rate. If interest rates remain low, your cash flows could significantly exceed those shown here.

10. For a similar point using a different time period, see Parker, "No Accounting for Gain," 49.

11. John Shoven, "The Retirement Security of the Baby Boom Generation," *TIAA CREFF Research Dialogues* (March 1995), 2.

12. Malkiel, *Random Walk*, 22–25.

13. Naturally, the 1981–2000 bull market encouraged such a view among the great number of investors and journalists with virtually no historical knowledge of the stock market—for example, "Historically, stocks have risen about 10% a year" Lynn Khalfani, "Six Reasons Investors Fire Their Brokers," *Wall Street Journal*, August 13, 2001, B7A.

14. E. L. Smith, *Common Stocks*, 17.

15. J. B. Williams, *The Theory of Investment Value* (Cambridge, Mass.: Harvard University Press, 1938), 3–4.

16. John T. Flynn, *Security Speculation* (New York: Harcourt, Brace, 1934), 40.

17. J. B. Williams, *Theory*, 6.

18. "The 100 Top Brands," *Business Week*, August 6, 2001, 60.

19. Viewed historically, with a highly diversified portfolio, no one should expect more. Prospectively, the 7% figure may prove optimistic.

20. Burton Malkiel, "Don't Sell Out," *Wall Street Journal*, September 26, 2001, A20.

21. J. B. Williams, *Theory*, 30.

22. J. Siegel, *Stocks for the Long Run*, 78.

23. Ben Graham and David Dodd, *Security Analysis*, 5th ed. (New York: McGraw-Hill, 1988), 565.

24. Hoffman, "Opening Your Nest Egg," 92–93.

25. Ibid., 92.

26. Every Wednesday the *Wall Street Journal* includes its Property Report section. You will see advertised there dozens of income properties yielding unleveraged *current* net income (no growth assumed, no appreciation assumed) returns of 9% to 11%.

27. Patrick Barta, "Your Money Matters," *Wall Street Journal*, August 10, 2001, C1.

28. Mara DerHovanesian, "Seniors, Beware of a Thief Called Inflation," *Business Week*, July 30, 2001, 96.

29. David Schumacher, *The Buy and Hold Real Estate Strategy* (New York: Wiley, 1992), 296.

30. Weinberg, "Rescuing Your Retirement," 112.

31. Patrick Hare, *Creating an Accessory Apartment* (New York: McGraw-Hill, 1987); Doreen Bierbrier, *Living with Tenants* (New York: McGraw-Hill, 1986); Ruth Rejnis, *Squeeze Your Home for Cash* (Chicago: Dearborn, 1995); Jan Stankus, *How to Open and Operate a Bed and Breakfast* (Old Saybrook, Conn.: Globe Pequot Press, 1995).

32. Eldred and McLean, *Investing in Real Estate*, 211–252.

33. John Bogle, *Common Sense on Mutual Funds* (New York: Wiley, 1999), 67–81.

34. Jonathan Clements, *25 Myths You've Got to Avoid* (New York: Simon & Schuster, 1998), 167–68.

35. Hawaii might prove the exception because its real estate prices were buoyed up (and let down) because of its close ties with the Japanese economy, more so than the continental United States.

36. John Witty, "Hot Housing Debate," *Bloomberg Personal Finance*, December 2001, 28.

37. This is not to say that apartment rents and concessions don't soften. Of course they do, as is now occurring in Atlanta and Silicon Valley. But cyclical softening in no way compares to the recurring collapses of stock prices and corporate earnings.

38. Clements, *25 Myths*, 123.

39. Douglas Sease and John Prestbo, *Barron's Guide to Making Investment Decisions* (Englewood Cliffs, N.J.: Prentice Hall, 1998), 139.

Chapter 4 Real Estate Risks and Returns

1. For a critical review of this idea, see Robert A. Haugen, *The Inefficient Stock Market* (Upper Saddle River, N.J.: Prentice Hall, 1999), 15–28. See also R. Haugen, *The New Finance: The Case for an Over-reactive Stock Market* (Upper Saddle River, N.J.: Prentice Hall, 1998).

2. Larry E. Swedroe, *What Wall Street Doesn't Want You to Know: How You Can Build Real Wealth Investing in Index Funds* (New York: Dutton, 2000).

3. Malkiel, *Random Walk*, 16.

4. Obviously, stockbrokers, managed funds, stock-picking newsletters, and personal-investing magazines would lose much of their market if the theories of modern finance became generally accepted among the investing public.

5. Charles D. Ellis, *Investment Policy* (Burr Ridge, Ill.: BusinessOne Irwin, 1998).

6. Swedroe, *What Wall Street*.

7. Bruce Greenwald et al., *Value Investing from Graham to Buffet* (New York: Wiley, 2001).

8. Harry Browne, *Why the Best-Laid Investment Plans Usually Go Wrong* (New York: Fireside, 1989).

9. Kenneth Fisher, "I Hate Funds," *Forbes*, August 20, 2001, 170.

10. Graham, *Intelligent Investor*, xiii.

11. Ibid.

12. Haugen, *Inefficient Stock Market*.

13. Ellis, *Loser's Game*.

14. Stephen A. Ross et al., *Corporate Finance* (New York: Irwin McGraw-Hill, 1999), 208–270.

15. Ellis, *Loser's Game*.

16. Ross, *Corporate Finance*, 229–240.

17. Graham, *Intelligent Investor*, 61.

18. In other words, the stated amounts are being discounted for a total of 30 and 40 years, respectively.

19. Siegel, *Stocks for the Long Run*, 159.

20. Ibid., 162. Also, as to stock prices and inflation, "Indeed, at this writing [1992], the DJIA adjusted for inflation (although not for dividends) has not matched the peak it reached in February 1966." Marshall Blume, Jeremy Siegel, and Dan Rottenberg, *Revolution on Wall Street* (New York: W. W. Norton, 1993), 56. This book also includes a highly readable review of the efficient market debate (85–104).

21. Siegel, *Stocks for the Long Run*, 59.

22. Parker, "No Accounting for Gains," 49. One reader of this article dismissed Parker by saying that "dividends were antiquated due to tax inefficiency." (Letters, *Barron's*, November 12, 2001, 29). However, in the aggregate, corporations have not displayed any long-term superior ability to create shareholder value through higher retained earnings. Witness the collapse of profits and massive write-offs of investments that occurred during 2001. In total, NASDAQ firms in the aggregate declared losses in 2000–2001 that more than offset the previous five years of reported earnings.

Moreover, dividends are far more tax efficient today than they were from the 1940s up through the 1981 TRA. Not only are marginal tax rates much lower today (30% to 40% versus the earlier 70% to 90%), but also since 1981, tax-deferred individual retirement accounts and tax-free pension funds hold an increasingly larger proportion of stocks.

23. J. Siegel, *Stocks for the Long Run*, 167.

24. Ibid., 59.

25. Although most assumable mortgages have disappeared, many ARMs for investors and home buyers and all VA and FHA mortgages for owner-occupant home buyers can be assumed at the contract rate. Thus, even in a future high-interest-rate environment, you may be able to find properties with assumable less-than-market interest rates.

26. For a dissenting view, see Gary Shilling, *Deflation: How to Thrive and Survive* (New York: McGraw-Hill, 1999).

27. Witty, "Hot Housing Debate," 28. Also see Peter Lynch, "What's Next?" *Barron's*, October 15, 2001, 2–3. Lynch says, "The price of the average house [nationwide] has not fallen over the last 30 years. In fact, [rising homeowner equity] . . . offsets a large portion of what individual investors have lost in the stock market in the last 2 years" (3).

28. Brendan Moynihan, "Market Wise," *Bloomberg Personal Finance*, December 2001, 20–21.

29. For a typically wrongheaded discussion of disinflation and housing prices, see "Will House Prices Ever Go Up Again?" in Roger Bootle, *The Death of Inflation* (London: Nicholas Brealy, 1996), 66–77. On the eve of our great housing boom due to low inflation and a strong economy, Bootle wrote, "It looks as though the [housing] market is set to continue in the doldrums. . . . [Property] should be viewed solely on its merit as a provider of housing services, not as a source of profit" (67, 85).

Chapter 5 The Enterprising Investor

1. Graham, *Intelligent Investor*, 73–93.

2. Tales of investor stock market losses didn't begin with the dot-bombs and tech wreck. They go back more than 150 years. "I have been in business in Wall Street 38 years. During that time 98 out of every 100 who have put money in the street have lost it." Cited in M. H. Smith, *Bulls and Bears*, 52.

3. Alfred Cowles, "Can Stock Market Forecasters Forecast the Market?" *Econometrica* (July 1933), 309–324. More recently, Swedroe, *What Wall Street*; also, Charles D. Ellis, *Investment Policy: How to Win the Loser's Game* (Burr Ridge, Ill.: BusinessOne Irwin, 1993).

4. Janet Lowe, *Ben Graham on Value Investing* (New York: Penguin, 1996), 83–84.

5. Graham, *Intelligent Investor*, 287.

6. Ellis, *Winning the Loser's Game*.

7. Charles Mackay, *Extraordinary Popular Delusions and the Madness of Crowds* (London: Richard Bentley, 1841). Reprint available from Harmony Books, 1980.

8. Shiller, *Irrational Exuberance*, 183–190.

9. Even the worst real estate recession would not cause an aggregate loss of property values anywhere approaching the magnitude of losses experienced by the S&P 500, DJIA, or NASDAQ circa March 2000 through September 2001.

10. Some nothing-down gurus advise their readers to tell a seller, "You name the price, I'll set the terms." That's a very expensive and dangerous way to buy real estate.

11. Graham, *Intelligent Investor*, 61.

12. For example, "Home Foreclosures Reach Near Record Highs in Atlanta," *Atlanta Journal and Constitution*, July 28, 2001, A1.

13. Herb Cohen, *You Can Negotiate Anything* (Secaucus, N.J.: Lyle Stuart, 1980); Roger Dawson, *Secrets of Power Persuasion* (Englewood Cliffs, N.J.: Prentice-Hall, 1992); Bob Woolf, *Friendly Persuasion* (New York: G. P. Putnam, 1990).

Chapter 6 The Ins and Outs of Market Value

1. Here we ignore the bid-asked spread as well as the purchase or sale of abnormally large blocks of a company's stock.

2. *The Appraisal of Real Estate* (Chicago: Appraisal Institute, 1996), 43.

3. Of course, securing such information is far easier for value investors in real estate than it is for value investors in stocks. Individual value investors in stocks often forget that both Warren Buffet and Ben Graham could access far more insightful information than they can. Is there a major CEO in the country who would refuse to take a telephone call from the Sage of Omaha?

4. Greenwald et al., *Value Investing from Graham to Buffet*, 35–47.

5. "Only a true value stock can stand up to [our] 160 relentless variables." Andrew P. Pilara Jr., "Fidelity Investments Advertisement," *Wall Street Journal*, November 2, 2001, C15.

6. Richard Babcock, *The Zoning Game Revisited* (Boston: Lincoln Institute, 1985), 234–253.

7. Developers must file a plat plan with the local government's land records office (typically the property tax assessor). To verify boundaries, some mortgage lenders require a site survey prior to closing. But you should at least make a preliminary determination before making an offer to buy.

8. Faith Popcorn popularized the term cocooning to indicate periods when many people would rather spend time at home than go out. Faith Popcorn, *The Popcorn Report* (New York: Harper Business, 1991), 27–34.

9. Dodge Woodson, *100 Surefire Improvements to Sell Your House Faster* (New York: Wiley, 1993), 121–129.

10. Ibid.

Chapter 7 Is the Property a Good Buy?

1. During the next 20 years, many demographers expect the U.S. population to grow by more than 50 million people—in total, a growth figure equal to the current population of both Florida and California.

2. The same is true for office and hotel space. See, for example, Jerry Adler, *High Rise: How 1000 Men and Women Worked Around the Clock for 5 Years and Lost $200 Million Building a Skyscraper* (New York: Harper Collins, 1993).

3. Also, as markets begin to suffer overbuilding, mortgage lenders tighten (sometimes shut down) their construction lending.

4. The most widely available cost manual is the *Residential Cost Handbook* (Los Angeles: Marshall and Swift). A monthly loose-leaf service keeps their cost figures current.

5. Tom Schachtman, *Skyscraper Dreams* (Boston: Little, Brown, 1991), 289–290.

6. James Tobin, "A General Equilibrium Approach to Monetary Theory," *Journal of Money, Credit, and Banking* (February 1969): 15–29.

7. Smithers and Wright, *Valuing Wall Street*.

8. Some say that corporate book values and replacement costs poorly measure intangibles such as patents, copyrights, brand names, and various other sources of intellectual capital. Perhaps so. But if that's the case, then corporate return-on-equity figures are greatly overstated. Moreover, in a world of fast-paced technological change, intangibles may not be worth the stock price premium that their enthusiasts think they are. The real issue is whether a firm can strongly protect itself from substitute products and services offered by other companies—or, even more troublesome, changes in consumer tastes, preferences, and buying patterns. Few companies command these types of market power.

9. Stephane Fitch, "The Gentrification Play," *Forbes*, January 8, 2001, 250–251.

10. Lauren Young, "Value Rules: The Best Strategy Ever," *Smart Money*, August 2001, 90.

11. See Gary W. Eldred, *Real Estate Analysis and Strategy* (New York: Harper & Row, 1987), 483–487. Also Greenwald et al., *Value Investing from Graham to Buffet*, 48–50.

12. See, for example, John Reed, *Aggressive Tax Avoidance for Real Estate Investors* (Danville, Calif.: Reed, 1998); Vernon Hoven, *Real Estate Investors Tax Guide* (Chicago: Dearborn Financial, 1998).

13. Stock enthusiasts who compare real estate returns throughout the 1950s up to 1987 (1986 TRA implemented) never cite the fact that most real estate investors not only paid no income tax on their realty earnings, but also were able to write off real estate "losses" against other earned income. The 1986 TRA has diminished (but not eliminated) these tax advantages of real estate over stocks.

14. John A. Mullaney, *REITs: Building Profits with Real Estate Investment Trusts* (New York: Wiley, 1997).

15. Since the decline of the S&P 500, the personal finance literature has rediscovered REITs for their dividend yield, appreciation, and portfolio risk attributes. See, for example, Sean Cronin, "Adding Property to Your Portfolio Can Boost Yield and Reduce Risk," *Wall Street Journal*, October 10, 2001, B15.

16. Tom Lauricella, "Real Estate Fund Gains Show their Value in Diversifying," *Wall Street Journal*, November 2, 2001, C1.

17. One such unusual event was the terrorist attack of September 11, 2001. With the travel industry greatly hurt, many hotel REITs did see their share prices plunge.

Chapter 8 Look Beyond Market Value

1. As of November 12, 2001, Amazon.com was trading on the NASDAQ at $7 per share.

2. "We didn't think we could lose." The more things change, the more they remain the same. California went through a previous boom and bust just 10 years earlier. How could any intelligent home buyer not realize the appreciation party had to quickly end?

3. Stephane Fitch, "What If Housing Crashed?" *Forbes*, September 3, 2001, 76–80.

4. Martin Ableson, "Will California Home Prices Crash," *Barron's*, February 14, 1989, 44. This right-on-target analysis compared high mortgage payments to relatively low rent levels to show the outsized financial disadvantage of buying or investing in houses.

5. When asked what problem would most plague the stock market, Jeremy Siegel has answered, "The unrealistically optimistic expectations of stock investors." Jeremy Siegel, "Going Long," *Kiplinger's Personal Finance*, December 2001, 70.

6. Andrew Bary, "Not Just Dot.bombs—Solid Stocks Have Been Marked Down 75%," *Barron's*, October 15, 2001, 19. But does that mean they're now a bargain? No, says Jean-Marie Eveillard in "Where's the Value?" *Barron's*, October 15, 2001, 29. "Despite the pounding stocks have taken, only a few bargains beckon," says Eveillard (29).

7. "Inflation cures all mistakes," say many real estate investors. Yes, but why not avoid the mistake in the first place? But more importantly, the cash-strapped investor may not survive the price cycle.

8. Fitch, "What If Housing Crashed?," 78.

9. You can find these figures in the real estate section of your local newspaper, or in local specialty papers that are written for the real estate and mortgage loan industry. Also, local Realtor and mortgage broker associations will keep track of these and similar data.

10. Patrick Barta, "Banks Tighten Standards for Mortgages," *Wall Street Journal*, November 12, 2001, C1.

11. Be sure, though, that you understand that vacancy rates vary greatly among a myriad of locational and property submarkets.

12. Gregory Mankiew and David Weil, "The Baby Boom, the Baby Bust and the Housing Market," *Regional Science and Urban Economics*, 19 (1989): 235–238.

13. Gary W. Eldred, *The 106 Common Mistakes Homebuyers Make—and How to Avoid Them*, 3d ed. (New York: Wiley, 2002), 147.

14. If you see a turnaround play (or can engineer one), such units may prove quite attractive to a value investor.

Chapter 9 Predict the Future

1. Stephane Fitch, "Gentrification Play," 250–251.

2. Gary W. Eldred, *Yes! You Can Own the Home You Want* (New York: Wiley, 1996), 135.

3. Ibid.

4. Cited in Gary W. Eldred, *Stop Renting Now* (Washington, D.C.: National Initiative for Home Ownership, 1998), 162–163.

5. Ibid.

6. Banks that fail to show that they have affirmatively responded to community reinvestment are denied the right to merge and can suffer other penalties.

7. Eldred, *Stop Renting Now*, 88.

8. Gary W. Eldred, *The Complete Guide to Second Homes for Vacations, Retirement, and Investment* (New York: Wiley, 1999), 18.

9. All these quotes are from Eldred, *The Complete Guide*, 153–154.

10. "A Frog in the Throat of Development," *Business Week*, April 9, 2001, 10.

11. Robert Gavin, "Rethinking Community Growth Management," *Wall Street Journal*, October 10, 2001, B13.

12. Tracey Kaplan, "List of Housing Needs in San Francisco Spawns Controversy," *San Jose Mercury News*, November 26, 2001, C1. Typical attitudes express, "We don't need more housing in Piedmont."

Chapter 10 Create Value Now

1. Parts of this chapter have been adapted from Eldred and McLean, *Investing in Real Estate*, 93–108.

2. Many books are available to help you fashion ideas for property improvements. Several that I recommend include: John Reed, *How to Increase the Value of Real Estate* (Danville, Calif.: Reed, 1999); and Wallace Kaufman, *Finding Hidden Values in Your Home* (New York: Collier, 1987).

3. Eldred, *Real Estate Analysis and Strategy*, 493–516.

4. Millions of the "nothing down" genre of real estate books have sold. But nearly all of their readers fail because the authors of these books imply that if you're able to buy, you're able to make a lot of money. Sadly, the world of successful real estate investing doesn't make life quite so easy as that pictured in the Carleton Sheets infomercials.

5. Thomas Stanley and D. Danko, *The Millionaire Next Door: The Surprising Secrets of America's Wealthy* (New York: Pocket Books, 2000).

6. R. Kiyosaki and S. Lechter, *Rich Dad, Poor Dad* (New York: Warner, 1999).

7. Stephen R. Covey, *The 7 Habits of Highly Effective People* (New York: Fireside, 1989).

8. Eldred, *106 Most Common Mistakes*, 132.

9. For the best discussion of government regulation of property, see Babcock, *Zoning Game Revisited*. For a very practical treatment, see Cora Jordan, *Neighbor Law* (Berkeley, Calif.: Nolo Press, 1998).

10. Eldred, *106 Most Common Mistakes*, 139.

11. Ibid., 139.

12. Harry Koenig, *How to Lower Your Property Taxes* (New York: Fireside, 1990), 15.

13. Steve Carlson, *The Best Home for Less: How to Drastically Reduce Your Taxes, Utility Bills, and Construction or Remodeling Costs* (New York: Avon, 1992).

14. Cynthia Barnett, "City Slickers," *Florida Trend*, August 2001, 60–64.

15. Ibid., 60.

16. Cynthia Draper, "Parents Fight for Better Schools," *Wall Street Journal*, August 23, 2001, A1.

17. Stephanie Mann and M.C. Blakeman, *Safe Homes, Safe Neighborhoods* (Nolo.com, 1993).

Conclusion You (Not Everybody) Ought to Be Rich

1. Samuel Crowther, "Everybody Ought to be Rich: An Interview with John J. Raskob," *Ladies Home Journal*, August 1929, 9, 36. Interestingly, Samuel Crowther, the interviewer-

journalist cited, also wrote a piece on buying real estate the following month. In this article he said, "On the purely financial side, it will be found that the purchase of a house is not only a most excellent way of saving money, but also is as sure a way of making money as can be found." "To Have and to Hold," *Ladies Home Journal*, September 1929, 186.

2. Raskob had been instrumental in numerous stock operations and was frequently referred to as one of the "Big Ten" that also included William Durant, Jesse Livermore, and the Fisher brothers.

3. Crowther, "Everybody," 9.

4. Assuming wages of a then good amount, $150 per month.

5. Imagine, work 20 years at around $150 per month, and then retire for life at $400 per month. True stock market magic; yet the stock market magicians are preaching a similar message today, albeit in not so grand proportions.

6. The DJIA fell from its high of 381.17 (1929) to its low of 41.22 (1932).

7. Of course, these figures still assume the impossible: a shifting portfolio that shuns losers and picks up winners, dividend reinvestment, and no payment of income taxes or transaction costs.

8. J. Siegel, *Stocks for the Long Run*, 4.

9. That is, of course, the fundamental problem with stocks for retirement. Without sufficient income, how much capital can you draw down each year? No one can confidently answer this question. See, for example, "The Cost of a Comfortable Retirement," *Kiplinger's Retirement Guide 2000*, October 2, 2000, 32–37.

10. In other words, this investor worked and bought stocks for 10 years longer than forecast. Yet he still collected 50% less than the amount promised. Undoubtedly, many (if not most) of today's "stocks for retirement" investors will experience similar shortfalls.

11. Naturally, these calculations (as all such stock market calculations must) could vary significantly according to the exact stocks purchased, the exact dates of purchase, and the specific dividend yields paid. I am using the DJIA.

12. The most heavily praised retirement planning Web site is www.financialengines.com. This commercial Web site is run by William Sharpe, a winner of the Nobel Prize in economic science for his contributions to the development of the efficient market theory. Yet no matter how fancy the computer spreadsheet and its associated numerical probabilities, all such results leave great room for error. No one can predict the stock market. Ironically, that's precisely what the efficient market theory attempts to prove.

13. WWW.Amazon.com, *Stocks for the Long Run*, 2d ed., Customer Reviews, A Reader from New York USA, June 3, 2001. Nearly all other customer and editorial reviews heap praise on Professor Siegel for (ostensibly) proving that stocks are the surest and safest way to build long-term wealth.

14. "The personal fortunes of this country have been made not by saving, but by producing." Crowther, "Everybody," 36.

15. Amazing! Throughout his life Karl Marx argued that capitalist profits kept the workers poor. Raskob (and latter-day stock enthusiasts) have argued that capitalist profits will make workers wealthy.

16. Look at any of the recent wealth statistics for the United States. The top 10% account for more than 90% of all individually held stock ownership. We're not even coming close to the "people's capitalism" or "bloodless revolution" that many stock enthusi-

asts have promised. Prior to 401(k)s, ESOPs (Employee Stock Ownership Plans) were the promised vehicle. Will Americans ever simply accept the truth that in a free market economy great inequalities will persist regardless of government or private schemes to effect otherwise?

17. Stock enthusiasts are still saying that you should be able to earn a long-term, essentially risk-free nominal rate of 9% to 12%. For example, " . . . [S]tocks should be able to match or slightly outpace their long-term average return of about 12% a year. Michael Sivy, "A Bear of a Different Color," *Money*, December 2001, 108. But such a high nominal rate presumes inflation at 4% to 6% a year. If long-term inflation remains low, say 2% to 3% per year, then such high nominal returns from stocks become even more tenuous.

18. Even stock enthusiast Jonathon Clements now admits that he dropped his critical guard. "Before the bear market," writes Clements, "I didn't spend much time contemplating likely stock market returns. Why bother? [For I am confident that] stocks will triumph in the long run. Nevertheless, I now believe it is important to have [a more cautious] sense for likely long-run stock performance." See "How the Stock Drop Has Schooled Me," *Wall Street Journal*, December 4, 2001, C1.

19. Unbelievably, in their quest for income, Americans are increasingly buying annuities. Yet, not only do annuities fail to protect against inflation; they dissipate your estate. Yet, quite naively, Fidelity Investments executive Farrell Dolan overlooks the superior attributes of income properties and says, "[Annuities are] the only thing that can bring lifetime income other than a pension or Social Security." Quoted in Carol Marie Cropper, "A Paycheck in the Mail Every Month," *Business Week*, December 10, 2001, 97. This article is subtitled "For Lifetime Income, Seniors Should Look at Annuities."

20. In an interview, Professor Siegel admits, "I've never been particularly good at picking individual stocks . . . very few people have what it takes to beat the market consistently." Kosnett, "History Takes a Detour," 42. If a world-class professor of finance can't pick stocks, what chance do you have?

21. If I still haven't convinced you to diversify away from stocks, see William Bernstein, "Riding for a Fall," *Barron's*, November 26, 2001, 36. This article is subtitled "The 401(k) Is Likely to Turn Out to Be a Defined-Chaos Retirement Plan." Right on point!

Index